LEGAL C.

MW00387700

Being a Concise Practical Exposition with Illustrative Examples

for

Corporation Lawyers,
Financial Officers and Accountants

as well as

Law and Business Students With and Without Accounting Backgrounds

of the

CURRENT STATE OF CORPORATION LAW REGULATING
Stated Capital, Par and No Par Stock,
Distributions to Shareholders, Equitable Contribution by Shareholders,
Corporate Capital Accounts, Promoters' Liability

and

Related Mysteries

THIRD EDITION

By

BAYLESS MANNING

Formerly
Dean: Stanford Law School
Partner: Paul, Weiss, Rifkind, Wharton & Garrison
New York

with

JAMES J. HANKS, Jr.
Partner: Weinberg and Green
Baltimore

Westbury, New York
THE FOUNDATION PRESS, INC.
1990

Foundation Press, a division of West Group, has created this publication to provide you with accurate and authoritative information concerning the subject matter covered. However, this publication was not necessarily prepared by persons licensed to practice law in a particular jurisdiction. Foundation Press is not engaged in rendering legal or other professional advice, and this publication is not a substitute for the advice of an attorney. If you require legal or other expert advice, you should seek the services of a competent attorney or other professional.

COPYRIGHT © 1977, 1981 FOUNDATION PRESS, INC.
COPYRIGHT © 1990 By THE FOUNDATION PRESS, INC.

        395 Hudson Street
        New York, N.Y. 10014
        Phone Toll Free 1–877–888–1330
        Fax (212) 367–6799
        fdpress.com

 TEXT IS PRINTED ON 10% POST CONSUMER RECYCLED PAPER

1st Reprint — 2002

ACKNOWLEDGEMENTS

I am happy to dedicate the Third Edition of this book, like the first two, to Sam Cross and Ernie Folk, authors respectively of the definitive works on the Connecticut and Delaware corporation laws. In respect of the First Edition, they helped me up and over the high wall that separates an almost completed manuscript from a completed one.

With respect to this Edition, I owe much more than thanks to Jim Hanks, corporate law practitioner, rigorous professional, thoughtful scholar, energetic reformer of the law, critical editor and unmatched *bon vivant*. Rapid and widespread changes in the laws obviously called for a Third Edition to be produced; but without the drive, scholarship, expertise, persistence and written contributions of Jim Hanks as a colleague, the job never would have got done.

Along the way I have also leaned on the knowledge, skill and good humor of a good many other people. Among them were professors of law Gordon Scott and Junius Hoffman, who early disciplined my legal analysis, Gordon Tasker and Robert Granow, C.P.A.s, who weeded out my more egregious accounting gaffes, and Brad Ritter, lawyer, who furnished valuable research and bibliographical assistance in connection with the Third Edition.

BAYLESS MANNING

New York, New York
1977, 1981, 1990

*

NON–PREFACE

I always read prefaces. I have found that what authors have to say in their prefaces is often more consequential than what they offer in the main body of their works. Whoever reads these words will, by that act, have shown that he, too, is a Preface Reader. He will, to his dismay, find this page virtually blank. But he should take heart. There really is a Preface to the Third Edition, as there were prefaces to the two earlier editions. The Preface text has just been shifted to the Introduction.

BAYLESS MANNING

*

SUMMARY OF CONTENTS

*

TABLE OF CONTENTS

TABLE OF CONTENTS

TABLE OF CONTENTS

SUBPART TWO: THE REVISED MODEL ACT— ILLUSTRATIONS

THIRD PART. STATE OF PLAY—1990: YESTERDAY AND TOMORROW AS CONTEMPORARIES

*

LEGAL CAPITAL

*

INTRODUCTION

The reader had as well learn straightaway that almost everything about the subject of this book (and therefore about the book itself) is a little peculiar. This Introduction is designed to prepare him [1] for that experience, to disclose in advance what the book is (and is not) intended to do and to furnish a walking guide to the unusual groundplan of the text. It could also provide the reader an informed basis for deciding not to read further.

First, for whom is the book written?

The anticipated users of this book are corporation law practitioners, corporate financial executives, accountants and judges, as well as law and business students aspiring to become such. The development of the analysis in the book will be found to demand the reader's concentration. But despite its forbidding title, the book is specifically written to be understandable not only by the accounting maven but by the reader who has no accounting background.

Second, what does the book seek to do and why does that need to be done?

The Preface to the First Edition of the book answered,

It is a textbook to be read . . . without the aid of an instructor.

*   *   *

The subjects treated here include the development and current state of corporation code provisions and common law governing stated capital, par and no par stock, reductions of capital, statutory restrictions on distributions to shareholders, impairment of capital, the shareholders' problem of equitable contribution, stock watering and promoters' liability. *   *   * [T]hese subjects are simply not amenable to usual instruction methods.

Case law in the field is spotty and incoherent. Most of the relevant material is statutory and the statutes themselves display a considerable variety. Classroom discussion of the law in the field invariably comes apart at the seams as the instructor engages in a losing effort simultaneously to teach instant accounting to those members of the class who do not know a debit from a credit, to sophisticate those students who

---

1. This first occurrence of a personal pronoun affords the opportunity to declare in the style of the corporation lawyer: "As used in this document, un-less the context otherwise requires, any personal pronoun signifying the masculine signifies the feminine as well."

1

already know some accounting (the most difficult group), and to philosophize with those who have a strong and modern accounting background.

But awkward as these factors are, the basic pedagogical problem in this field lies elsewhere. The real problem is that the game is not worth the candle. The complexity and novelty of the material involved require an investment of classroom time that is wholly incommensurate with the value of the educational return to the student. * * *

[S]tudents who have endured this experience fall into three groups. The first group—recollecting weeks of classroom work devoted to par, stated capital, and the like— believes the subject is very real and very important. It is not. The second group remembers that the end product of the elementary instruction was the instructor's analytic devastation of the whole topic; this group sneers at the subject as trivial and not to be taken seriously. Later, as lawyers, they will get a client and themselves in trouble. The third group remembers only that the whole matter seemed terribly complicated at the time, they didn't understand any of it, and they haven't thought about it since. Each of these groups needs a brief, readable, inclusive and critical reading source to go back to.

The book is addressed to that need. It is analytically rigorous. But it is not a treatise or encyclopedia. It is an explanatory guide through an intellectual wilderness. *The reader who has a particular legal capital problem to deal with must always find his answer in the applicable state statute and cases.* But, if he has read this book, he is considerably more likely to understand his problem and to be able to work his way through the applicable statute and cases to a practical solution.

Third, what is the book's groundplan?

The book has three parts, each quite different.

The First Part presents the substance of legal capital doctrine. It contains two Subparts. Subpart One is an analytic lay-out of the labyrinth—the inherited corpus of legal capital statutes and related concepts and doctrine. Subpart Two walks through a sequence of typical corporate financial transactions to illustrate traditional legal capital law at work. Subpart Two is specifically designed for the reader with no accounting background, and such a reader will—probably to his surprise—find it quite comprehensible.

The two Subparts of the First Part are interdependent. Neither is likely to be well understood without the other.

The Second Part reviews recent movements to demolish the labyrinth of legal capital. The Preface to the First Edition of this book included the following observation:

> Unfortunately, the worst charge that can be brought against these laws is that they are ineffective. No persuasive case can be made that the statutory provisions on par, stated capital and equity distributions are vicious, and no organized segment of American society is gored by them. As a result, the existing scheme shows prospects of great durability.

That prophecy turned out to be a dud. Tremors of change were felt in California when in 1975 a new General Corporation Law substantially revamped that state's stated capital provisions. Then, contrary to all expectations, a full-scale revolutionary act was committed by the American Bar Association's Committee on Corporate Laws (the "Committee"). That Committee, composed of 25 corporation lawyers from private practice, corporate law departments and law faculties, is the guardian of "the better view"— the Model Business Corporation Act (the "Model Act"), all or parts of which make up the corporation law of more than 30 states. In 1980, the Committee, on the basis of a long and painstaking study, calmly threw out of the window substantially all of the doctrinal propositions with which this book is concerned—if not lock, stock [2] and barrel then at least lock and barrel.

In 1984, the Committee went farther in the same direction in the course of its general overhaul of the Model Act that became the Revised Model Business Corporation Act (the "Revised Model Act"). Additional amendments in 1987 moved still farther away from traditional stated capital doctrines. At least a dozen states have now substantially enacted the Revised Model Act. Many more have enacted important parts of it.

Perhaps there would be a degree of hyperbole in the suggestion that these developments have been as sudden and startling as the recent collapse of East European regimes—but that does convey the general idea.

The Second Part, like the First Part, is made up of a Subpart One of exposition and a Subpart Two of transactional illustrations.

The Third Part of the book reviews the state of legal capital doctrine in the new era. Regrettably, the latter-day changes— bold, drastic and sound though they be—have not made the problems discussed in this book go away. Nor will they do so, at least for a very long time. In the field of legal capital, (1) the new generation of law cannot be understood without the base of the earlier law and (2) the battlefield continues still to be largely

---

2. See pp. 32–33, infra.

occupied by the older generation. That is why the Third Part is titled "State of Play—1990: Yesterday and Tomorrow as Contemporaries."

* * *

This Third Edition was born out of a need to update its predecessor. Along the way, it has, in addition, benefitted from substantial reworking, correction, editing and general improvement throughout.

And now, to commence.

First Part

LEGAL CAPITAL DOCTRINE—
CONSTRUCTING THE LABYRINTH

Subpart One

LEGAL CAPITAL DOCTRINE—
EXPOSITION

Chapter I

THE PROBLEM—CORPORATE CREDITOR
AND CORPORATE SHAREHOLDER

The interests of creditors of a corporation and the interests of shareholders of a corporation are adverse whenever assets of shareholders are to be committed to the corporation's treasury and whenever assets are to be distributed to shareholders from the corporate treasury. Shareholders like to minimize the former and maximize the latter; creditors like the opposite. The legal apparatus built by common law and statute around the concept of "legal capital" is fundamentally aimed at striking a partial accommodation of that conflict of interests.

A. THE CREDITOR'S PERSPECTIVE

1. Creditors—General

The legal term "creditor" expresses a single basic proposition. A creditor has, subject to the special terms of the credit, a higher and prior claim to the assets of his debtor than the debtor has himself (leaving aside extraordinary circumstances as when, for example, a debtor has received a bankruptcy discharge or holds a homestead exemption). When a loan or other class of creditor's claim has become due and payable, the creditor may, in normal course, enlist the engines of the law to compel his debtor to pay the debt, regardless of the consequent diminution of the assets that "belong" to the debtor.

Though the term "priority" is usually reserved in the law to describe relationships among claimants other than the debtor, in a basic sense it may be said that the creditor's claim against the assets of his debtor is "prior" to the debtor's own claim to "his" assets. "Prior" in this sense has no relationship to the concept of time; it relates to hierarchy of claim. If the debtor has just enough assets to pay the creditor's claim, the creditor gets them all, *i.e.,* his claim is "prior," and the debtor gets nothing.

General creditors are those creditors who are not secured creditors. A *secured* creditor is a creditor who, in addition to his creditor's claim, has "collateral"—a mortgage or other security interest in particular assets of the debtor. Since all claims of all creditors to the assets of the debtor have priority over the debtor's claim, the secured creditor does not by force of his security interest in particular assets of the debtor gain in priority vis-à-vis his *debtor.* The purpose and effect of the collateral obtained by the secured creditor is to achieve a preferred position as against, not the debtor, but other creditors. If, at the critical time for payment, the debtor has enough assets to pay all creditors, the secured creditor's security is irrelevant since he will be paid in any case. But if the debtor's assets are not sufficient to pay all the creditors' claims outstanding against him, some creditors will come out short. The creditor who has in some manner obtained a lien on particular assets of the debtor has the opportunity to claim those assets for the full payment of the debt owing to him, even if they are the only assets around so that the application of the collateral to his debt means that other creditors will receive nothing at all. Until paid, the secured creditor is "prior" to general creditors to the extent of the value of the assets that are subject to the secured creditor's lien. The general creditors have no claim against the assets under the secured creditor's lien except to the extent that the value of the assets exceeds the secured creditor's claim.

Creditors compete among themselves not only for an interest in specific assets of the debtor but also, to the extent they are unable to achieve a fully-secured position, for priority among themselves in right of payment. The creditor, or class of creditors may, of course, be negotiated into agreeing (in advance or later) that its claim against the debtor's assets will rank below that of some or all other creditors or classes of creditors—though always, of course, ahead of the debtor's claim to the assets. Such a creditor is said to have "subordinated" his claim, he is referred to as a "subordinated creditor" and his claim is "subordinated debt." Reflecting this relative priority of claims, creditors are often referred to as "senior" or "junior".

Thus, from the perspective of any single *general* creditor:

- he is more likely to be paid and is thus better off the more assets the debtor has on the payment date;
- he is adversely affected by an increase in the aggregate of outstanding claims of general creditors against the debtor

since, in any ultimate showdown, all the general creditors will share equally in the finite assets of the debtor; and

- he is more adversely affected still by the creation or existence of *secured* creditors, for in the showdown, the secured creditors will, to the extent of their security, be able to assert a claim prior to all general creditors.

2.   The Creditor of the Individual Proprietorship or Partnership

When a creditor lends money to an individual, or allows him otherwise to become indebted to the creditor, the assets to which the creditor may generally look for payment of his claim are made up of the aggregate of the debtor's assets that have not earlier been placed under lien to some secured creditor.   The creditor, may, of course, insist as a condition of his loan that he be empowered to pursue assets in addition to those owned by his debtor; he may, for example, require some commitment by a third party, such as a guaranty, letter of credit, endorsement, or pledge of assets of the third party.   Occasionally, too, the law will step in to help a creditor reach assets beyond those in the hands of his debtor;   thus a creditor may in some circumstances be able to reach the assets of a father for an indebtedness incurred by a child, or those of a husband for indebtedness incurred by a wife or assets the insolvent debtor just shoveled out to friendly hands in a so-called "fraudulent conveyance" or a "preference".   But except for such special situations, (i) the creditor's *only* resort is the pool of unencumbered (unsecured) assets belonging to the debtor and (ii) *all* of the unencumbered assets of the debtor are at jeopardy for payment of the creditor's claim.

The second of these two propositions is more significant and less inevitable than may appear.   Suppose B, a wealthy man, holds net unencumbered assets worth $1,000,000 made up of $950,000 in real property and a $50,000 sole proprietorship interest in a small suburban barber shop.   Suppose, further, that the barber shop needs $20,000 worth of new furnishings and that, for whatever reason, B decides to borrow the money to pay for them. L, the lender, fully understanding that the money is to be used for the barber shop fixtures, and having satisfied himself that the profit potentials of the barber shop are such as to give promise that the loan can be paid off out of the proceeds of the barber shop business, thereupon lends B the $20,000.

In these circumstances, it could be plausibly argued that, when the time for payment comes, L should have no resort to B's assets beyond his property interest in the barber shop.   But the law is to the contrary, and *all* of B's unencumbered assets—his "personal" as well as his "business" assets—will be held equally answerable to pay off L. L's claim is not limited to the assets of the enterprise for the use of which the loan was made. All of B's assets are at jeopardy. B is said to have "unlimited liability".

The term "unlimited liability" is not a particularly apt one; B's liability is in fact limited in two ways—first by the size of the creditor's claim and second by the aggregate unencumbered assets that B has. But no matter. L, in considering whether to make the loan for purposes of the barber shop business, may assume that, unless L and B otherwise agree, whatever unencumbered assets B may have when the loan becomes due (or, indeed, acquires thereafter) will be available to L for payment of his claim (and to other general creditors for payment of their claims).

In substance, the same situation obtains, and the same result follows, if the borrower is a business enterprise conducting its affairs in the form of a partnership having partners P, Q, and R. Even though the loan be exclusively for the business enterprise, the law of partnership treats the loan as though each partner had been an individual borrower of the full amount of the loan. The lender may therefore, on the day of reckoning, look for payment not only to the assets held in common in the business enterprise but also to all unencumbered assets owned by each of the partners.[1] Again, the liability of each of the partners is said to be "unlimited".

In the case of a loan by L to B who has an individual proprietorship interest in an enterprise, or a loan by L to a partnership enterprise, L has an obvious and vital interest in seeing to it that the assets of the individual or of the partners are not dissipated before he is paid off. L will therefore not only investigate the present and likely future asset condition of the individual, and of the partners, before he makes the loan, but he may also seek to obtain a security interest in B's assets and/or seek to limit in some way his borrower's power to put assets beyond L's reach. L can do little or nothing to insure that B's investment portfolio will retain its market value, or that his other holdings will retain their value; but he may have at least a chance, by contract, to prevent B from engaging in certain trans-

---

1. Of course, the lender who gave credit for the uses of the partnership enterprise may well, on maturity date, find himself locked in a struggle with personal creditors of the partners if the sum of the partnership assets and the partners' assets is insufficient to meet both kinds of claims. Out of this situation arises the equitable procedure of "marshalling assets" and the principle that partnership creditors have prior claim to partnership assets, and personal creditors of the partners have prior claim to personal assets—embryonic recognition of the enterprise as an independent entity. See Uniform Partnership Act § 40(h), 6 U.L.A. 469 (1969) (codifying the rule of *Rodgers v. Meranda,* 7 Ohio St. 180 (1857)); see generally Bromberg and Ribstein, Law of Partnership § 3.05(d) (1988).

actions that could have the effect of leaving L high and dry at the critical moment. L would like, for example, to prevent B from transferring all of his assets to his wife or children; and L will be very unhappy if B is left free to borrow more money from another lender or, worse, to pledge or mortgage his assets to another lender as security for another loan. Finally, L might like to try to keep B from living too high on the hog pending payment of the debt; enough yachts, trips around the world, and visits to casinos, and B's assets will have likely shrunk to nothing by the time L pounds on the door to collect his debt.

Of course, what L really hopes is that B will have sufficient cash on hand and available to repay the loan when it comes due. Fixed or capital assets in B's hands, such as farmland or an oil tanker, may well be very valuable but are difficult and expensive for L to take over and convert—"liquidate"—into cash to repay the debt. L will also be much happier if B is engaged in a profitable operation that will lead B's total assets to grow over time. But L will often be even more interested in B's cash flow. Even if an enterprise is continuously unprofitable so that its net worth is steadily declining, it may generate a large and steady cash flow for a long period of time; conversely, a business may be very profitable but generate very little cash. L's intention will be to be paid out of current cash flow long before the unprofitable enterprise finally has to shut down. The prudent lender therefore investigates not only B's assets but *also* his current and projected profitability *and* liquidity.

Nevertheless, L wants to be able to pursue B's pot of general assets in case B does not repay. L's ultimate right to do that will protect L not only if B's business collapses altogether but also if B is able to keep his doors open but unable to repay all of his obligations as they fall due. In the latter case, often known as a "work-out", the creditor with the greatest protection is in a better position to negotiate with the debtor and with the other creditors.

To generalize, L knows that he may have to look to B's assets for payment. From L's perspective, it is important that the assets in that pool be substantial when the loan is made and that, so long as the loan is outstanding, B's uses of the assets be limited in a way that will prevent their being dissipated, leaving L holding an empty bag. A prudent creditor will seek to protect himself by close investigation before the loan is made and by extracting from B some restrictions on B's power to dispose of his assets during the period of the loan. L cannot, and will not try to, protect himself against all the risks to which he subjected himself by making the loan; he accepts as inevitable what may be called the business risks inherent in the situation—the risk that the barber shop will go broke as young men suddenly decide to let their hair grow long, like their ancestors, or the risk that the bottom will fall out of the real estate market as people conclude that it is more pleasant to live in the sea, like their ancestors.

3. The Creditor of the Corporation

Much is usually made of the proposition that the hallmark of the corporate form of business enterprise is "limited liability". The statement is not untrue, but it deserves somewhat closer attention than is usually given to it.

As a matter of history, it is at least worth noting that the feature of limited liability, so much emphasized today, played little or no part in the development of modern corporation law. The law of corporations grew up not out of the law of commerce but as an offshoot from the public law area of municipal government. The device of the corporate charter, and of the implied separate corporate entity, found its appeal as a device for (i) providing a continuity of enterprise and of property ownership that would legally survive the death of individual participants in the enterprise, (ii) providing a semi-political vehicle for the grant of monopolies, such as the fur trade in a particular area, or a toll bridge, and (iii) providing a functional administrative structure that could simultaneously mobilize capital investments from many individual investors while offering a machinery for centralized decision-making. Even when the corporate form had advanced so far as to be embodied in general corporation laws in the middle of the 19th century, limited liability for shareholders was not uniformly provided for in the general corporation laws in this country, and in England the Companies Act did not provide for generalized limited liability for corporate shareholders until 1862.

History aside, the key point is not that the shareholder has been granted some special thing called limited liability. The real point is that in the case of creditor claims against an enterprise in corporate form, *the corporation is the debtor,* not those persons who hold claim to the proprietorship capital in the enterprise. Once that conceptual step is taken, the creditor law of the corporation exactly parallels the law of individual indebtedness and of creditors of individuals. The corporation has no limited liability at all. As in the case of any debtor, the creditors of the corporation have a claim to the assets of the corporation that is prior to the corporation's own claim as "owner". The creditors' claim to the corporate assets is thus automatically prior to the claim of the proprietorship investors—the shareholders. And the creditors' claim extends to *all* the assets of the debtor corporation. If necessary, the entire assets of the corporation must be devoted to payment of creditors of the corporation, even though nothing is left for the corporation or, *a fortiori,* its proprietorship owners.

Furthermore, as in the case of almost all debtors, the creditors of the corporation must, in usual course, find their payment from the pool of assets that belong to the debtor corporation. If the assets of the corporation are insufficient to pay the claims, then, in the absence of some special guaranty, a creditor can no more expect to pursue assets beyond the debtor corporation's assets than a creditor of an individual can expect that payment of a debt owed by that individual can be extracted from some other individual.

Thus, the creditor of a corporation has the same kind of economic interest as the creditor of a human being and is subject to the same kinds of risks as the creditor of the individual. Similarly, the corporate creditor tries to resort to many of the same devices to enhance the likelihood that his corporate debtor will have sufficient funds in hand to pay off the debt when maturity comes. As a part of the bargain negotiated when the corporation incurs the indebtedness, the creditor may, of course, succeed in extracting from a shareholder (or someone else who wants to see the loan go through) a third-party pledge agreement, guaranty, endorsement, or the like that will have the effect of subjecting non-corporate assets to the creditor's claim against the corporation. Such protective arrangements are common when the corporation is closely-held and not well-funded. But in the general conduct of corporate enterprises, the creditor will not be able to negotiate such extra protection. In the usual case, therefore, it will be a matter of major concern to the creditor of the corporation to seek four objectives—precisely as in the case of the lender to an individual debtor.

(1) The creditor will be happier if his corporate debtor has substantial assets in the corporate till at the time he extends credit and thereafter;

(2) The creditor will want to restrict the corporation from incurring debts to other general creditors with whom he might have to share the corporation's limited assets;

(3) The creditor will want the corporate assets to be free and unencumbered of any lien interests of a prior (secured) creditor; and

(4) The creditor will want to preserve a cushion of protective assets, and will want to see to it that no claimants who rank junior to him (usually shareholders, but sometimes subordinated debt holders) make off with assets of the corporation while the creditor's claim is still outstanding and unpaid.

Note again that even if the creditor should happen to be so fortunate as to achieve all four of these protections—which he will seldom be able to exact in full measure—still he has, by making the loan, put his funds at risk of the basic *commercial* vicissitudes of the debtor enterprise. If the market for the enterprise's product disappears, or the market value of the assets it holds drops through the floor, the creditor is apt to be left to whistle for his claim. Absent some special arrangement for recourse to assets lying outside the corporate enterprise, as through a shareholder's personal guaranty or a bank letter of credit, the creditor has no protection against such commercial risks except his own skill in predicting whether an enterprise will or will not make enough return to pay out the loan with interest. In the long pull, there is no security for enterprise creditors (or any other investors) other than the initial capital unspent and profitability of the enterprise. This uncontrollable, inherent commercial risk of the enterprise stands in marked contrast to the creditor's other risks—the risk that the corporate debtor might incur additional debt, or might distribute assets to the junior proprietorship investors, the shareholders. Those managers who control the business affairs of the corporate enterprise cannot determine what will happen to the general market, but they can determine whether indebtedness or distributions occur. Since the occurrence or non-occurrence of these events *are* amenable to managerial decision, they can be proscribed or limited by contract or by general law. And they often are.

To summarize the perspective of the lender to the corporation—he is willing to make the loan on the terms negotiated and assume the commercial risks that are inherent in it. But if he could have things all his way: The pool of corporate assets would be large and growing; there would be no other creditors senior to or who rank equally with him (that is, as the lawyers say, "pari passu"), the only other claimants to the pool would be the shareholders, whose claim is junior to his; the corporation would be forbidden from incurring later indebtedness, and especially secured indebtedness; and no assets of any kind would be permitted to be distributed out of the corporate pool to shareholder investors until the creditor had been paid off in full.

The legal doctrines revolving around the concept of "legal capital" developed as a partial response to, and were mainly attributable to, this perspective of the creditors of corporations. Before the accommodation reached by the legal capital system can be appreciated, however, it is necessary to take a look at the shareholder's perspective of the matter.

B. THE SHAREHOLDER'S PERSPECTIVE

1. Payouts to Shareholders

The ideal world as conceived by the creditor of the corporation is a world that is normally wholly unacceptable to the shareholder. The investor who buys shares of stock in the incorporated enterprise and the investor who lends money to the incorporated enterprise, are, as a matter of economics, engaged in the same kind of activity and are motivated by the same basic objectives. They are both making a capital investment; they both expect or hope to get their investment back in the long run, either by liquidating pay-out or by sale of the security; and they both expect and hope to receive income from their investment in the interim before their capital is returned to them in full.

In the stereotypic model transaction, the investor who chose to take a shareholder's position rather than a creditor's position in a particular transaction simply made a calculated economic judgment that was different from the creditor's. The shareholder estimated that he could make more money by relinquishing to creditor investors a "prior" claim for interest and a fixed principal payment on maturity, and, by opting for uncertain "dividends" and the residual claim to the assets of the enterprise that would remain after all creditors, with their fixed claims, had been paid off.[2]

The shareholder is willing to admit the "priority" of the creditor's interest claim and claim for principal payment on maturity. That does *not* imply, however, that the shareholder is willing to stand by chronologically until such time as the creditors have been paid in full. The shareholder will usually insist, that if, as he hopes, the enterprise makes money (and perhaps even if it does not), the shareholders will receive some return on (or of) their investment from time to time, regardless of the fact that there are

2. This stereotypic model, like the other illustrative models used here, is grossly oversimplified.

In the first place, it groups together as a unitary interest all those characterized as "shareholders". Even as creditors may be arrayed along a spectrum of claim from secured to subordinated, shareholders are often divided among themselves into subclassifications of hierarchical claim by the creation of different classes of stock, each class having a differentiated claim to dividends, liquidation payments, voting rights, etc. In usual parlance these classes are spoken of as either "preferred" or "common", but the usage is misleading, since the various classes (or series) may be almost infinitely varied in their terms and still remain "stock" so long as their claim to liquidation payment falls hierarchically below the lowest ranking creditor's claim in liquidation. As a result, clashes of interest *among* shareholder classes may in some circumstances be as intense as, or even more intense than, the more general-ized clash of interest between share-holders as a whole and creditors as a whole.

Second, the investor's choice as be-tween the debt or equity position will be influenced as well by his tax position, marginal preferences as to growth po-tential versus current income, concern with voting power, estimates about in-flationary or deflationary trends, equi-ty-debt leverage, and many other con-siderations. Moreover, in the hands of sophisticated financial lawyers, the eq-uity-debt difference itself blends into a grey continuum in the cases of converti-ble debt, debt with warrants, income debentures, etc.

Finally there is no necessary correla-tion in any case between the lawyer's characterization of the security and the economic deal that underlies it; for ex-ample, the corporate structure of the Carolina & Clinchfield RR Co. is de-signed so that a dividend of $5 per share, no more and no less, is paid each year on the "common stock."

creditor claims outstanding. Such periodic payments to shareholders are characterized as "dividends"; and, in the usual and
normal case of the healthy incorporated enterprise, it is assumed
that some assets will be regularly distributed out from the corporate treasury to the shareholder investors in dividend form.

Simple as this observation may be, its implications are far-
reaching. If it were the case that all creditors had to be paid off
before *any* payment could be made to shareholder investors, and if
shareholders received nothing until ultimate liquidation of the
enterprise when they would divide the residuum left after payment of all creditors—if, in other words, the terms "prior" and
"before" were chronological as well as hierarchical—the creditor
would not have to worry about assets being drained away into the
hands of junior claimants and he would sleep better at night. But
that arrangement would be wholly unacceptable to shareholders.
Shareholders insist—and ultimately creditors must concede—
that, *during the life* of the creditor's claim, assets may be passed
out to an investing group that hierarchically ranks below the
creditors. The question becomes unavoidable: How much of the
assets in the treasury of the incorporated enterprise may be
distributed to shareholders, when, and under what circumstances?

While "dividends" are the most common form in which distributions are made to shareholders out of corporate assets, the
distributive process is potentially Protean. If it is decided that an
incorporated enterprise should be broken up, or that some of its
assets or separable operations should be sold for cash, extraordinary cash distributions may be made to shareholders; these will be
referred to as liquidating distributions, or distributions in partial
liquidation. Similarly, the decision-makers in a going economic
enterprise may conclude that the company has more cash or other
liquid assets on hand than it needs, that no interesting investment
opportunities are visible, and that the best thing to do is to
distribute the excess assets to the shareholders; such a transaction may be referred to as a partial return of capital. Substantially the same transaction may occur where, for one reason or
another, it seems desirable to those who are making the decisions
to transfer a major nonliquid asset (such as a parcel of land or a
separable business operation) to the shareholders, either by transferring to each shareholder a proportionate undivided interest in
the asset, or by putting the asset into a subsidiary and distributing
the subsidiary's shares to the parent's shareholders. Or those in
control of an incorporated enterprise may decide to "buy in" or
"repurchase" some of the outstanding stock of the corporation—a
transaction that pays assets out of the corporate treasury to
shareholders but brings in to the corporation nothing but pieces of
paper in the hands of the corporation. If, for example, a corpora-

tion has three shareholders, each of whom owns twenty shares of stock, and the corporation offers to "buy in" ten shares from each of them at $1,000 per share and all three accept the offer and the "buy in" is consummated, the consequence will be that each shareholder will continue to own and control one-third of the enterprise, but there is $30,000 less in the corporate treasury to meet the claims of creditors and $30,000 more in the hands of the shareholders. Whether the stock bought in is said in lawyer's talk to be cancelled, or to be retired, or to be held as treasury shares, the result is identical as seen from the creditor's standpoint: $30,000 has been funneled off to the junior claimants, the shareholders, just as though a dividend in that amount had been paid out.

These instances do not exhaust the numbers of ways in which assets can be transferred by corporate managers out of the corporate till into the hands of shareholders. Distributions of corporate assets to a shareholder may be denominated as "salary payments" though in excess of a compensation level that would be reasonable for the services performed for the corporation by the shareholder. Corporate assets can be sold to shareholders for less than their market value. Corporate assets can be loaned to shareholders, or leased to shareholders, on terms that in effect reduce the aggregate resources of the corporate treasury. If the corporation guarantees the debt of a shareholder to a third party, the corporation's credit is put in jeopardy to the benefit of the shareholder. Corporate assets can be pledged or mortgaged to shareholders through arrangements under which, upon nonpayment of the loan by the corporation (at the decision of the board), the assets will be forfeited to the shareholders.[3] These same transactions, with the same consequences, can be carried out through dealings between the shareholders of the corporation and subsidiaries of the corporation. In all these instances, and others, the problem of the creditor of the corporation is the same. Assets have left the corporate pot, have gone beyond his reach, and, worst of all, have been paid out to that group of investors whose claim to the assets of the corporation is junior to his.

Finally, it must be observed, there are two other factors that contribute to the creditor's unease. It is not just that there are many ways by which corporate assets *can* be channeled out of the corporate pot and into the shareholders' pockets. More worrisome is the shareholders' keen desire and incentive to do just that. The

---

3. In addition, of course, one who is a shareholder can legitimately lend money to the corporation and thus become both a creditor and an equity owner. In that case, however, a payment made by the corporation on the loan is not, as an analytic matter, a distribution to shareholders, but a payment to a creditor.

Manning Leg.Capital 3rd Ed. UTB—2

shareholder knows that so long as his money is at stake in the enterprise he will be the last one paid—or will not be paid at all—if the weather gets stormy. His instinct is to limit that risk by arranging for some kind of payout of at least his initial investment as soon as possible.

A closely related consideration is the dynamic known as "leverage". The creditor wants a thick equity cushion under him; the equity investors tend to prefer a thick debt slice in the company's capitalization, up to the capacity of the enterprise to meet the carrying charges of the debt. The shareholder sees an obvious advantage in a funding plan under which he puts in $1 and the lender puts in $2, the lender agreeing to a fixed return of 5¢ for each dollar loaned; if the enterprise earns 10¢ on each of the three dollars invested, the end result is that the creditor's $2 investment yields him 10¢ while the shareholder's $1 investment yields him 20¢. Shareholders greatly relish such leveraged arrangements under which the entrepreneurial harvest, if any, will come to them while the risk of capital loss is largely that of lenders.[4]

The second thought that disturbs the sweet slumber of the creditor is the knowledge that virtually all responsibility and power for the conduct of the enterprise is in the hands of the members of the board of directors, who are elected by and mainly interested in the shareholders, and of corporate officers selected by the board. As the creditor sees it, hungry goats have been set to watch the cabbages.

Out of the conflict between the creditor's desire to keep corporate assets from being distributed to shareholders, and the shareholder's insistence upon receiving asset distributions despite the existence of outstanding creditors' claims, arises the major problem to which the par and stated capital provisions—the legal capital provisions—of state corporation codes are directed.

4. Again the real world proves more complex than the stripped-down model. The desires of particular classes of investors will not always conform to the generalizations. Some creditors may, for example, have a view toward leverage that parallels that of the shareholder. A creditor, though normally fearful that the corporate debtor might create senior debt ranking ahead of him, may see an advantage in the corporation's incurring new senior debt if the new money can be brought in at low cost so that the profits generated by the new capital will be greater than the cost of the new capital, the excess redounding to the advantage and payment of the junior creditor's claim. Moreover, if the enterprise is in sufficiently dire straits, the junior creditor may be happy to see senior debt created, regardless of the terms, where the new money may keep the enterprise going and where the only prospect for the enterprise in the absence of new investment would be bankruptcy.

Finally, some investment securities are hybrids, designed to enable the holder to run with the foxes and hunt with the hounds; an example is the convertible debenture, a debt instrument that can be swapped by the holder for shares of stock.

2. Equitable Contribution Among Shareholders—A Separate Problem

Taken as a class, the shareholders of a corporation have in common a conflicting interest with that of creditors of the corporation. But within the class of those denominated "shareholders" clashes of economic interest also exist.

Even in the simplest case of a corporation having a single class of stock, contention can arise between shareholder S1 and shareholder S2 as to whether each one made a fair and proportionate contribution of assets into the corporate pot in exchange for the share interest he received. Other things being equal, S1 will be very unhappy if he put up two-thirds of the total assets invested by shareholders into the corporate till and received only one-third of the total stock issued, while S2, who invested only one-third of the total equity input, received two-thirds of the stock issued.

It is easy enough to recite in black letter hornbook style: "Shareholders should contribute equitably in proportion to their shareholdings." But this abstract principle is of little utility in dealing with any real situation. What is an equitable amount? What are equitable amounts when S2 buys his shares from the corporation at a different time from S1? What is an equitable amount for S2 to pay if he buys from the corporation an issue of shares of a class, or series, different from that held by S1? And if S1 puts in cash while S2 puts in a computer software program of conjectural value or a promise to provide a service tomorrow? These, and many other related questions, constitute the problem of equitable contribution. Some of them are referred to in a later chapter and a number of illustrations are given in Subpart Two. For the present, it is enough to note the existence of the topic and to observe that one strand in the development of the law of par and stated capital has been an effort by the courts (often only dimly perceived or even unconscious) to develop a working solution to the problem of equitable contribution among shareholders.

C. THE CREDITOR'S AND SHAREHOLDER'S PERSPECTIVES COMBINED

It will now be seen that a corporate financial "model" has begun to appear. That model will be substantially elaborated in later pages. It is well to pause here, however, to emphasize again the point made in passing in two earlier footnotes—that the analytic corporate financial model discussed here is just that. The model does not purport to be fully descriptive of reality—of the actual way in which corporate creditors and shareholders go about their business of making investment decisions and protecting their positions. Reality is much more complex, often involving special factors that are determinative in the particular situation.

Moreover—and this point deserves special underscoring—the whole model we are using here presents a fundamentally skewed picture because of its emphasis upon the creditor's concern about the *ultimate* payment of his claim out of his debtor's assets in liquidation or bankruptcy. Creditors *are* concerned about that of course. And debtors *do* sometimes wind up in liquidation proceedings that set all the claimants against one another in a Donnybrook over who gets what from the insufficient carcass. But such events are not normalcy in the conduct of business. They bear the same relationship to daily business as a train wreck bears to a train trip. It *could* happen; one may do well to carry some travel insurance against it, perhaps even sit in the middle of the car; but if one knows, or seriously suspects, that a train may wreck, he does not usually take extra protective precautions—he stays off the train.

In the usual case, creditors expect to be paid, and are actually paid, on an ongoing basis out of the cash flow of the enterprise. The depression of the 1930's and the repeated wipe-out of gold-plated "fully secured" bond issues of blue chip railroads drove the point home at last; enterprise debt is not ultimately paid out of balance sheet assets but rather out of cash, which usually means operating profits. Security interests, mortgages, liquidation preferences and the like, are disaster remedies—like emergency exits. When an enterprise asks to borrow money, the prospective lender's primary interest will be in the economic prospects of the enterprise—the *dynamics* of the enterprise—the estimated cash flow, the chances of profitability, quality of management, markets for the product, competition, assembly of production components, labor relations, adequacy of financing, technological leads—to name but some. The model outlined here is distorted, for analytic purposes, in its pervasive implication that balance sheet assets are foremost in the creditor's mind, and in the essentially static character of the model.

In defense of the use of the model employed here, one can say two things:

(1) In some degree the creditor *does* look at static assets and consider the possiblity of an ultimate liquidation Armageddon; to that degree the model is substantially accurate.

(2) We have no choice but to develop and understand this model if we are to understand the corporate code provisions on stated capital, for, whatever its deficiencies, it is the model on which the statutes are based.

Accepting the model as given, how should corporation law, statutory or judge-made, regulate the activities of businessmen and lawyers so as to deal with the combination of the creditor's perspective and the shareholder's perspective—namely:

(1) The creditor of the corporation desires that the enterprise have large quantities of assets against which the only other claimants are those who rank junior to him, i.e., the shareholders. Shareholders, by contrast, would like to have as little as possible of their own assets tied up in the enterprise and exposed to the jeopardy of creditors' claims.

(2) The creditor does not ordinarily welcome the creation of additional creditors' claims against the limited assets of the enterprise. The shareholder investor will often (not always) be willing for the incorporated enterprise to incur further debt in order to benefit from leverage, especially when his own equity investment position is small.

(3) The creditor would prefer that the junior investment claimant, the shareholder, receive nothing as a return on his investment for so long a time as the creditor's claim has not been paid. The shareholder, on the other hand, would prefer a concurrent return paid out to him as the enterprise earns profits.

(4) The creditor wants protection against all manner of asset distributions to shareholders—particularly since he sees the board of directors as a creature of the shareholders. The shareholder wants maximum freedom to receive such distributions.

(5) Each shareholder wants assurance that each other shareholder has contributed to the corporate pot a proprietorship investment proportionate to his shareholdings.

The provisions of state corporation codes dealing with legal capital are addressed to resolving, or at least accommodating, these conflicts.

Chapter II

LEGAL CAPITAL—DEVELOPMENT OF THE KEY CONCEPT

This chapter is devoted to tracing the development of the concept of legal capital—the key concept that our corporation codes have evolved to deal with the problems outlined in Chapter I. The ways in which the concept is used by the statutes, and the consequences of that use, are reserved for discussion in later chapters.

The legal capital scheme contained in our modern corporation codes is the direct product of nineteenth century legal history. Legal capital provisions are comprehensible (to the extent they are comprehensible at all) only in the context of that history.

At the same time, one must not demand too much clarity or coherence from the record of the past in this field. During the latter half of the nineteenth century, when industrial capitalism was maturing in the United States and finance capitalism was beginning to emerge, the profession of accounting was in its infancy. Accounting concepts that seem both elemental and indispensable today had not yet been perceived or crystallized; terminology had not yet been settled upon; and, outside a very small group of emerging professionals, double entry bookkeeping had not penetrated the consciousness of the public, the bench, or the bar. Nineteenth century judicial opinions dealing with par values, stock issues, capital, and stock subscriptions, are nearly always analytically incoherent. But repetitive demonstration of the point by case analysis is unseemly; it is to shoot fish in a barrel.

The field of corporate finance was too embryonic to have assumed shape, and courts and advocates of that era were not yet equipped and could not have been equipped with the conceptual tools required to deal with it. In large degree, therefore, it is an error to attempt a precise reconstruction of the way in which the nineteenth century looked at such matters. The truth is that there simply was no coherent view of these matters in the nineteenth century. And while each generation must write its own history of the past, we should not try to attribute to nineteenth century courts an integrated set of analytic theorems that they would have been incapable of understanding, much less inventing.

A. THE STANDARD OF EQUITY INVESTMENT— WHAT AMOUNT OF WHAT ASSETS MUST SHAREHOLDERS PUT INTO THE CORPORATE POT?

1. Minimum Pay-in Requirements

As noted in Chapter I, a corporate creditor will be happiest if the corporation to which he extends credit has a substantial quantity of assets that are free of the claims of other creditors— assets whose only claimants are of the lowest priority rank, the shareholders.

The question of what amount of assets must be paid in to an enterprise by its shareholders before it will be permitted to enter the market place has never been candidly addressed in American corporation law. For a governmental agency to prescribe minimum capital standards for particular enterprises or economic sectors has been considered wholly impractical as well as antithetical to the way in which we go about our economic process. There are exceptions to this statement, and they are significant ones; banks, insurance companies, and corporate trustees offer instances of enterprises where, as we have learned painfully, undercapitalization can be a public menace and in those instances a combination of statutes and regulations compels a minimum pay-in of equity assets. But the only fields of endeavor in which our law seriously undertakes to set minimum standards of capitalization are those we view as industries affected with a special public interest, and which we regulate in a number of other ways as well.

Until very recently state corporation acts genuflected to the desirability of requiring a minimum amount of assets to be paid in to a new enterprise as a prerequisite to achieving corporate status, or at least before commencing business. But these provisions were always *pro forma* only, typically requiring a *de minimis* pay-in on the order of $1,000 or less, and with no provision precluding an immediate return of this amount to the shareholders. In the last few years, however, most state statutes have eliminated even these *pro forma* requirements for initial pay-in by shareholders.[1] In general, therefore, the creditor has received little or no direct protection through legislative or regulatory prescription requiring an incorporated enterprise to have a minimum amount of assets at its inception.[2]

1. See 2 Model Bus. Corp. Act Annot. § 54, ¶ 3.03(7) (2d ed. 1971). See also 1 [Rev.] Model Bus. Corp. Act Annot., § 6.21, Annot. ¶ 2 (3d ed.) (1989 Supp.)

2. Here and there a legal commentator or a judge will be found to say that shareholders may not enjoy the corporate shield of limited liability where the corporation is "grossly undercapital-

2. The Prototypical Model and Par

Nonetheless, the corporate creditor's desire to have a well-funded debtor has played a part in the development of the legal capital scheme contained in our corporation codes. To see the connection, it is necessary to reformulate the statement of the creditor's interest. To do so, it is necessary to run the statement through two transformations and, as a prototypical model, to consider a very simple business situation.

Consider a newly formed corporate enterprise at the stage of its initial financing by the issue of shares; the only assets in the corporate treasury are those which the shareholders have just put in for their stock, and the enterprise has done no business. If, at that time, a prospective lender asks the question, "How much assets does the corporation have free and clear after claims of creditors?" the answer will be the same as the answer to the question, "How much did the shareholders put in?" Similarly, if a loan is then made to the corporation, the question, "How much assets did the corporation have at the time of the loan?" has the same answer as the question, "How much assets have the shareholders put in over *all* time?" On this simplistic model, the statutory stated capital scheme is based. The scheme assumes that the key to protection of the creditor lies in the answer to these two questions which, taken together, become, "How much assets have shareholders put into the corporate treasury for shares since the formation of the corporation?" Whether or not that question is one that really interests a creditor, it is the elemental question to which the statutory legal capital scheme is addressed.

The nineteenth century pattern of corporate financing provided a ready suggestion to judges and statutory draftsmen for a way to gauge the quantity of assets that shareholders had, at some time or another, put into the corporate treasury. According to that pattern of corporate practice, an entrepreneurial organizer, the "promoter," who had conceived of an idea for a new business, would make the rounds of people who had money to invest ("capitalists" all, whether little grey widows or sturdy yeomen), and seek to persuade them to invest in stock of the proposed enterprise. If the idea had appeal, and if the promoter was persuasive, he would succeed in obtaining commitments from them to buy stock. Such commitments, called subscription agree-

ized." And intuitively one wonders particularly about the situation of the tort victim of outrageous corporate negligence: Would it really be possible to build a downtown culture center for bacterial warfare experiments and to immunize the equity investors from liability through formation of a corpora-

tion with an initial capitalization of $1,000? But, the concept of "gross undercapitalization" is too ill-defined a concept to afford creditors any predictable protection from the default of corporate enterprises capitalized on a shoestring, and actual judicial holdings on the point are, at most, scant.

ments, had a number of features about them that were jarring to nineteenth century concepts of contract law and their assimilation into contractual jurisprudence proved very awkward.   But its essence was simple enough: The subscriber agreed that if enough other subscribers were found within the time period specified in the subscription agreement, and if a corporation was formed for the purposes of the enterprise envisioned by the promoter, he, the subscriber, would, on call of the future board of directors of the corporation when organized, put in a set amount of money, or other assets, and would receive a set number of shares of the newly-formed corporation.

Given this practice, it was to be expected, and was perhaps inevitable, that in drawing up the subscription agreements for any single enterprise, a fixed mathematical relationship would be set between the amount of dollars to be invested by a subscriber and the number of shares he would receive: so many dollars to be put in for each share to be issued.   That relationship produced the concept of the "par value" of the stock to be issued.   In the normal situation, no equity investor could expect to obtain a share of stock for less than the par value of it, since presumably all other purchasers were paying that amount.   Similarly, no share subscriber could be persuaded to agree to pay more than the par value for a share since other investors were receiving a similar share by paying in the par value.

If the promoter was successful in obtaining subscription commitments in an amount that appeared sufficient to provide the basic equity financing for the enterprise, he would then see to it that papers were prepared for obtaining a corporate charter under the local state law, often naming the subscribers (or a few of them) as the "incorporators".[3]   The incorporators-subscribers were then brought together for an initial meeting, directors of the corporation were elected, by-laws were adopted, the board of directors made a call upon subscribers to ante up all, or a part of, the dollar amount to which they had committed themselves under the subscription agreements, those dollars were paid into the corporate treasury by the subscribers, and stock certificates for an appropriate number of shares were delivered to the subscribers—now shareholders.   The stock certificates were formal and elaborate, and, in analogy to paper currency or bank notes, bore upon their face as the most dominant feature, the share's "par value" stated as a fixed number of dollars, typically $100.   This number represented the amount the shareholders had agreed to pay for each share according to the subscription agreements.   In time, the par

---

3. Sometimes the charter would have already been obtained, with only the earliest subscribers, or associates of the promoter, named as "incorporators."

value of the stock was required by statute to be stated as a provision in the corporate charter.

The essentially arbitrary character of this number must be understood. If, for example, each of three investors agreed to invest $10,000 in stock of a new company, the number of shares to be issued, N, and the par value, $P, could be anything—could be any numbers that the promoters might set so long as N × $P = $30,000. Further, so far as the shareholders in this case were concerned, it was immaterial what "par" was so long as each one received the same number of shares for his $10,000 investment.

Against this familiar background of practice, however, it was easy for the courts—and legislatures—to take a next assumption, and it early became a matter of common understanding, that the "par value" was what the shareholder *ought* to have paid for his stock. Stock which was issued without a corresponding pay-in of assets valued at an amount equal to par was called "watered stock"—stock issued not against assets but against water. (The term also echoed an ancient sharp practice in another field, the aquatizing of livestock before weighing them in for sale.) The term "bonus shares" was reserved to describe shares that were issued to someone who had paid in nothing for them. Bonus shares and watered stock obviously gave the recipient shareholder a free, or cut-rate, ride, to the disadvantage of the other shareholders who had put more assets per share into the corporate pot.

It must be emphasized that concepts of watered stock and bonus stock, and the doctrines that came to surround them, were and are limited in application to the *issue* of stock, that is, sales by the *corporation* of its own stock. The doctrines do not in any way inhibit the *shareholder's* freedom to sell his stock at any price he can get, or to give it away if he wishes. Similarly, a corporation holding shares of another corporation may, like any other shareholder, dispose of them at any price it wishes or can get.[4]

3. "Par," "Capital" and the Creditor

It will be clear to the reader that the development of the "par" concept just described arose as a response to the problems of assuring equitable contribution among shareholders. But development of the shareholders' par payment obligation served, in a somewhat fortuitous and naive way, to further the corporate creditor's interest in seeing shareholder assets committed to the enterprise. One can spin at least a hypothetical argument as to why this should be and how it came to be.

---

4. See p. 49, infra, as to "resale" of treasury shares.

The argument would go in this wise: If a creditor extends credit immediately after the incorporation of the new enterprise and if he has been informed that the par value of the shares is $P per share and the number of shares that have been issued is N, it is not unreasonable for him to assume that the shareholders have collectively contributed into the corporate treasury an amount of dollars equal to the par value of the shares issued multiplied by the number of shares that were issued, or $PN. In a kind of rough and ready way, assuming that there have been no other transactions, the creditor might infer that the number $PN is an approximation of the total assets of the corporation, and on that basis might conclude that he could safely lend a certain amount of funds to the enterprise.

Did any rational creditor ever in fact act that way or extend credit on such a naive basis? The answer has to be "no." But two things did occur.

First, in lawyers' discourse the number "$PN" came to be called the corporation's "capital". (*number of shares × par value*

Second, if the enterprise ultimately went broke, and the creditor did not get paid, and he found out at that later time that some shareholder had *not* in fact paid into the corporate treasury an amount of assets equal to the par value of the shares he had received, the creditor's lawyer would certainly *argue* in a suit against the shareholder that: (i) Everyone knows that shareholders should pay into the corporate treasury assets equal to the par value of the shares issued to them; (ii) the defendant shareholder did not pay in that amount; (iii) the corporation is insolvent, creditors are unpaid, and the shareholders are not liable for the corporation's debts; (iv) therefore the court should require the defendant shareholder to pay over to this energetic suing creditor, to the extent of his claim against the corporation, the amount by which the defendant shareholder failed to pay into the corporation assets equal to the aggregate par value of the stock he received; and (v) if (iv) does not appeal to the court as the appropriate remedy, then the defendant shareholder should be required to pay into *the corporate treasury* now for the benefit of all corporate creditors, the full amount by which he failed earlier to pay into the corporate treasury assets of a value equal to the aggregate par value of the shares he received.

As will appear later, a number of serious analytic problems flaw this argument, as they also flaw contractual theories and other approaches that litigants and courts tried in efforts to assert shareholder liability to contribute capital to the incorporated enterprise. And all sorts of remedial and procedural questions

arose, as are discussed in Chapter III. But in time, this much
became clear:

> (1) The courts came to recognize that purchasers of
> shares from the corporation have some obligation to
> invest in the corporate enterprise;
>
> (2) It came to be understood (perhaps "assumed" is a
> better word) that the measure of the investment
> liability of such a shareholder was the number of
> shares issued to him times the par value of the
> shares; and
>
> (3) It came to be recognized that at least some creditors
> could in at least some circumstances enforce this
> obligation of the purchasing shareholder in some
> way.

Statements may be occasionally found in the literature to the
effect that the *reason* why shareholders were held to pay in the
par value of their shares is that that was the price exacted by the
law for the corporate advantage of limited liability. While some
such idea may have occurred to some nineteenth century court or
legislative draftsman, the history of the matter will not bear out
this theory. Limited liability arose in American corporation law
as an almost incidental by-product of corporateness, and did so
independently of the development of the par and stated capital
scheme in the statutes.

4. The Going Enterprise: A Change in the Model

On the whole, the concept of par as a standard for shareholder
investment did not work badly in the prototypical model of the
corporate enterprise since par was nearly always the subscription
price and since everyone agreed that a subscriber-shareholder
should as a matter of contract be held to do what he had agreed to
do. The system may not have helped the creditor very much, but
at least it had a plausibility to it and could be made to work. But
as the enterprise moved from the stage of initial financing to that
of an ongoing enterprise, the system lost both plausibility and
workability.

If an incorporated enterprise had navigated in the stream of
commerce for ten years after its initial incorporation, and had
undergone ten years of economic vicissitude, why would a prospective creditor in the company's eleventh year consider it relevant to
his credit decision to enquire whether subscriber-shareholders had,
ten years before, paid fully for their stock? Perhaps the shareholders had invested heavily but the company had lost all its
assets, perhaps they had paid nothing but the company had
prospered. For that corporation, the passage of time destroyed

the prototypical proposition that the assets in the corporation were the assets that had been put there by the subscriber-share-holders. Plausibility for that proposition had departed.

The problem of workability arose a little differently. Suppose that the original promotor, ten long years before, had set the par of the shares at $100 and the original subscriber-shareholders had paid in that amount per share. It is now the eleventh year, and the board of directors decides that it would be desirable—perhaps necessary—for the company to sell additional shares of stock in order to raise money to buy inventory and make it possible for the company to obtain additional lines of credit. Assume finally that the current market value of the stock is $52. What is to be done? The statute says that a purchaser of a newly issued share of stock with a par value of $100 must pay at least $100 for it; under that principle, any person who buys a share of the new stock from the issuing corporation for its fair market value of $52 may someday be held liable for an extra $48, an untempting prospect for a new investor. Something must give way in the face of economic reality. Of course, it turns out to be the principle of par payment.

In *Handley v. Stutz,*[5] a company that was on the verge of bankruptcy managed to bail itself out for a while by attracting new money through the sale of bonds; to make the bonds saleable, the company gave a certain number of free shares of newly-issued stock to each purchaser. Action was brought by a judgment creditor of the corporation to hold the new shareholders liable for payment of the par value of the shares they had received. With no support of any kind in the statute, the Supreme Court came out with the common sense answer fitted to the circumstances before it. It held that if a company is in a state of economic emergency it may, without generating risk of liability to new stock purchasers, issue stock at the best price it can get, whether or not below par.[6]

A legal prophet at the time would have predicted that because courts are by and large sensible, they would gradually expand the *Handley* concept of "economic emergency" to cover any situation where the going market value of the stock was below the par value. But in fact that proposition never fully developed, for other ways were found to deal with the problem.

It will be recalled that though the par value of a share of stock appears upon the stock certificate its roots lie in the corporate charter. In the example given above, would it not have been possible through the normal avenues of shareholder meeting and vote to amend the charter so as to reduce the $100 par of the company's stock to a figure below $52 and thereby make it feasible to issue shares on the current market and to do so compatibly with

5.   139 U.S. 417, 11 S.Ct. 530 (1891).   6.   139 U.S. at 435.

the requirement that the sale price must at least be equal to par? The answer was "Yes," and thus was opened another way by which the problem was—and is—handled under the corporation acts.

By this point, however, it is clear that concern about the economic worries of the creditor has moved to the edges of the universe and is receding at an ever-increasing speed. With par alterable by charter amendment, the switches, levers, and throttles are all in the hands of the very group whose interests conflict squarely with those of the creditors—the shareholders and corporate management.

5. Low Par Stock

In the nineteenth century pattern of corporate financing, it was simply assumed that good companies—respectable companies—solid investments—would have stock with a high par value.[7] It is a tribute, indeed, to the power of mythology and folklore, that still today the buying market, the investment bankers who feed it, corporate managements, and their legal counsel cannot say "penny stock" without a sneer. And it remains true today that most "preferred" stocks continue to carry a high par value.[8] Nonetheless, eventually the practical argument prevailed and the invariable practice of using high par value common stock gradually gave way to the use of low par common stock as it came to be perceived that if the stock has a low par from the beginning, it might never be necessary to amend it or rely upon the vague license of *Handley v. Stutz.*

With this shift made, a typical transaction might see a promoter (i.e., his lawyer) set a par of $10 per share and a *higher* subscription price, say, $50 per share. What difference does it make to any shareholder that the par is lower than the purchase price, so long as each initial equity investor pays in the same amount per share? With this development, however, the prototype corporate model outlined earlier is reduced to splinters.

If the subscription agreement calls for $50 per share for the $10 par stock, but the subscriber-shareholder pays in only $5 per

---

7. Many general corporation statutes in the late nineteenth and early twentieth centuries went even further and either limited corporate debt to a percentage of equity or required shareholder approval for increases in corporate debt. See McDaniel, *Bondholders and Stockholders,* 13 J.Corp.L. 205, 214–17 (1988).

8. A recent historical analogy: As Britain moved to a decimal currency system, a major question was whether to retain the pound as the basic unit or to adopt as the basic unit the shilling, a currency unit of a conveniently commensurate order of magnitude with the Swiss franc, the French franc, the German mark, the Dutch guilder, the Danish crown, etc. The decision, of course, was made in favor of the pound. Despite the awkwardness of its size, it had a more prestigious "par".

share, should a subsequent unpaid corporate creditor be able, at a later time, to force an additional payment of $5—to bring the shareholder's contribution up to the par value of $10—or should he be able to enforce a liability of $45—the balance the shareholder had agreed to pay under the subscription agreement? At this point it becomes conceptually critical whether the creditor is suing on a theory of statutory obligation of the shareholder to pay par, or on a contractual theory of enforcement of the shareholder's obligation to pay the corporation in accordance with the terms of the subscription.

More important for present analytic purposes, the separation of par and purchase price has the effect of opening a chasm between the lawyer's perspective and the economist's concept of the entrepreneur's capital investment. If there are ten subscribers in a newly incorporated enterprise each of whom buys ten shares of stock at a price of $50 per share, the economist, or the businessman, would say that the company's beginning "capital" is $5,000. But the lawyer (and later the accountant) will tell the economist or the businessman that the "capital" is determined by par, and in this case is the number of issued shares, 100, multiplied by the par value of each share, $10, for a total of $1,000; the other $4,000 is something else, about which we will hear more later.

With the evolution of low par stock came the evolution of that strange lawyer's convention and the title of this little book—"legal capital"—the $1,000 in the example just given.

6. No Par Stock

If a corporation may have stock with a par value of 1¢ per share, why not abandon the par concept entirely and permit the issuance of stock with no dollar amount printed on the share certificate? Why not have no par stock?

It was not until 1912 that analysis of the matter had reached a sufficiently wide circle to produce the first statutory authorization of no par stock. The advent of no par stock did not, however, have the effect of eliminating the concept of legal capital. It was, and still is, statutorily necessary to designate some dollar number on the corporate balance sheet as "capital". Since, with no par stock, it is no longer possible to calculate what the "capital" is by multiplying the number of shares issued times the par value, a "capital" number can be arrived at for this purpose only by fiat— by declaration—by stating it. The responsibility for making that statement, and the power to make it, is placed by corporation statutes with the board of directors, and the dollar number declared by them made in the customary form of a board resolution, is the "stated capital" of the corporation. It remains so until such time as it is changed to something else by means set forth in the corporation act. The accountants accept this designation of "stated capital" and it appears on the lower right hand side of the corporate balance sheet.

No par stock is common in the world of contemporary corporate finance. It is interesting, however, that it has not preempted the field, and par stock continues to be in majority use. This is true for several reasons. For a long time, the computational method of the federal stamp tax on stock issuance favored par as against no par stock and some state franchise tax provisions still do. Additionally, for a careful lawyer concerned about such things, it is appealing that a low par value on a share of stock sets the outer limit of liability of a subscriber-shareholder as against a creditor's claim, whereas in the case of no par stock the subscriber's liability would appear inevitably—for want of any other criterion—to be measured by the full amount that he agreed to pay for each share of the stock.[9] The use of low par values, and the ease of shareholder amendment to reduce par in situations where the par proved not to have been low enough, combine to make par stock a usable tool in the hands of the experienced corporate practitioner—and the market is used to it.

7. Legal Capital

The discussion so far dealing with pay-in requirements for shareholders has yielded the rudiments of the concept of "legal capital" or "stated capital", as it is more often called today. For further refinement of the concept, we turn to the other side of the coin, corporate pay-outs to shareholders.

B. DISTRIBUTING CORPORATE ASSETS TO THE SHAREHOLDERS

1. *Wood v. Dummer*—The Classic Case

What does the law do to prevent shareholders of a distressed company from pulling assets out of the corporate treasury just when the creditor needs them? The problem is not hypothetical. Indeed, from an historical point of view, the entire range of subjects to which this book is addressed may be seen to emerge

---

9. Interestingly, the 1967 Delaware corporation law obliterated this long-standing distinction between par and no par stock, so that the subscriber to par stock is now also liable for the subscription price rather than the par. See Del. Gen.Corp.Law § 162(a). See also, e.g., Md.Gen.Corp.Law § 2–206(c), (d). In a further decomposition of classic concepts, Maryland provides that stock may be issued as full paid for a price *less* than its par value. See id. § 2–203(e).

from a single 1824 opinion of Justice Story, *Wood v. Dummer*.[10] The case could not be more elegant in its purity. The corporation was a bank that went broke. Just before the bank went under, the board of directors distributed most of its bank's liquid assets to the shareholders. Certain of the creditors of the bank sued some of the shareholders, claiming that in the circumstances the distribution of assets was illegal and that the shareholders should be made to pay the claims of the creditors. In an opinion that is simple, clear and wholly adequate for the particular problem with which he was confronted, Justice Story ordered the defendant shareholders to pay to the plaintiff creditors a proportionate share of the debt owed by the bank to the plaintiffs.[11]   (At this point, the

10.   30 F.Cas. 435 (no. 17,944) (C.C.D. Me.1824).

11.   Bill in equity brought by the plaintiffs . . ., as holders of the bank notes of the . . . Bank, against the defendants, as stockholders . . . for payment of the same notes upon the ground of the asserted fraudulent division of the capital stock of the bank by the stockholders.

· · ·

The case is full of difficulties. The bill is drawn in a very loose and inartificial manner. It proceeds principally upon the grounds of a gross over issue of bank notes, and other violations of the charter, and of a fraudulent dividend by the stockholders with a knowledge of their insolvency; grounds, which are denied by the answers, and are not in the slightest degree established in the proofs. It does not directly proceed upon the ground, that the defendants hold a trust fund applicable to the payment of the debts of the corporation; but leaves this to be picked up in fragments by a minute analysis of the bill.

· · ·

The next consideration is, whether the bill makes out a case, which upon the facts proved or admitted, entitles the plaintiffs to relief. I have already adverted to the loose structure of the bill. It primarily charges the case, as a case of fraud: that is now abandoned. If it can stand at all, it must be simply on the fact, that the defendants have the funds in their possession. That alone could not entitle the parties to relief, without allegations of insolvency on the part of the corporation or of the non-existence of other funds. Now the bill does not allege, that the corporation is insolvent, nor that it is dissolved, nor

that there is no other corporate property, out of which the debts can be paid. These are extraordinary omissions; and if there had been a demurrer to the bill, it would be difficult for the court to have strained hard enough to support it. But these defects are in some degree helped by the answers, which admit the insolvency of the corporation, and show, that in fact no sufficient funds for payment of its debts are in existence, independent of the capital stock. Then again the bill (notwithstanding the intimations thrown out by the court on a former hearing of the cause) does not charge, that the capital stock is a trust fund, appropriated by law and the charter to the payment of the debts, and that the surplus only, after such payment, belongs to the stockholders. Such an allegation was most fit to have been made upon the grounds, on which ultimately the plaintiffs concluded to rest their case at the hearing. The court is therefore compelled to thread it out by inference and intendment and exposition of the charter, as made part of the pleadings. Then again the bill charges the new Hallowell and Augusta Bank to be possessed of large funds of the old bank, which ought to be applied to the payment of the debts of the latter; and without attempting to bring the new bank to a hearing, the bill has, by the plaintiffs, been dismissed as against the new bank, leaving all the inferences, deducible from the charge in the bill, in full force against the plaintiffs. This ought to have been cured by an amendment of the bill.

I advert to these defects, not in the spirit of censure, (for I am well aware, that an apology is found in the fact, that chancery proceedings have, hitherto, but in a slight degree engaged the

reader will, it is hoped, pause to read the passages set forth in the margin below from the learned justice's opinion in the *Wood* case and deem its inclusion a favor to the reader and not a vexatious digression. Justice Story sat as the trial judge on the *Wood* case while riding circuit in Maine; from his paragraphs below, much can be gleaned about jurisprudence in action, about lawyering, about the schooling of the bar of that day and about Justice Story, as an intellect, as a scholar and as a person.)

The eminent jurist's innovative legal theory underlying his decision—the so-called "trust fund" theory—and its subsequent fate are discussed in later pages.[12] But a point of Justice Story's terminology in his opinion in *Wood v. Dummer* invites special attention. Throughout the opinion, the Justice refers to "the capital stock" of the corporation; it is evident from the context that in his usage "capital stock" means the *assets* that had been put into the company by the stockholders, the "capital stock" that in the Justice's view should not be withdrawn and returned to the proprietary investors until all creditors of the bank had been paid. The word "stock" in this phrase rings oddly to the modern ear. But Justice Story's use is the original etymological Old English meaning of "stock"—the root or trunk of something growing, or a basic central supply. This meaning of "stock" continues today in many terms, such as "soup stock", "stockroom", "stock in trade", "gunstock", "root and stock", "good stock", "stocky" and many others.[13]

Our concept of "corporate stock" has moved so far away from its original meaning that we are startled to hear Justice Story use

attention of the bar in this district), but in a spirit of regret, because they have been most embarrassing to the court in every step of its progress, and distressed it by creating a perpetual struggle between the desire to do justice to the parties after so prolonged and expensive a controversy, and the difficulty of overcoming technical principles.

The exception as to parties ranges itself under this head. There is no allegation in the bill, that the old corporation is defunct, so as to dispense with its being made a party. The answers do not deny, that it yet has a legal existence, and therefore afford no help to cure the defect. Now, if in existence, nothing can be more clear, than that it ought to have been made a party to the bill. It is the original debtor; its funds are to be applied in payment of debts, and it would be wrong to touch those funds without the most plenary proofs, that the debts were due, and the corporation had no defence. Id. at 435–6.

One wonders how the lawyers for both parties explained these comments of the judge to their respective clients. Perhaps their best course was to be sure the clients never saw a copy of the opinion.

Other aspects of this early bank case are interesting, foreshadowing the bank regulations of a later era. Not only did the directors pay out most of the current assets to the shareholders, thus precipitating insolvency, but it also appeared that at least some of the share subscription money had never been paid in by the shareholders and that the bank had used much of the money it had borrowed (from plaintiffs and others) through its bank notes to lend to the bank's own directors—who were at the time of the lawsuit also bankrupt.

12. See infra pp. 50–51.

13. See Introduction, supra, p. 3.

"stock" as a synonym for the assets put in by the shareholders, and to hear him describe the events in *Wood v. Dummer* as an illegal return of the "stock" to the shareholders. But the usage was standard at the time. It appears, for example, in the 1784 newspaper announcement that led to the establishment of The Bank of New York:

> It appearing to be the disposition of the Gentlemen in this City, to establish a BANK on liberal principles, *the stock to consist of specie only;* they are therefore hereby invited to meet Tomorrow Evening at six o'clock, at the Merchant's Coffee House, where a plan will be submitted to their consideration.
>
> fm: New York Packet,
> February 23, 1784

(Emphasis added.)

As perceived by our most learned of judges in 1824, the terms "capital" and "stock" pointed to the top left-hand side of the balance sheet, close to the modern businessman's concept of current assets. But, as will appear subsequently, in the eyes of the law, both "capital" and "stock" were defined to jump over to the right-hand side of the balance sheet, and slide down to the bottom.

Whatever the ultimate validity of Justice Story's theory in *Wood v. Dummer,* his decision on the facts in the case was unimpeachable. But it was certain to lead to a series of next questions that were much less susceptible to simple, or even sensible, answers. In *Wood v. Dummer,* the corporation was insolvent. It was easy to say that in such a case no assets should have been returned to the shareholders. But the *Wood* opinion gave only a general suggestion as to what limits there might be on distributions to shareholders if the bank had been a healthy ongoing enterprise.

2. The Key Proposition—"Legal Capital" as a Measuring Rod

As pointed out in Chapter I, there would be little or no problem about distributions to shareholders if corporate enterprises were periodically and routinely liquidated, creditors paid off, and only then the residuum of "velvet" returned to the equity investors. The problem of limiting distributions to shareholders arises fundamentally out of the economic pressure to make some distributions to shareholders while some creditors' claims remain outstanding and unpaid. That condition arises from the reality of the ongoing enterprise operating over time. The company in *Wood v. Dummer* was not, however, such an ongoing enterprise. The situation was static—the pathological case of an incorporated insolvent enterprise at one point in time—the moment of dismemberment by its creditors. Similarly, the prototypical model transaction on which the nineteenth century conception of par value was predicated was also a static instant-of-time concept—the instant when the equity money was first put in and the stock certificates first issued.

Nonetheless, however static these models, they were the ones from which the courts and legislatures drew as they sought to develop a standard by which to judge the legal propriety or impropriety of distributions of assets to shareholders by an ongoing enterprise. The courts and the statutes combined the principle of *Wood v. Dummer* and the par value concept to produce an answer. Two basic propositions slowly emerged:

1. The measuring rod for judging the propriety or impropriety of distributions to equity holders is the corporation's "capital"; and

2. "Capital" refers not to assets but to that abstract number that is obtained by multiplying the number of shares of stock outstanding by the par value assigned to each share. In due time, the emergence of low par and no par stock expanded this second proposition so that "capital" came to mean "stated capital", or "legal capital".

3. The Classic Example: High Par

A general idea of how these propositions work can be demonstrated by simplified balance sheets of a hypothetical corporation with high par stock at three stages in its corporate life—immediately following its organization and funding; at the end of its first year of operations; and at the end of its second year of operations.

The general idea of the legal capital scheme is that no distribution may be made to shareholders unless, after the distribution, the corporation has not only enough assets to pay its creditors but also an additional specified amount. This amount is called "stated capital". Anything over the sum of stated capital and liabilities is known as "surplus", that is, an amount greater than the sum of (a) the amount needed to pay creditors and (b) the "stated capital". If the accounting entries representing the enterprise's assets do not total to a figure equal to the indebtedness of the enterprise plus the "capital", the capital is said to be "impaired" and the stock is said to be "under water". In the case of a corporation in a condition of "capital impairment", if the figures on the assets side of its balance sheet actually reflected their selloff value, and if all the assets were sold off for cash, and if all the creditors were paid off, the money that would be left over for the equity investors, the shareholders, would be less than the "capital" they put into the enterprise in the first place. Where that is the condition, the statutory scheme forbids the incorporated ongoing enterprise to distribute assets to shareholders by dividend or otherwise.[14]

Assume that the shareholders of a new enterprise, Laminated Thumbscrew, Inc., pay in $50,000 in cash and take back 500 shares of $100 par common stock. The company's assets are $50,000 in cash; the corresponding entry on the right hand side of its balance sheet is the company's "legal capital", or "stated capital", the number of outstanding shares times the par value, $50,000. The balance sheet would read:

Balance Sheet of Laminated Thumbscrew, Inc.,
Immediately Following Organization and Funding

ASSETS		LIABILITIES	
Cash	$50,000		–0–
		SHAREHOLDERS' EQUITY	
		Capital: $100 par	
		common, 500 sh.	$50,000
		Surplus	–0–
	$50,000		$50,000

In the circumstances of this balance sheet, there is no "surplus" and a distribution of any assets to shareholders would be "illegal." [15]

Now consider the same company's balance sheet at the end of a year of active business operations and a variety of transactions.

Balance Sheet of Laminated Thumbscrew, Inc.
Year End After One Year of Operations

ASSETS		LIABILITIES	
Cash	$20,000	Bank loan	$10,000
Accounts receivable	6,000	Accounts payable	2,000
		Liabilities	$12,000
Inventory	10,000	SHAREHOLDERS' EQUITY	
Land	5,000	Capital: $100 par	
		common, 500 sh.	50,000
Patents	1,001	Surplus (Deficit)	(19,999)
		Shareholders'	
		equity	$30,001
	$42,001		$42,001

14. This drastically oversimplified introductory description assumes a so-called "balance sheet surplus test" statute. Other statutory variations are reviewed in Chapter IV and at length in the series of transactions in Subpart Two.

15. Deferred to Chapter III are all questions of who might be held liable, how, to whom, and for how much where an "illegal" distribution is made to shareholders.

This balance sheet shows that during its first year the corporation has incurred debt, that the accounting figures reflecting its assets have gone down and the enterprise suffered a loss during the year. The balance sheet in this condition shows—to use a common anomalous term—a "negative surplus" and the stock is under water. It will be observed that the corporation has a major net worth ($30,001), has far more than enough assets to pay off the $12,000 owed to its creditors and, indeed, is in a position to pay them all off at once in cash. Nonetheless, the "stock is under water" and distribution by the ongoing enterprise of any assets to shareholders would be illegal because there is no surplus above the legal capital figure of $50,000, the bench mark of legality of distribution.[16]

Suppose now the following balance sheet at the end of the *Year 2* company's second year of operations.

Balance Sheet of Laminated Thumbscrew, Inc., Year End After Two Years of Operations

ASSETS		LIABILITIES	
Cash	$16,000	Accounts payable	$ 3,000
Accounts receivable	8,000	Liabilities	$ 3,000
Securities	54,000	SHAREHOLDERS' EQUITY	
Inventory	15,000		
		Capital: $100 par	
Land	5,000	common, 500 sh.	50,000
Patents	1,001		
		Surplus	46,001
		Shareholders'	
	$99,001	equity	$96,001
			$99,001

As a result of the second year's operations, according to this accounting record, the company has acquired additional assets (most likely as a result of profitable operations during the year), has paid off the bank debt, overcome the deficit it had at the end of the preceding year, and generated a balance sheet surplus of

---

16. While we speak of the inhibition as lying within the balance sheet, even the reader least familiar with accounting will be aware that the directors are not free to solve the problem by simply running up the numbers representing assets, or running down the figures representing debt. Accounting entries are made in accordance with so-called "generally accepted accounting principles" considered respectable and proper by the accounting profession and, in some respects, public agencies. These "principles" are often vague or conflicting or ambiguous, and the institutional sources of their legitimation are not yet fully identified. But the "principles" are sufficiently crystallized, sufficiently accepted as norms of behavior, and sufficiently recognized as a basis for fraud liability, that the accountant is not free to accept just any numbers the directors may wish. Application of the legal capital scheme inevitably entails a host of accounting problems, some of which are discussed later and especially in Subpart Two.

$46,001 above its "capital" and debt. Under the general statutory scheme of many corporation codes, the company may now legally distribute to shareholders assets having a "book value" of $46,001 or less. Thus if the company should distribute all its cash ($16,000) to its shareholders, there would still be a surplus of $30,001, and the distribution would be in conformity with the statutory scheme. If the company sought to distribute to share-holders all its securities, however, the accounting effect would be to remove a $54,000 asset, wiping out the surplus, and generating a capital deficit of $7,999; distribution of all the securities would thus "impair" the capital, drive the stock under water again, and violate the typical legal capital statutory scheme.

4. Legal Capital as a Bench Mark—Some General Observations

Even at this preliminary stage of introduction to the legal capital scheme in its balance sheet version, several of its basic features are immediately visible.

1. As an analytical matter, the scheme is utterly dependent upon the way in which the assets and liabilities of the enterprise appear on the books of the company. Accounting decisions on write-ups and write-downs, on depreciation, on amortization, on cost or market valuation, and the like, will determine the total figure assigned to the asset side of the balance sheet, and in consequence the bottom-line entry on the right hand side and therefore the legality of the shareholder distribution. Equally, the answers provided by the balance sheet are wholly dependent upon the accounting conventions governing the recognition of liabilities. All accounting conventions are exactly that: every accounting-literate person will agree that economic verity and the accountant's depiction are often unrecognizably dissimilar. Inherently, the efficiency of the legal capital system can rise no higher than the level of verity that can be achieved through "generally accepted accounting principles" and the consistency with which they are followed.

2. One result of the perspective adopted by the legal capital scheme is that lawyers and judges often speak of making a distribution "out of surplus", or of "paying out the surplus" to shareholders. There is no special harm in this manner of speaking so long as the speaker and all their listeners are fully con-scious that the statement is hash. "Surplus" and "deficit" are concepts invented by lawyers and accountants. They refer to an arithmetic balancing entry on a balance sheet, to the number that is the resultant of all the other numbers on the balance sheet and that is dictated by the basic mandate of the double entry book-keeping convention—that the left side and the right side must at

all times balance. Distributions are never, and can never be, paid "out of surplus", they are paid out of assets; surplus cannot be distributed—assets are distributed. No one ever received a package of surplus for Christmas. A distribution of assets will produce accounting entries that reduce assets and also reduce something on the right hand side of the balance sheet—often surplus—but that is quite another statement.

The enterprise that wishes to make a distribution to its shareholders must use assets to do it. It will usually find that only a small fraction of its total assets are in a form suitable for the purpose. Dividends are typically paid in cash. Occasionally, distributions are made in kind, as by parceling out security holdings or, to recall a famous World War II instance, through the distribution of warehouse receipts for whiskey.[17] In special circumstances, a distribution may sometimes be made by distributing fractional undivided interests in a major asset, such as an oil well working agreement.

But, to take the example of Laminated Thumbscrew, the directors would find it difficult as a practical matter to distribute the patents, the land, the inventory or the accounts receivable; only in unusual circumstances would it wish to distribute the securities; and it cannot distribute all the company's cash since it needs cash for running its operations. The practical choices that will face the Laminated Thumbscrew board of directors are, therefore, to make no distribution, or to make a small cash distribution, or to sell off some of the securities to generate cash for distribution, or to borrow cash for the purpose of distributing it to shareholders (which of late has been resorted to as a device to reduce the company's attractiveness to takeover predators).

Except for an enterprise that is unusually cash heavy, or an enterprise that is in liquidation, the form and character of the assets, the need of the enterprise for operating cash, and the restrictions of outstanding debt covenants against payments to shareholders will be much more of an inhibition on shareholder distributions (assuming that the management *wants* to make such distributions) [18] than the arithmetic statement on the right hand side of the balance sheet called "surplus".

17. See *In the Matter of Ira Haupt & Co.*, 23 S.E.C. 589 (1946).

18. Retained earnings are today the largest source of new capital investment for American business enterprise. The fraction of after-tax profits paid out as dividends (commonly called the "payout ratio") tends to be held to about one-third; the other two-thirds being committed by management to growth and research. Institutional Investor, Study Report of the Securities and Exchange Commission, Vol. 1, Ch. III at pp. 72, 80 (Table III–5) (1971); Standard & Poor's Trade and Securities Statistics, Security Price Index Record at p. 132 (1976).

3.   It is obvious that "legal capital", or "capital" as used by the corporation statutes, has little or no relationship to the word "capital" as the economist, or even the businessman, knows it. Nor is it the block of assets that Justice Story had in mind.

The following statements may now be made about "legal capital".

a.   Legal capital is a number expressed in dollars.

b.   That number is initially the product of par value—itself an arbitrary dollar amount printed on the stock certificate and recited in the certificate of incorporation—multiplied by the number of shares "outstanding".[19]

c.   Legal capital is a number that appears on the *right-hand,* or claimant's, side of the balance sheet, *not* on the left-hand asset side.   "Legal capital" is *not* an asset, a fund, or a collection of assets.   And it does not refer to an asset, a fund, or a collection of assets.   (The same is true of "surplus.")

d.   Legal capital is a number that implies that a valuation of at least that amount was placed upon some indeterminate assets that were transferred to the corporation at some indeterminate past time in exchange for shares then issued.   Legal capital can at best be read to convey a message by implication—a message about a historical event.

Legal capital is entirely a legal invention, highly particularized in its meaning, historical in reference, *and not relatable in any way to the ongoing economic condition of the enterprise.*   For most purposes, it is best thought of simply as a dollar number—a number having certain consequences and derived by specified statutory procedures, but just a number.

4.   The law makes use of the concept of "legal capital" in two ways:

a.   It is the maximum number of dollars up to which someone might, in certain circumstances, be able sometime to hold some shareholders liable if the implied statement in 3(d) above could be proved to be false.

b.   It is a datum line, or water table, or bench mark, or nock on a measuring stick laid alongside the total number on the asset side of the balance sheet, on the basis of which lawyers will—or will not—sign an opinion that a proposed distribution of corporate assets to shareholders is valid

19.   Legal capital where no par stock is involved is discussed later, as are situations in which the stated capital may be higher than the product of par times shares outstanding.

and legal, and generates no liabilities either for the board of directors that declares it or the shareholders who receive it.

And here is the real bite. In the world of corporate finance, the closure of any significant transaction is utterly dependent upon written opinions of legal counsel that are delivered at the closing, stating that the transaction is valid and legally enforceable. Whenever a corporate financial transaction requires the lawyers to inquire into a company's legal capital position, the impact of the statutory schemes of legal capital is enormously magnified by the Go/No-go function performed by opinions of counsel. The lawyers, in turn, are compelled to develop an understanding of the statutory scheme and of its application. From that state of affairs, "legal capital" draws its perverse vitality, and this small book draws its functional relevance.

5. The Classic Example Modified: Low Par

As described earlier, in the typical corporation financing of the nineteenth century, the stock had a high par value, such as $100, and the subscribers did not agree to pay in more per share than the par value printed on the certificate. As promoters and investors became more sophisticated, however, low par stock came into use with the end in view of lowering the liability exposure of shareholder investors and of simplifying later issuance. If Laminated Thumbscrew was to receive $50,000, and was to issue 500 shares, as in the earlier examples, but the stock was to have a par value of $10 rather than $100, how then would its legal capital structure operate and with what consequences?

Balance Sheet of Laminated Thumbscrew, Inc.
Immediately Following Organization and Funding

ASSETS		LIABILITIES	
Cash	$50,000		$ –0–
		SHAREHOLDERS' EQUITY	
		Capital: $10 par	
		common, 500 sh.	5,000
		Capital surplus	45,000
	$50,000		$50,000

Since on this balance sheet the "capital" is only $5,000, there is, in some sense of the term, a "surplus" of $45,000. If the only limitation on distributions to shareholders is the aggregate of debt plus legal capital, it is apparent that this company could lawfully distribute to its shareholders up to $45,000 of the cash that has just been put into the enterprise treasury. If, for some reason it is thought desirable that the statutory scheme prohibit such a distribution, the statute can do so only by going beyond the concept of capital as a restriction and by differentiating between one group of surpluses that may be properly charged when shareholder distributions are made and another group of surpluses that may not. The more modern accountant would characterize the particular surplus here as "paid-in surplus" or "contributions in excess of capital" or "amount paid-in in excess of par"; older terminology, and most statutory provisions on legal capital, would call it "capital surplus". The status of such paid-in surplus, or capital surplus, under various alternative statutory schemes is discussed later.

The possible significance and impact of the use of low par stock and the creation of paid-in surplus may be seen by returning again to the Laminated Thumbscrew balance sheet at the end of its first year of operations, but with $10 par rather than the $100 par stock assumed earlier. Making that one change, the balance sheet at the end of the first year would look like this:

Balance Sheet of Laminated Thumbscrew, Inc.,
Year End After One Year of Operations

ASSETS		LIABILITIES	
Cash	$20,000	Bank loan	$10,000
Accounts receivable	6,000	Accounts payable	2,000
		Liabilities	$12,000
Inventory	10,000	SHAREHOLDERS' EQUITY	
Land	5,000		
		Capital: $10 par	
Patents	1,001	common, 500 sh.	5,000
		Capital surplus	25,001
		Shareholders'	
	$42,001	equity	$30,001
			$42,001

The difference in the par, the capital accounting and the statement of the legal capital has changed a $19,999 negative surplus to a $25,001 surplus. If a capital surplus account is legally chargeable for equity distributions under the corporation law of the corporation's state of incorporation,[20] Laminated Thumbscrew, which with $100 par could pay no dividends, may, with $10 par, pay up to $25,001.

6. The Classic Example Further Modified: No Par Stock

Statutory provisions authorizing the use of no par stock, and a corresponding sophistication of the money market making no par

---

20. All matters of legal capital, shareholders' distributions and the like (including the liability, if any, of directors for assenting to an unlawful distribution) are governed by the law of the corporation's state of incorporation.

stock acceptable, pulled one of the pintles out of the statutory scheme for controlling corporate capital and equity distributions. If "capital" was supposed to be the par value of the shares multiplied by the number of shares outstanding, what was capital to be if there was no par to multiply by? The only available answer was to say that the "capital" was whatever the board of directors "stated" it to be. The removal of the "par" printed on the stock certificate brought to visibility the arbitrary character of the process by which the number called "capital" was developed.

No other changes in the operation of the statutory machinery were required by the advent of no par stock, and no analytic problems were solved by it. If the capital account of Laminated Thumbscrew was to be made up of 500 shares of no par stock, the board of directors at the time of the issue would simply assert by resolution that $X of the $50,000 entry on the right hand side of the balance sheet should be allocated as "capital" and $50,000 minus $X as capital surplus. From there on, the matter would be handled as in the case of par stock.

7.   Changes in Capital Structure of the Ongoing Corporation

The simplified models examined so far have assumed that Laminated Thumbscrew has a static capital structure that was set once and for all at the time the company was organized and funded. In fact, of course, the capital structure of a corporation is altered from time to time to conform to the evolving needs of the enterprise in response to the business conditions in which it finds itself. Additional stock may be issued; stock may be bought in by purchases paid for with funds in the corporate treasury, after which it may be cancelled, or retired to the status of authorized but unissued stock, or, as is said, "held in the treasury"; so-called stock dividends may be paid out, or the stock outstanding may be split; reverse splits are not unknown through which, for example, each two outstanding shares are converted into one; stock options may be granted and subsequently exercised; new stock subscription agreements may come into being; stock or debt instruments with convertible privileges or exchange rights may be turned into newly-issued shares, or in some circumstances in some states, even into debt instruments; new classes of stock may be created; by amendment of the certificate of incorporation, the par value of one or more classes of stock may be altered; the board of directors may wish in a particular circumstance to increase the stated capital or reduce it without altering the par of the outstanding class; or a merger may eliminate, or radically alter, any existing capital structure.

Every one of these transactions, and others, can have the effect of altering the stated capital figure on the company's balance sheet. The effects of these changes, and the corporate procedures required to bring them about, are considered in more detail later, especially in Subpart Two. For the present it is enough to note three points. First, changes in the capital structure of a company are commonplace and may be frequent. Second, the procedures required for particular changes are usually specified in detail in the applicable corporation code. Third, almost any change affecting the number of shares "outstanding", or altering their particular characteristics of par, will require an adjustment in the stated capital account and will, under the typical legal capital statute, have direct repercussions upon the legality of distributions to its shareholders.

C. LEGAL CAPITAL AS A CONCEPT: CONCLUSION

The purpose of this chapter has been to develop a general understanding of the concepts of par value and legal capital. With the general concepts in hand, the next two chapters consider the way in which these concepts are used by the law to regulate shareholder investment and corporate pay-outs to shareholders.

Chapter III

REGULATING THE SHAREHOLDER'S CONTRIBUTION

It is generally agreed that shareholders have an obligation to pay for their shares, and everyone knows that bonus shares, discount stock and watered stock are Bad Things frowned upon by the law. But the corporation statutes and the courts have had great difficulty in translating that general notion into practical terms. There are few cases and most of them are old. The statutes are not well worked out. In this untidy field, many more questions are open than are resolved, not only as to procedural pragmatics but as to basic theory as well.

A. THE SHAREHOLDER'S PAY-IN OBLIGATION

1. How Much Assets?

As earlier observed, state corporation laws make no effort to require that an incorporated enterprise be funded adequately for the business operations contemplated. Until recently the corporation statutes typically gave a general mandate to the effect that a corporation may not commence business until a minimum amount of assets have been paid in; but the minimum was always trivial ($500 or $1,000) and it was seldom clear who would be liable to whom for what if the assets were not in fact be paid in. Today, even this token requirement has been abandoned in most states. As a practical matter, therefore, the shareholder's only general legal obligation to contribute to the corporate pot is that he pay in assets in an amount equal in value to the par value of each share issued to him. Where no par stock is involved, his obligation is to pay in assets in an amount equal to the "stated capital" attributed on the balance sheet of the corporation by the board of directors in respect of each share of the newly-issued stock.

Let it be emphasized that the topic at hand is the shareholder's obligation imposed by general corporation law; a shareholder may, of course, incur additional enforceable obligations to pay in assets to a corporation through stock subscription or other contract.

See Second Part, infra, for recent developments.

2. What Kinds of Assets?

Apart from the question of amount, what *kind* of asset payment will be considered effective to discharge the shareholder's obligation to pay in to the corporate treasury? What kinds of assets will qualify for the purpose?

Cash has never posed a problem. Real and chattel property may also obviously be used by the shareholder to discharge the payment obligation imposed by the law. If the shareholder has already performed services for the benefit of the corporation prior to the issuance of the stock, those services, too, are accepted by the law as a medium of payment. Similarly, payment for stock in forms of property that involve an element of future performance by a third party has also caused the courts no problem. Thus, for example, the shareholder may pay for his shares by transferring to the corporation a General Motors bond.

But where the purchasing shareholder himself undertakes a future obligation, the courts and traditional statutes have balked.

a. *Future Services*

To a businessman or an economist, a contract for future performance by a talented athlete, famous entertainer or high-powered executive is of immense value and commands an enormous price in the marketplace. Courts and statutes, however, have traditionally taken the view that an agreement to perform services in the future is not acceptable as a medium of payment to discharge the shareholder's obligation to pay for his shares; stock issued in exchange for such an agreement for future services is watered stock.[1]

b. *Promissory Note*

Similarly, the economist or businessman will readily attach economic value to a promissory note signed by John D. Rockefeller. But the courts have said that if X Corporation issues stock to Rockefeller for his note, the note will not qualify as "property" for purposes of meeting the shareholder's pay-in obligation. The note, delivered to the issuer by Rockefeller, is seen not as payment but only as a promise to pay. By the same token, General Motors cannot pay for X Corporation shares with a General Motors bond. In Rockefeller's hands, of course, a General Motors bond would be "property", and he could pay for the newly-issued X Corporation stock with it; and in the hands of General Motors, Rockefeller's

---

1. This has been overwhelmingly the prevailing American view, although an occasional court has taken the contrary position. E.g., *Petrishen v. Westmoreland Finance Corp.*, 394 Pa. 552, 147 A.2d 392 (1959).

note is "property" with which GM could pay for its X Corporation stock.

From an economist's point of view, the value of most goods is made up precisely of a present market valuation of a future return—the patent license, the lease, the computer software royalties agreement, the coal production contract, the bond, and the contract for future services being fundamentally all alike in this respect. But in the strange land of legal capital, the law has, for reasons none too evident, sought to distinguish the sheep from the sheep.[2]

c. Future Earnings

Particularly foggy has been the use of capitalized future earnings of an enterprise as a basis for meeting the shareholder's obligation to pay for his stock. Suppose a board of directors wishes to issue stock to acquire a going enterprise which has substantially no physical assets but has large annual earnings. Setting aside the question of the rate that should be used to capitalize the earnings in arriving at a valuation, may the capitalized earnings be considered at all as a medium for effective discharge of the shareholder's obligation to pay for the newly-issued shares?[3]

In the frequently cited New Jersey case of *See v. Heppenheimer*,[4] decided in 1905, creditors of an insolvent corporation sought to hold defendant shareholders liable for the debts of the corporation, arguing that they had not paid for their stock since the valuation of the property they had transferred to the corporation in exchange for their stock was based upon a capitalization of future profits. The court held the shareholders liable, and in the course of the opinion stated that the word "property" must evidently be construed by its context which refers to something visible and tangible.[5] A later New Jersey case[6] looks the other way as do other

2. The Delaware statute has for some time permitted promissory notes for any part of the consideration in excess of the par value of par stock or the stated value of no par stock—an obvious incentive to attribute as little of the consideration as possible to "stated capital." Del.Gen.Corp.Law § 152 (as amended in 1974). California's 1975 statutory revision forbids promissory notes of the purchaser "unless adequately secured by collateral other than the shares acquired" or unless the shares are issued through a stock option plan. Cal.Gen.Corp.Law § 409(a)(1).

3. As the example grows slightly more complex, it may be well again to note that the only matter under discussion here is the application of the legal capital provisions of a corporation law. As a matter of contract or sales law, of course, the corporation is free to issue its stock for whatever kind of consideration, in whatever amount, it wishes or can command.

4. 69 N.J.Eq. 36, 61 A. 843 (1905).

5. 61 A. at 847.

6. *Railway Review v. Groff Drill & Machine Tool Co.*, 84 N.J.Eq. 321, 91 A. 1021 (1914), *aff'd mem. sub nom. Sloan v. Paul*, 84 N.J.Eq. 508, 96 A. 1103 (1915).

cases, and it is hardly conceivable that a modern court would take quite so unsophisticated and non-economic a view, but the *Heppenheimer* case serves as a reminder and illustration of the literal-minded, antique flavor that besets much of the law of legal capital and, more specifically, the difficulty that courts have had in this field with payments that explicitly identify a future element in the valuation of the property paid in.

This doctrinal result should be contrasted with the courts' unquestioning acceptance of the practice of issuing stock "against surplus". If a corporation with a stated capital of $50,000, representing 500 shares of $100 par value each, declares a stock "dividend" of an additional 50 shares, issuing one new share to each shareholder for each 10 shares he already holds, it is uniformly assumed by courts, practitioners and commentators that the demands of the legal capital laws will be fully met if the stated capital account is raised from $50,000 to $55,000, representing now 550 shares of $100 par value each, and the surplus account is correspondingly reduced by $5,000. While it is true that that procedure generates a satisfactory looking balance sheet conforming to the statutory par scheme, it is also true that the new stock was issued without any new property of any description being paid in to the corporate treasury. To contend in support of their result, as some courts have, that the transaction is permissible under the statute because the "surplus" is "property", and to say that the accounting entry is a "pay-in", is meaningless on so many levels that it betrays the truth that the concern of legal capital law is frequently no more than formal in character.

See Second Part, *infra*, for recent developments.

3. Valuation

If the shareholder who buys a new issue of shares pays cash for them in the legally-required amount, and there is an appropriate record of the transaction, he runs no risk of later assessment or liability. But when the payment is in the form of other property, or services rendered, an issue of proper valuation is inevitably introduced.

Many of the old cases that disqualified certain kinds of assets as a medium of exchange for newly-issued stock in fact involved problems of valuation—situations in which it could be seen in hindsight that the consideration paid in had been overvalued. The *Heppenheimer* case offers an example: The capitalized prospective earnings had never materialized. Case law in the field typically arose from situations in which the corporation had become insolvent, and creditors were pursuing shareholders whose pay-in had been in the form of overvalued speculative real estate, contract rights, or services purportedly performed. From these cases there developed, as would be expected, varying doctrinal pronouncements as to the proper way to judge the propriety of the valuation.

Some courts declared themselves in favor of the "true value" rule, under which the value of the shareholder's contribution would be judged with the wisdom of judicial hindsight;[7] others opted for a "good faith" or "reasonable prudence" rule under which the shareholder was safe from later attack if the valuation put upon the property was one that a reasonably prudent man would have put upon it in the light of the facts known at the time of the valuation.[8]

Eventually, however, pressures for certainty and predictability led most state legislatures to add provisions in the corporation codes declaring that "in the absence of fraud" the valuation placed on the property by the board of directors at the time of the pay-in is conclusive and determinative of the valuation question. These provisions have virtually eliminated the valuation problem today as a subject of litigation.

As assets are paid-in and par stock is to be issued, the well-advised board of directors adopts a resolution prepared by counsel valuing the assets at a level that at least matches the par value of the stock being issued for them; once that is done, the shareholder can cease to worry about the risk of later suit by creditors, "in the absence of fraud", whatever that may be.[9] Thus, again, the statutory legal capital scheme that was born out of an impulse to protect creditor claimants has arrived at a state of affairs in which the purchasers of the shares and the board of directors of the issuing corporation are in a legal position to head off any potential objection by creditors.

Where no par stock is being issued, experienced counsel will give a special twist to the valuation question. Since the shareholder-purchaser's only statutory obligation in the case of no par stock is to pay in whatever he agreed to pay in, the board resolution authorizing the issue will be drafted to state simply that the company will issue N shares of the no par stock for particular described assets and will make no mention of any valuation for the property. If the share purchaser then delivers the assets described, he has, by definition, fulfilled his obligation in full. The board (or at least the company's accountant) will eventually have to assign a value to the assets to enter them on

7. See *Clinton Mining & Mineral Co. v. Jamison,* 256 F. 577 (3d Cir.1919).

8. *Coit v. North Carolina Gold Amalgamating Co.,* 119 U.S. 343, 7 S.Ct. 231 (1886).

9. E.g., Del.Gen.Corp.Law § 152 ("[i]n the absence of *actual* fraud in the transaction . . ."); Md.Gen.Corp.Law § 2–203(b) ("actual fraud"); N.Y.Bus. Corp.Law § 504(a) ("fraud").

the balance sheet, and the board will also have to set some dollar number for entry as the "legal capital" attributable to the newly issued no par shares. But the shareholder who paid in the assets is safely out of the controversy once he turned over the assets he agreed to turn over—whether or not they have significant value.[10]

See Second Part, infra, for recent developments.

B. QUALIFICATIONS ON THE PAY–IN OBLIGATION

1. Transferees of Watered Shares

Does the shareholder's obligation to pay in run with the shares, so that subsequent transferees of watered shares risk later suit by creditors? Absent complicity, the courts and statutes have said no.[11] The creditor's remedy, if he has one at all, must therefore be against the initial stock purchaser who underpaid—if the creditor can find him.

2. Treasury Shares

But what if the subsequent transferee of the watered shares is the issuing corporation? If shares are issued for less than par, then "reacquired" by the corporation, "held in the treasury", and later "sold" by the corporation? Should the second transaction be treated (a) as a transfer from one shareholder to another, and thus free the purchaser from worries about the legal capital provisions, or (b) as an "issue" by the corporation and therefore subject to the pay-in rules? The law has historically been consistently baffled by the mirror of treasury shares, and once again on this question the cases and almost all the statutes have opted for the conceptual instead of the sensible answer. As a result, the corporation that has reacquired a block of its shares, and held them "as" treasury shares rather than "retiring" or "cancelling" them, is free under the statutes to sell those shares for whatever it can get for them and can at the same time assure the purchaser that he runs no risk of later claims by creditors.[12]

See Second Part, infra, for a review of recent developments.

3. The *Handley* Doctrine

Earlier reference has been made to the doctrine announced by the Supreme Court in *Handley v. Stutz* that shareholders will be

---

10. If the assets paid in are worth less per share issued than the value per share of the shares already outstanding, the transaction, of course, dilutes the interest of the preexisting shareholders. Their remedy, if any, is discussed infra.

11. E.g., Del.Gen.Corp.Law § 162(c); Md.Gen.Corp.Law § 2–215(b)(1).

12. E.g., Del.Gen.Corp.Law § 153(c); La.Bus.Corp.Law § 12:52(A); Me.Bus. Corp.Act § 506(3); Pa.Bus.Corp.Law § 603(A).

exempted from the obligation to pay in assets equal to the par value of newly-issued stock where the corporation is in financial trouble and the market value of the stock at the time of issue is less than par.[13] It is difficult to assess the continuing vitality of the *Handley* doctrine under modern corporation statutes. The statutes never refer to it. And the courts have not been called upon to pinpoint the implications or scope of the doctrine because modern techniques of corporate financing give rise to simpler and more reliable ways to predetermine the scope of the shareholder's obligation. Nonetheless, no general statement of the shareholder's obligation to pay par is complete without noting that the *Handley* rule may, in some situations, be invoked to qualify the absoluteness of that obligation.

C. ENFORCING THE PAY-IN OBLIGATION— CREDITOR AS PLAINTIFF

How, and to what extent, can the creditor make avail of the shareholder's statutory obligation with respect to share purchase? At least *five* approaches may be found in the cases!

1. Three Theories for Creditor Enforcement of the Obligation to Pay Par

a. The Trust Fund Theory

Justice Story in his landmark opinion in *Wood v. Dummer*[14] said that shareholders are not permitted to take their assets out of a corporation, thus rendering the company insolvent, because the shareholders' equity (the "capital stock") is in the nature of a "trust fund" for creditors. Later creditors' lawyers and courts took up the term "trust fund" and sought to build from it a basis for a judicial remedy requiring shareholders to pay assets into the corporation to the extent of the par value of their shares.

Though one still hears occasional reference to the "trust fund" theory, the idea spawned an inconsistent and unsatisfactory jumble of case law. The fault cannot be laid at the door of the learned Justice Story. In his opinion in *Wood v. Dummer,* he had been talking of assets that had been paid in, while the later "trust fund" cases were addressed to an asserted obligation to pay in funds that had not been paid in. Part of the problem lay in the difficulty of applying the notion of a "trust fund" where there was no "fund", and where there were none of the usual concomitants of a trust. And part of the problem lay in the fact that Justice Story's reference to a "trust fund" had been addressed to corpo-

13.   139 U.S. 417, 11 S.Ct. 530 (1891).

14.   30 F.Cas. 435 (No. 17,944) (C.C.D. Me.1824). See pp. 30–33, supra.

rate assets while later usage was addressed to the emerging new concept, "legal capital", on the right-hand side of the balance sheet.

b.   *The Holding Out or Fraud Theory*

In 1892 the Supreme Court of Minnesota in *Hospes v. Northwestern Mfg. & Car Co.*[15] boldly announced that the "trust fund" theory was a shambles and proclaimed as a substitute a "holding out" theory of shareholder liability.   Though foreshadowed by some earlier decisions purporting to follow the trust fund theory, the *Hospes* case was the first to make explicit the idea that the basis of the shareholder's liability to pay in the par value of his shares was grounded in the tort of misrepresentation.   The basic rationale of the *Hospes* court was that the creditor had somehow received a representation from the *corporation* to the effect that the shares had been fully paid for; if in fact the shares had not been paid for, and if the company later became insolvent the creditor could claim that he had been misled and could compel shareholders who had not paid in the par value of their shares to do so.[16]

The most immediate effects of this beautifully representative expression of late nineteenth century jurisprudence were to make it absolutely clear that (i) the creditor had no cause of action against shareholders unless the company became insolvent (since no damage had been shown to the creditor) and that (ii) any creditor who extended credit to the corporation *before* the relevant stock was issued was barred from complaining.

There are obvious problems with the opinion of the Minnesota court in the *Hospes* case.   On its face, the opinion shows itself as less than serious in its talk of misrepresentation and reliance as the gravamen of the action, for the court explicitly says that the creditor need not show that any representations had been made *to him* about the paid-in equity, or that he *knew* anything about the balance sheet, or that he had in fact *relied* on such statements; these are all simply "presumed" by the law.   The court did not even try to explain why a shareholder should be held liable for a misrepresentation made not by him but by the corporation.   Moreover, like other earlier courts, the Minnesota court in the *Hospes* opinion continued to be confused, and confusing, by its failure to perceive the elemental difference between the question whether the shareholder had originally paid for his shares when they were issued and the question whether the corporation had assets in that amount in its treasury at the time the creditor made his loan.[17]

15. 48 Minn. 174, 50 N.W. 1117 (1892).

16. 50 N.W. at 1121.

17. "The capital of a corporation is the basis of its credit. It is a substitute for the individual liability of those who

But whatever the difficulties in the analysis, the holding in the *Hospes* case was clear: the shareholder will not be held liable unless the company is insolvent and unless the complainant is a creditor who extended credit after the issuance of the shares. The *Hospes* doctrines have exerted great influence in other courts.

c. The Statutory Obligation Theory

A smaller group of jurisdictions has in more recent times taken another approach—one that, not surprisingly, has a more modern jurisprudential ring to it. Abandoning both the trust fund theory and the holding out theory, a few courts have held that creditors of an insolvent corporation may compel shareholders to pay in full for their shares because the applicable corporation statute says so.[18]

2. Two Other Theories for Creditor Enforcement of the Shareholder's Obligation to Pay In

a. Stock Subscription

One way to approach a legal characterization of the shareholders' pay-in obligation is to view it as a matter of contract law. In this perspective, the shareholder should be held to the terms of the subscription agreement he entered into with the corporation, and an unpaid corporate creditor should be able to pursue satisfaction for his debt by enforcing through the locally-available third party procedure the corporation's unpaid claim against the subscriber. When shareholder subscriptions were a common method for financing corporations, and when the subscription price was the par value of the stock (which was the usual case), a creditor's action based on the contractual theory of subscription enforcement was substantively (though often not procedurally) the functional equivalent to an action to compel the shareholder to pay the par value for his shares under one of the three theories just reviewed.

b. Balance Sheet and Other Misrepresentation

In rare circumstances, a creditor might successfully contend that the facts in his case gave rise to a classic action for actual misrepresentation. Suppose a creditor, before making his loan to

own its stock. People deal with it and give it credit on the faith of it. *They have a right to assume that it has paid in capital to the amount which it represents itself as having;* and if they give it credit on the faith of that representation, and if the representation is false, it is a fraud upon them; and, in case the corporation becomes insolvent, the law, upon the plainest principles of common justice, says to the delinquent stockholder, 'Make that representation good by paying for your stock.' " Id. at 1121. (Emphasis added.) Note, too, the court's shifting uses of the word "capital."

18. See Second Part, Subpart One, Chapter II, infra. E.g. *Harman v. Himes*, 77 F.2d 375, 379 (D.C.Cir.1935).

a corporation, had asked the board whether certain shares had been paid for; they had not, but the board answered untruthfully. Or suppose the prospective lender had requested and been given the corporation's balance sheet and that, as the shareholders knew, the balance sheet listed as corporate assets properties which the shareholders had not in fact paid in to the corporation. In such rare cases, the classical action of common law fraud would be available and could, depending upon the misrepresentations involved, provide the creditor with an action against a shareholder participating in the fraud that would be substantially equivalent to an enforcement of the shareholder's obligation to pay in the par value of his stock.

3. Hybrid Theories

It must not be thought that the five theories separated and isolated here for identification have been scrupulously thought through by the courts, or that the cases in the field (there are not very many) can be neatly stacked into five piles. As often as not, a judicial opinion in this field will be found to have adopted some hybrid theory, and it would not be startling for a court in a single opinion to refer dimly to a "trust fund", to advert to the shareholder's subscription contract, and to suggest that creditors may have relied, or may be presumed to have relied, upon the fulfillment by the shareholders of their statutory obligation.[19]

4. Procedural Pitfalls—The Significance of the Creditor's Theory

With five theories and their permutations to work from, the courts and corporation statutes have not been notably successful in solving the procedural problems that are inherent in the legal capital exercise upon which corporation law embarked a century ago. On the whole, the legal capital statutes themselves have been of little help, for they merely assert that shares shall not be issued except upon the payment designated, and are silent as to who may do what to whom if that mandate is not followed. The

---

19. For example, the former California Corporation Code on its face laid down an absolute statutory prescription for shareholders to pay in at least the par value of their shares, and commentators on the code, including the draftsman, Ballentine, had identified California as a statutory obligation jurisdiction. The Supreme Court of California, however, when called upon to apply the statute, interpreted it as being for the benefit of creditors who had actually relied on a representation about the shareholders' pay-in—thus blending the statutory obligation theory, the holding out theory, and the balance sheet misrepresentation theory. *Bing Crosby Minute Maid Corp. v. Eaton,* 46 Cal.2d 484, 297 P.2d 5 (1956). (The case and its underlying statutory provisions were superseded by California's new corporation code in 1975.) See Second Part, infra.

discussion that follows is illustrative—but surely not inclusive—of the kinds of procedural problems encountered.

In the first place, the statutes do not usually even make it clear that creditors may invoke the legal capital scheme for their benefit at all. The courts have simply assumed that they may— reasonably enough, if the engine is to have any function whatever. In developing that assumption, however, the courts have added another—equally without statutory basis—namely, that the corporation must be insolvent before the creditors may pursue the purchasers of the watered or bonus stock. The point is not insignificant. It means that the apparent injunction to the shareholder to pay in assets equal to the par value of his shares is in reality only a statement of a risk that may be remote. Insofar as the liability under legal capital provisions is concerned, it is open to the shareholder to hold back the pay-in of his own funds until insolvency comes—which, he hopes and believes at the time he acquires the stock, will be never.[20]

Assuming that "insolvency" is a prerequisite to suit by a creditor, by what standard shall insolvency be judged—by the equity criterion or by the bankruptcy criterion? [21] Through what procedure is "insolvency" to be determined? Before pursuing the shareholder, must the creditor first receive judgment against the corporation and obtain a return *nulla bona?* May he proceed immediately upon the institution of some form of voluntary or involuntary insolvency proceeding?

Then there is the question of *what* creditor has standing to enforce the shareholder's pay-in obligation. The holding out theory of the *Hospes* case eliminates as possible complainants those creditors who became such before the issuance of the watered stock.[22] As noted, the California Supreme Court managed to come to the same conclusion even in a state that had been thought to subscribe to the theory of statutory obligation.[23] On the whole, the courts have not been sympathetic toward the role of the creditor as avenging archangel or as policeman undertaking to enforce the general obligation imposed by the corporation codes upon the shareholders; the courts' tendency has been to think in terms of tort and injury (real or assumed) to the individual creditor plaintiff.

20. In such a situation, if the corporation's counsel is called upon to opine that the outstanding shares are fully paid and non-assessable, he will have to decline to do so; and that may trigger some corrective action. See FitzGibbon & Glazer, *Legal Opinions in Corporate Transactions: The Opinion that Stock is* *Duly Authorized, Validly Issued, Fully Paid and Nonassessable,* 43 Wash. & Lee L.Rev. 863, 888–90 (1986).

21. Most statutes prescribe the equity criterion. See Second Part, infra.

22. See pp. 51–52, supra.

23. See p. 53, n. 19, supra.

Division of creditors into those who may pursue (some) shareholders, and those who may not, increases the procedural complexity of the situation enormously. Since the corporation must be "insolvent" to ground the action at all, there will typically be a receiver for creditors or other creditors' representative in the driver's seat. If the receiver is thought of as representing "the corporation" rather than creditors, he will have no action at all under a *Hospes* analysis. Even if he is thought of as an agent representing and acting in the place of creditors, the misrepresentation or holding out approach compels the creditors' representative to discriminate among his principals and, correspondingly, determine which shareholders may be sued, how much they may be sued for, and what shall be done with the proceeds of the suit. The creditors' representative will obviously be much happier with a theory of the action that will enable him to force all shareholders who have not met their pay-in obligation to do so, and to add the proceeds to the assets available to all creditors.

Then there is the question of who may be sued. Each of the five theories outlined above will, if logically carried out, produce its own characteristic group of potential defendants as, over the course of the life of the corporation, shares will have been issued at different times to different shareholders under different arrangements at different prices while many shareholders who took originally-issued shares will have disappeared from sight in favor of transferees who are not liable.

Through what kind of proceeding shall a creditor, or a representative of a creditor, pursue the shareholder defendants? Must each one be sued individually? Will some kind of class action be possible? May all of the actions be consolidated into some sort of plenary insolvency proceeding? What about service of process? And the jurisdiction of the court? Res judicata? Collateral estoppel? Notice to other creditors? Settlement? Collusive settlement?

What is the measure of the amount for which the shareholder may be sued? Again different theories of the action will produce different answers. Consider the case of the creditor who is owed $100 by the corporation and who sues a shareholder whose liability under the local prevailing theory is $1,000; presumably, the plaintiff's own judgment will be limited to $100, but will other creditors have to bring separate suits against the shareholder in order to collect the other $900?

If judgment is obtained against a shareholder, to whom does he make payment? To the complaining creditor alone; does the race go to the swift? To the corporation for the benefit of all creditors similarly situated; if the recovery will be shared by all creditors of the bankrupt corporation, what incentive has the individual creditor to bear the costs of pursuing the delinquent shareholder? May the shareholder defend on the ground that the plaintiff creditor is a junior creditor whose claim against the corporation would not have been collectible in any case because of the prior claims of higher ranking creditors? What is the effect of the intervention of bankruptcy proceedings or state insolvency proceedings?

How about actions over? If a shareholder has been compelled by creditors' action to live up to his pay-in obligation, may he then turn to other shareholders similarly situated and compel contributions from them?

The statute of limitations is likely to impose a problem and, again, the characterization of the shareholder's pay-in obligation as being essentially contractual, or tortious, or statutorily prescriptive, will point to a choice among the potentially applicable statutes of repose and determine the time when the statutory period starts, ends, and is tolled.

What about suit by the creditor on the basis that he is somehow a third party beneficiary of a contract—express or implied—between the non-paying shareholder and the corporation? Efforts by creditors to pursue shareholders on the theory of enforcement of their stock subscriptions became hopelessly snarled in the theology of nineteenth century contract law. Suppose the board of directors of a corporation simply refused to make the call on the subscriptions; was not the call a necessary precondition to the subscribers' contractual liability? Or, suppose the directors had, for a trivial consideration, waived or cancelled the subscriber's liability? Was that not a defense for the subscriber? Finally, how could the corporation, after it had become insolvent, perform its part of the subscription bargain—that is, the issuance of shares in accordance with the subscription agreement; would the subscriber be getting what he bargained for, i.e., shares of a viable business enterprise, and if not, was the subscription agreement enforceable against him?

Out of these and similar problems, the courts amassed a doctrinal slag pile of subscriptions, subscription agreements, stock purchase agreements, agreements to purchase stock, options, estoppels, constructive conditions, and the like. This jumble will never be sorted out for, with the development of different forms of corporate financing, the subscription agreement largely faded away, the law took another turn, and today the pile molders, forgotten and decreasingly visible under the green cover of time.

* * *

So much for procedural problems of the creditor. They are seldom relevant anyway, it must be reemphasized. In the real world, the creditor will almost always find that he has no basis under the legal capital provisions to pursue shareholders since the stock issuance will usually have been carried out in formal compliance with the statute. It is so easy to comply with the legal capital requirement that only the most careless lawyering will botch the stock issuance in a way that will leave the purchaser open to risk from this source. But in the unusual circumstance in which the shareholder has been left open to risk, the creditor who seeks to take advantage of that delinquency will find his way beset with one procedural pitfall after another, and almost no statutory or judicial chart to guide him.

D. ENFORCING THE PAY-IN OBLIGATION— SHAREHOLDER AS PLAINTIFF

1. The Legal Capital Scheme

Development of the concepts and procedures of the legal capital machinery is traceable entirely to a judicial and legislative concern with the problem of creditor protection. In some situations, however, the shareholder may have benefited from the legal capital scheme.

The interest of a shareholder in having other shareholders make a contribution to the corporate pot equitably commensurate with his own has already been noted in earlier discussion. In the days when high par value stock was commonly used, and when the mores of corporate financing did not contemplate purchase of initially-issued shares at a price higher than the par value, the par machinery at least tended to produce an incidental equitableness of contribution (although this same end could have been achieved by contract). Of course, once the enterprise is underway, the par value of the stock is irrelevant to its economic value and is therefore useless as a standard for measuring the equitableness of subsequent shareholder contributions. And, as low par and no par stock came into common use, the fortuitous protective effect of the par scheme largely disappeared even in the context of an initial stock offering.

What of the possibility that a shareholder might be able to rely upon the par payment obligation to implement his interest in equitable contribution in a case where bonus, discount or watered shares had been issued to the shareholders? There is apparently only one case on the books in which a shareholder has been able to invoke in his own behalf the statutory par scheme. In *Scully v.*

Automobile Finance Co.,[24] the enterprise had prospered. An original shareholder who had not fully paid for his stock was sued by other shareholders, not to compel him to pay in the par value of the shares he had received, but to cancel the shares he had received, a remedy that would have immediately and dramatically raised the value of the other shares outstanding. The Delaware court gave judgment for the plaintiffs, but, at the request of the *defendant,* refused to cancel the shares and instead permitted the defendant to pay in the full par value and retain his fractional share of the enterprise.[25]

2. Promoter's Liability

There was once, and in a sense there still is, a substantial body of law grouped together under the rubric "promoter's liability". Enough cases were litigated in the vocabulary of "promoter's liability" to generate, if not justify, treatises in the field.[26] Though the courts of the day almost never perceived it, the main problem that gave rise to this litigation (other than simple misrepresentation and fraud) was the problem of equitable contribution among shareholders. Corporate promoters in these cases had put little or nothing into the corporate pot except their "services", often of dubious value, while other shareholders had paid in the par value of the shares in cash or property; the promoters wound up owning a substantial fraction of the corporate shares, and the other shareholders' proportionate share in the corporate assets was correspondingly diluted.

The courts of earlier day were either unable or unwilling to embark upon the development of a jurisprudence spelling out the obligations of promoters to individual purchasing shareholders (including *later* shareholders) or to tackle the problem of establishing disclosure standards or developing economic standards for determining the fair price of newly-issued shares. Instead, the judges tried to deal with the question in terms of a breach of fiduciary relationship between the promoter and "the corporation." The essence of the courts' theory was that the promoter was some kind of special fiduciary vis-à-vis "the corporation" and, as such, owed "the corporation" a duty not to obtain secret or "unconscionable" profits.

That theory may have been better than nothing in a day that was innocent of securities regulation, but the effort could not possibly succeed. In the "promoter's liability" cases, the problem was not one of injury by the promoter to an abstract "corporation"

24. 12 Del.Ch. 174, 109 A. 49 (1920).   **26.** E.g. M. Ehrich, *The Law of Promoters* (1916).
25. 109 A. at 54.

but dilution of the economic and political power of full-paying shareholders by the issuance of cheap or free shares to other shareholders—i.e. the promoter. Inter-shareholder conflicts cannot be resolved in legal categories that treat the "corporation" as a collective unity. When Shareholder group A and Shareholder group B of the same corporation are at odds, neither the promoter, nor the board, nor counsel, nor a court will find guidance for behavior in pronouncements about someone's duty to "the" corporation. Intra-corporate factional dispute called for molecular corporate jurisprudence to be supplanted by atomic or sub-atomic jurisprudence.

Sometimes the promoter's transactions with the corporation involved the issuance of shares for overvalued property, in which case there would be an overlap between the theory of the promoter's general fiduciary duties and his obligation as a shareholder to pay the par value of the shares. To that extent, situations giving rise to promoter's liability might also have given rise to liability under the requirement for the payment of par value; but the theory of the action, the measure of damages, the legal qualifications required of the plaintiff, and the legal requirements of corporate insolvency would be wholly different in a promoter's liability suit from those that would inhere in a suit to compel payment under the par value requirement.

In many other situations, however, there would be no such overlap of theory. For example, the promoter may not have taken stock but rather received money from the corporation in payment for alleged property or services. Or he might have made an undisclosed profitable sale of properties to the corporation. Development of a rational law of promoter's liabilities was stunted by the conceptualistic decision made by Justice Holmes in *Old Dominion Copper Mining and Smelting Co. v. Lewisohn* [27] that shareholders could not recover from a promoter on grounds of fiduciary violation if the promoter, at the time of the sale of overvalued property to the corporation, owned all the shares of the corporation, since "the corporation" had full "knowledge" of the inflated value of the land it had received from the promoter.

Though the promoter's fiduciary theory may have been of some help in restraining the most spectacular excesses of promoters, the doctrinal structure was a weak one and of little assistance to those who most needed help—subsequent-purchasing shareholders. The subject has today been taken over almost entirely by disclosure requirements under state and federal securities laws and by the development of modern securities fraud law.

27. 210 U.S. 206, 28 S.Ct. 634 (1908).

3. Equitable Contribution Doctrine

With the doctrines of legal capital largely inoperable to protect shareholders against dilution through the underpriced issue of shares, there has been some small tendency to develop specific doctrinal tools to deal with the matter. Some states, in their corporation codes, came to perceive the point as they required that a corporate issuer receive consideration for its stock in an equitable amount.[28] Some courts are developing a jurisprudence condemning the sale of stock at less than "fair" value as a breach of the board of directors' fiduciary obligation to "the corporation,"[29] though that of course is not the real problem. And occasionally a court appears accurately to perceive the issuance of stock to a particular shareholder at too cheap a price not as a problem of abstract "corporate waste" but as a dilution transaction that reallocates political power and economic return *among* shareholders.[30]

4. Disclosure and Securities Regulation

But by far the greatest protection the shareholder has today against stock issues at improper prices lies in the disclosure and filing requirements of state Blue Sky laws and of the federal Securities Acts. As a result of developments in twentieth-century securities law, the stock purchaser and the stock owner who care enough to enquire can today usually ascertain what fees were paid to promoters and how and what securities have been or are about to be issued by a corporation to whom, when, and for what. When contrasted with live, developing, economically-oriented disclosure requirements and with the rapidly-evolving rules of security fraud under modern securities laws, statutory stated capital machinery is seen to be an obsolete and seldom relevant mechanism for protecting shareholders threatened with dilution.

E. ENFORCING THE PAY-IN OBLIGATION— CORPORATION AS PLAINTIFF

As a matter of contract law, a corporation may by suit compel a stock subscriber to make payment to the corporation, on call, in

28. E.g., former Minnesota Bus. Corp.Act § 301.16(1) ("Shares . . . shall not be allotted for a cash consideration which is *unfair to the then shareholders* nor for a consideration other than cash upon a valuation thereof which is unfair to such shareholders; . . .").

29. Compare *Schoenbaum v. Firstbrook*, 405 F.2d 215 (2d Cir.1968), with *Popkin v. Bishop*, 464 F.2d 714 (2d Cir.

1972), and with *Schlick v. Penn–Dixie Cement Corp.*, 507 F.2d 374 (2d Cir. 1974), and with *Blue Chip Stamps v. Manor Drug Stores*, 421 U.S. 723, 95 S.Ct. 1917 (1975).

30. *Bodell v. General Gas & Electric Corp.*, 15 Del.Ch. 119, 132 A. 442 (Ch. Div.1926), *aff'd* 15 Del.Ch. 420, 140 A. 264 (1927). See also *Atlantic Refining Co. v. Hodgman*, 13 F.2d 781 (3d Cir. 1926).

accordance with the terms of the subscription agreement. But may the recipient of bonus, discount, or watered stock of a corporation be sued later by the corporation, while it is still solvent, to compel him to pay in the full par value of the shares? Under the holding out theory, there would obviously be no such liability, since there is no creditor even presumptively injured. While it would be arguable under the statutory obligation theory that the corporation should be able to pursue the shareholder to enforce the statutory requirement, such a suit would obviously be met by the defense that the corporation had, with knowledge, consented to the issuance and thereby specifically waived all right to collect the full par value. Except for one case in which one shareholder brought a *derivative* action against other shareholders who had not paid in full for their stock,[31] there has been no implication in the judicial opinions that the corporation may sue a shareholder to compel him to pay up the par value of the shares he received.

As noted earlier, the corporation's legal incapacity to enforce the shareholders' pay-in obligation has also proved an embarrassment to a corporate receiver where the receiver has been viewed as "standing in the shoes of" the corporate debtor.

F. THE CORPORATE PRACTITIONER: AN OUNCE OF PREVENTION

The perspective of the corporate practitioner is prospective. Litigation is usually the result of failure to perceive trouble in advance and to take appropriate steps at an earlier date. The corporate lawyer and the corporate accountant can have almost no excuse for letting a situation develop where there is any question about shareholder liability for violation of legal capital provisions.

The statutes place within the hands of the board, and their counsellors, almost unlimited opportunity to set par, or eliminate par, to prescribe the consideration paid, to value it, and to control the corresponding accounting entries. The issuance of stock can, of course, raise genuine and difficult problems; "fairness" of price and appropriate disclosure under developing doctrines of federal securities fraud are difficult to determine, as are assessments of the equitableness of the terms of mergers and exchanges of stock. But the statutory legal capital provisions, as such, are almost invariably manageable in advance through the application of rudimentary skill and attention in the design of the transaction. If there is an exception to this statement it arises from the annoying residual unreal doctrines that still prohibit the issuance

31. *Scully v. Automobile Finance Co.,* 12 Del.Ch. 174, 109 A. 49 (1920).

of stock in exchange for contractual commitments for future performance. The point is further discussed in Second Part, infra.

Given the vagueness and uncertainties that attach to all procedural aspects of the legal capital provisions, the corporate practitioner is well advised to invest the energy needed to comprehend the legal capital provisions under which he must work, however much fossilized or, worse, like the coelecanth, still alive. He will then be able to include in his prescription for a corporate transaction the ounce of prevention that will ward off trouble from that quarter. Subpart Two of this First Part of the text provides assistance in that endeavor, as it sets out a series of transactions involving stock and capital readjustments, with corresponding accounting entries under the legal capital provisions. The main focus of Subpart Two is upon regulation of pay-outs to shareholders, but the illustrations also provide representative guidance in the application of legal capital doctrines to share issuance and shareholder pay-ins.

Chapter IV

REGULATING DISTRIBUTIONS TO SHAREHOLDERS

Chapter III addressed the effort of legal capital doctrines to regulate pay-in of assets by shareholders. The legal capital scheme also undertakes to regulate the permissible flow of corporate assets out to shareholders.

As foreshadowed in the Introduction, the 1980s saw an astonishing wave of changes in the law in this field. Those changes cannot be understood without a general understanding of what it was that was being changed, or not changed. The mission of this chapter is to provide that background.

Where not otherwise indicated, the material in this chapter speaks as of the late 1970s. As such, the chapter, speaking at the beginning of the 1990s, recounts history. But, as with a geology text, it tells of history that is more than history, for much of that that was, still is.[1]

The statutory provisions regulating pay-outs to shareholders have long differed from state to state. When dealing with a specific problem, the lawyer must examine the applicable state statute carefully.

A. INSOLVENCY CRITERIA—EQUITY TEST

The basic thesis of *Wood v. Dummer* is incontestable. If the hierarchical relationship of creditor to shareholder is to have any meaning at all, then the management must not be left free to shovel all the assets in the corporate treasury out to the shareholders when the corporation has insufficient assets to pay its creditors or when the shareholder distribution itself renders the corporation unable to pay its creditors. The central point is to avoid insolvency.

"Insolvency" has, of course, long had a recognized duality of meaning. The first was developed over the centuries by the English chancery courts—the equity courts. In the equity courts, the test of a debtor's insolvency was whether he was unable to meet his obligations as they became due. This is often referred to as the "equity insolvency test", a term that will appear frequently hereafter in this book.

1. See Third Part, infra.

63

As was often the case, the English law courts across the street from the chancery court went their own way in developing a concept of insolvency for use in bankruptcy proceedings. In the law courts, the test for bankruptcy was whether the aggregate amount of the debtor's assets was less than the total amount of his liabilities. This is often referred to as the "bankruptcy test".

The difference between these two conceptions can be very great. The equity insolvency test is concerned with current liquidity of the going enterprise; the emphasis of the bankruptcy sense of insolvency is upon liquidation of the enterprise. It is easily possible for an enterprise to be short of cash and other liquid means of payment while at the same time holding illiquid assets of great value; such an enterprise may well fail the equity insolvency test. It is also a quite possible occurrence for an enterprise to have a large current cash flow while steadily operating at a loss and suffering a continuing erosion of its asset base; in time, such an enterprise will fail to meet the bankruptcy test of insolvency.

Those with any familiarity with accounting will recognize that the equity insolvency test is concerned with the income and cash flow statements of the enterprise while the bankruptcy insolvency test is focused on the balance sheet of the enterprise. For this reason, the bankruptcy insolvency test is frequently referred to as the "balance sheet" or "net worth" test.

These two concepts of insolvency play an important role in the corporation law provisions regulating the distribution of assets to shareholders.

All state corporation statutes contain as a restriction on shareholder distributions an equity insolvency test. Everyone agrees (whatever the statement may mean and however it may be interpreted or enforced) that directors may not lawfully distribute corporate assets to shareholders unless after doing so the corporation will still be able to pay its debts as they mature; or, as it is often put in the negative, no distribution can be lawfully made if it will put the corporation in a position where it cannot meet its obligations as they mature.

The substance of that equity solvency test prevails in all jurisdictions. It is commonly said that in one state—Massachusetts—the equity insolvency rule is the only statutory provision regulating shareholder distributions.[2]

The equivalent of the same rule may be found outside the corporation laws. The Uniform Fraudulent Conveyance Act may be interpreted to produce the same result, since it provides that a

---

2. See Mass.Bus.Corp.Law ch. 156B, § 61. See also *Brigham v. M & J Corp.*,   352 Mass. 674, 227 N.E.2d 915, 919–20 (1967).

conveyance without a fair consideration by a person who is rendered insolvent thereby is fraudulent as to his creditors.[3]

B. BALANCE SHEET–BASED TESTS

Excluding, perhaps, Massachusetts, all other jurisdictions employ, in addition to the equity insolvency test, some more stringent form of test for shareholder distributions. These tests are balance sheet-based. Any proposed distribution to shareholders must meet both tests.

The statutes in those states are customarily referred to in short hand as "balance sheet statutes". The term "balance sheet statute" is doubly unfortunate. First, as will emerge, it does not distinguish among a variety of different kinds of statutory tests that have as their base the balance sheet. Second, to characterize particular statutes as balance sheet statutes obscures the fact that *all* statutes include a parallel equity insolvency test, whatever else they may also contain. But infelicitous or no, the usage is deep-seated.

1. Accounting, Accountants and the Law

All balance sheet-based tests start by comparing the corporation's assets shown on its balance sheet with the liabilities shown there. By its very nature, any form of balance sheet test is inherently wholly dependent upon the accounting principles followed in constructing the numbers on both the assets and the liabilities sides of the balance sheet. The interplay of law and accounting that determine these numbers is exceedingly complex, subtle and difficult. Whether or not clearly perceived, several kinds of questions arise out of the relationship. Since that relationship provides the central predicate to all balance sheet tests—regardless of type—it is well to examine it before going further.

Should statutes and courts undertake to prescribe a corpus of accounting principles? Should legislatures and courts instead defer, and refer all questions to the accountants' own evolving common law—"generally accepted accounting principles"?[4] Or

---

3. Uniform Fraudulent Conveyance Act § 4. At least two courts have held that the U.F.C.A. applies to corporate dividends when the distribution triggers insolvency. *Powers v. Heggie*, 268 Mass. 233, 167 N.E. 314, 317 (1929); *In re Kettle Fried Chicken of America, Inc.*, 513 F.2d 807 (6th Cir.1975) (applying Delaware law).

4. The North Carolina Business Corporation Act formerly incorporated into the statute the concept of what it called

"generally accepted principles of sound accounting practice." See, e.g., former N.C.Gen.Stat. § 55–2(2), (7) (definitions of "assets" and "liabilities," respectively); § 55–49(b) (in determining legality of dividends, distributions, or "withdrawals of corporate assets," assets may "be carried on the books in accordance with generally accepted principles of sound accounting practice applicable to the kind of business conducted by the corporation"); § 55–49(d) (definition of

just refer some questions, and if so, which ones? Assuming that the guide is to be "generally accepted accounting principles", has the accountant in the particular situation followed those principles, or made an appropriate selection from among an array of different but equally permissible principles? And, finally, has the accounting principle in question been properly applied to the facts at hand?

A balance sheet-based scheme for restricting distributions to shareholders would, if seriously pursued, require the development of a full scale judicial jurisprudence of accounting. Nearly everyone agrees that that would be wholly impractical and a disaster. Courts do not have and do not claim to have the technical training to sit as accounting tribunals; the accounting profession would far prefer to be its own law generator through opinions of the Financial Accounting Standards Board and the development of "generally accepted accounting principles"; and the corporate lawyer has no desire to submit technical questions of this kind to a court. As a result, there is virtually no litigation in the field. And when there is occasional litigation, there is a strong tendency for the court to find that the accountant was acting in accordance with *some* generally accepted accounting principle.

After embarking bravely upon the adventure of regulating shareholder distributions in the interest of creditors, both courts and legislatures recoiled from actively carrying through with that enterprise as they came to realize, more or less consciously, the enormity and complexity of law building that would be necessary to make the system really work. That second judgment was undoubtedly a wise one; perhaps, too, it suggests that it was a mistake to embark upon the endeavor in the first place.

Generally accepted accounting principles have a reality, and do provide a usable general guidance. The professionally responsible accountant is not free to write down any number that occurs to him. But laymen who are neither trained nor experienced in accounting tend to assume that these principles have a certainty, precision and exclusivity which they do not in fact have. Financial statements are inevitably a composite of a myriad of judgmental decisions made by the accountants, or some combination of accountants, lawyers, and business management. What expenditures should be expensed and which ones "capitalized" [5] as an asset? When should the accountant's convention of carrying

"earned surplus"). Those interested in the interplay of law and accounting practice will find the financial sections of the former North Carolina statute a challenge, N.C.Gen.Stat. §§ 55–43 to –52. See also Md.Gen.Corp. Law § 1–402(2). The former North Carolina statute was repealed in favor of the Revised Model Business Corporation Act, effective July 1, 1990.

5. Note yet another variant meaning for "capital."

assets at cost be modified so as to write up or write down the figure at which the assets are carried? What allowances should be made for potential bad debts, and when? When should losses be recognized and written off? How should depletion, amortization, and depreciation be treated? To what extent and when should capitalization of anticipated earnings—so called "goodwill"—be carried or not carried on the balance sheet? On these, and similar questions of accounting arising in particular circumstances, accountants and industry practices will differ, and will claim support of generally accepted accounting principles.

On the liability side of the balance sheet similar questions will arise. When should guarantee obligations, loss contingencies (e.g., from pending or threatened litigation) and other contingent liabilities be recognized and entered as liabilities? The same question for bilateral contracts (e.g., leases) requiring future payments by the corporation. When should obligations thereunder be noted, and how? How shall unliquidated liabilities be quantified? How about long term pension liabilities? Indebtedness (and assets) held in fluctuating foreign currencies?

And what, if any, adjustments should be made for inflation?

More fundamentally still, it must be recognized that in most ongoing business situations, there is only a fractional relationship between the concerns of the creditor and the figures that show up on a corporate balance sheet. In part this is true because the creditor's primary concern is with his debtor's ability (cash flow) to pay the debt when and as it matures. In part, however, it is because the focus of the accountant's art is not to present a continuous picture of the "value" of the enterprise (whatever that may mean) but to apply with consistency a series of accounting conventions (which are recognized to be conventions) on a periodic basis and to achieve at least a satisfactory degree of disclosure of selected kinds of transactions and elements in the economic life of the enterprise. By force of the limitations of his function and his tools, the accountant offers a picture that is incomplete, is differently focused from that of the creditor, and is of a highly stylized character.

The reader will find it instructive in reading Chapter VI of this Subpart One to contrast the statutory balance sheet-based protection schemes, utterly dependent as they are upon formal accounting, with the operational techniques that sophisticated creditors and their lawyers have handcrafted for their protection.

2. Types of Tests

Against the backdrop of the preceding discussion of accounting, one can turn to a consideration of the subcategories within the generic category of balance sheet-based tests.

a. Tests Employing Stated Capital

Historically speaking, as recounted in earlier pages, the formula that evolved to provide for creditors a cushion of safety was, of course, our friend stated capital.

(i) Stated Capital/Surplus

The central idea of the simplest of the stated capital schemes is that (put negatively) a distribution is forbidden if after giving effect to it the total of assets would be less than the sum of liabilities plus stated capital; or (put affirmatively) a distribution is permitted to the extent there is a "surplus", with "surplus" defined as the amount by which assets are greater than the sum of liabilities plus stated capital.[6]

(ii) Stated Capital/Earned Surplus

More stringent would be a formula that would work just as in (i) above, except that a distribution could be made only to the extent that the corporation has a particular *kind* of surplus available—earned surplus—or, as it is usually called in contemporary accounting vocabulary, retained earnings. Such a statute is usually in shorthand referred to as an earned surplus statute; more precisely described, it is a balance sheet-based stated capital/earned surplus statute.

(iii) Stated Capital/Other

Other statutory variations of stated capital formulae are possible and are discussed below at pp. 82–84.

b. Tests Not Employing Stated Capital

(i) Net Worth

The simplest form of balance sheet-based regulation would wholly dispense with the concept of "stated capital" and set the corporation's net worth as the measure for shareholder distribution. That is to say (put negatively), a distribution would be forbidden if after giving effect to it the corporation's assets, as shown on the balance sheet, would be less than its liabilities, as

---

6. The reader was introduced to the perspective of this test in the earlier conceptual discussion at pages 33–34 and 37–40, supra.

shown on the balance sheet; or (put positively) a distribution is permissible to the extent that assets are greater than liabilities as appearing on the balance sheet. For purposes of applying this test, any "stated capital" entry on the balance sheet is simply irrelevant.

(ii) Adjusted Net Worth

It would also obviously be possible to construct any number of adjusted net worth tests. While continuing to operate independently of any concept of stated capital, such tests would adjust the standard net worth calculation by including or excluding certain assets or liabilities in a manner different from that employed by generally accepted accounting principles to arrive at net worth. For example, the test formula might require not only all liabilities to be deducted from total assets but also other contingent claims, such as the dollar amount of liquidation rights of outstanding preferred stock.[7] Or the test formula might not count as, or limit the inclusion of, assets that cannot be readily liquidated.[8] We shall return to this topic in the Second Part.

C. STATED CAPITAL—CENTRAL CONCEPTS

Before turning to a review of balance sheet-based stated capital statutes, it is advisable to examine the two key conceptual components that they share in common—stated capital accounts and surplus accounts. Those two components (with, of course, "total assets" and "total liabilities") are the heart of any stated capital mechanism.

1. Computation of Stated Capital; Increasing Stated Capital

One factor that must be used in the computation of "surplus" is a dollar figure designated as the corporation's stated capital. As we have seen, more than any other component of the balance sheet, "stated capital" is a lawyer's concept rather than an accountant's and a modern corporation statute will usually provide more guidance for its computation than for other balance sheet elements. But most statutes leave many questions open, and some questions are not answered by any of the statutes.

Computation of stated capital is simple if the situation is simple. Following the statutes, and history, an entry must be carried as "capital" in the shareholders' equity portion—the southeast corner—of the issuing company's balance sheet with regard to all shares "outstanding". To determine the amount of this entry, one multiplies the number of shares "outstanding"

---

7. See Second Part, Subpart One, Chapter III, pp. 182–84, *infra.*

8. See, e.g., Cal.Gen.Corp.Law § 500(b)(2).

times the par value prescribed in the certificate of incorporation for each share; if there is no par value, a "stated value" of each issued share is substituted by resolution of the board of directors. When additional shares are issued, if the company's existing stated capital is equal to the number of shares theretofore outstanding multiplied by their par value, stated capital is increased by an amount equivalent to the par value of the new shares times the number of new shares being issued.

So far, so good. But after that point, assignment of stated capital begins to become more difficult and uncertain.

For any number of reasons, the stated capital of a company may at any particular time be higher than the product of the par value of the shares multiplied by the number of shares outstanding. Most statutes permit the board of directors, acting without shareholder vote, to increase the company's stated capital and that step is sometimes taken.[9]

Suppose a corporation has on its books an aggregate stated capital of $750 attributable to an outstanding issue of 10 shares of $50 par stock, or an average of $75 per share, and that the corporation now issues one new such share for a price of $60. Should the issue of the new share be reflected in the stated capital account by an increase of $50 (the par), or $60 (the issue price), or $75 (the preexisting average stated capital per share), or some other arbitrarily assigned number greater than $50; or is *no* increase in stated capital needed to reflect the issuance of the new share since the existing stated capital of $750 is greater than the product of all shares outstanding including the new share (11), multiplied by the par value ($50)?

Similar questions arise in the case of a so-called "stock dividend" where the preexisting stated capital is greater than the par value per share times the number of shares outstanding; when the new shares are issued pro rata to existing shareholders, by what measure, if at all, must stated capital be increased, and surplus (of some kind) be correspondingly charged?

If there are outstanding subscriptions for shares, should the stated capital be increased to reflect the stock subscribed for at the time the subscription agreement is entered into, or when the directors call for payment, or when payment has been made in part, or when payment has been made in full? A similar question is raised where, as is specifically authorized by some corporation statutes, shares may for some purposes be considered to be "issued" though they are only partially paid for and the balance

9. See, e.g., N.Y.Bus.Corp.Law § 506(c). See also discussion infra pp. 72–74 on "reducing capital".

owing is expected to be received in installments? Current accounting practice regarding stock subscriptions would tend to write up the stated capital as soon as a subscription is entered into and correspondingly create an account receivable on the asset side, but that result is not inevitable. It is quite reasonable to argue that there should be no account receivable at least until the directors have called the subscription, and it is also possible that the statutory provision governing stated capital might be based upon a legal concept of "outstanding" shares that is independent of and different from accounting practice, i.e., is the subscribed-for share "outstanding" for some purposes but not others?

How should stock warrants and stock options be handled in the stated capital account? Contemporary accounting practice would probably not enter a stock option as part of the stated capital until the optionee exercised his option. But it is a separate question whether that practice, to the extent followed, should govern the statutory concept of stated capital.

How about convertible shares? Suppose an outstanding share of preferred stock with a par value of $100 is convertible into two shares of common stock each having a par value of $100: should the stated capital of the outstanding preferred be $100 or $200? Or take the example of a $1,000 convertible debenture that may be converted into three shares of common stock with a par value of $100 each. Should the accountant at the time of exercise of the conversion privilege reduce liabilities by $1,000 and increase stated capital by $300, thereby increasing surplus by $700? If this example is slightly modified, a peculiar by-product of the system becomes visible. If a $100 debenture is convertible into three shares of $100 par value common stock, the effect of the conversion is to reduce liabilities by $100 and increase stated capital by $300, thus further restricting shareholder distributions to the extent of $200; but why should the general creditor need extra protection as a result of a transaction that is entirely to his benefit, namely, the elimination of an outstanding creditor claim and the substitution of a lower ranking shareholder's claim?

And then, what of acquisitions by the corporation of its outstanding stock? If the company "buys in" a share of its $10 par stock and pays $40 for it at a time when the average stated capital per share attributable to that class is $20, what happens to the stated capital account? Analytically, there are at least the following options: the treasury share is considered still to be "outstanding", and no change is made in the stated capital account; or the share is considered no longer to be outstanding and the stated capital account is reduced by $10 (the par), or $20 (the average stated capital per share), or $40 (the price). Consider how the answers should be affected by the lawyer's distinctions between "holding the reacquired share as a treasury share", "retiring the reacquired share to the status of authorized but unissued stock", and "cancelling" the share, thereby eliminating it from the aggregate of authorized shares. Consider then what legal capital entry should be made when "the share" that has been "reacquired" by the corporation is not retired or cancelled but is "resold" for $30.[10]

Finally, is stated capital to be thought of as an aggregate concept, or should one instead think of separate stated capitals for each class of shares? This point is discussed subsequently in connection with limitations on distributions to shareholders and the differing interests of differing classes of shareholders, but it should at least be noted here. Where a company has a complex capital structure involving several classes and series of shares, and where stock dividends, stock splits, conversions, options, warrants, exchanges, new issues redemptions, repurchases and other sophisticated corporate transactions are routine events, this matter of the aggregate or componential character of stated capital can become very complex—and often indeterminable.

All of these transactions, and others like them, are discussed with illustrative examples in Subpart Two of this Part.

2. Reducing Capital

At this point the concept of "reduction of capital" must be addressed, though the discussion may entail a modest digression.

Frequent reference may be found in cases, statutes, and texts, to "reducing capital". Unfortunately, "reducing capital" has had, and still has, at least three wholly different meanings:

(1) In the era of *Wood v. Dummer,* and occasionally still today, "reduction of capital" referred to a distribution of corporate assets to shareholders. The assets—the "capital"—put at stake by the shareholders is reduced when a part of those assets is returned to them. This sense of the term is that of the economist or the businessman.

(2) In its second meaning, reduction of capital takes "capital" to refer to the outstanding shares, and a reduction to mean a decrease in the number of shares outstanding. The focus of this meaning is not upon an asset distribution but upon a legal step whereby the corporation by redemption, purchase, retirement,

10. See discussion of "treasury stock" in Second Part, Subpart One, Chapter IV, infra.

conversion, exchange, or cancellation cuts back on the number of shares that are legally characterized as "outstanding".[11]

(3) Finally, reduction of capital in its modern statutory sense refers neither to an asset distribution nor a decrease in the number of outstanding shares, but to a downward revision in the stated capital account on the lower right-hand side of the balance sheet.

The most direct way to bring about such a downward revision is through a lowering of the par value of the outstanding shares; this is usually achieved by a simple resolution adopted by directors and shareholders amending the certificate of incorporation to lower the dollar figure prescribed as the par value of the shares of a particular class, and filing with the state corporation authority a suitable certificate of such amendment. If, for example, a corporation has outstanding 100 shares of $100 par value each, and the certificate of incorporation is amended to provide for a par value of $5 per share, the minimum stated capital is thereby changed from $10,000 to $500, and so, by appropriate corporate procedure the stated capital can be written down on the corporation's books to $500. This reduction in the stated capital produces a corresponding increase in a surplus account, sometimes denominated "reduction surplus".

If and to the extent that such reduction surplus may, under the governing statute, be charged in conjunction with a distribution of assets to shareholders, the reduction of capital that creates the reduction surplus bears a potentiality for a shareholder distribution and a consequent weakening of assets available to creditors; but that risk is a potentiality only, and the reduction of capital itself affects no one economically in any way. It is simply an accounting entry. But the hangover effect of the older meanings of reduction of capital continues to tincture the atmosphere, and in statutes, judicial opinions and legal commentary, it is usual to find that "reduction of capital" is viewed as a drastic event with ominous overtones.

It is not uncommon to find two or more of these wholly different meanings of "reducing capital" used within a single statute, judicial opinion or commentary. This practice does not bring added clarity to a topic already technical and confounding.

Reduction of capital in its sense as a downward revision of stated capital can obviously be brought about by a number of ways in addition to lowering the par value of shares. A conversion of

11. Once in a while, but fortunately not often, one also hears reduction of capital used to refer to an amendment to the certificate of incorporation reducing the number of shares *authorized* to be issued by the corporation.

$100 par value convertible preferred stock into three shares of $10 par common could lead to such a reduction, as noted above. Different avenues for reducing stated capital typically call for different voting and filing procedures under the applicable corporation statute.[12] In this connection, see the later discussion of reacquisitions of shares by a corporation, and of distributions in liquidation.[13]

3. Surpluses of Various Hues and Flavors

Given a balance sheet on which assets, liabilities, and stated capital are designated by specific dollar figures, deducting the sum of the latter two from the first yields the "surplus". When the total of corporate assets is decreased by a distribution to shareholders the left-hand side of the balance sheet is reduced and the amount of surplus shown on the right-hand side goes down correspondingly. Under the simple stated capital/surplus statutes, assets may lawfully be distributed to shareholders up to the point where the decline in assets consequent upon the distribution reduces the surplus account to a zero balance. Under many statutes, however, analysis must not be permitted to stop at this point.

When corporate accounting was in its infancy, accountants customarily used only one surplus account. They did not seek to explain *how* the surplus had come to be there. Statutes following a strict stated capital/surplus test approach have not moved past that stage in accounting analysis. Over the last 20 or 30 years, the accounting profession has, however, moved steadily in the direction of sub-categorizing surplus in an effort to have the balance sheet identify the way by which the surplus was generated. A modern balance sheet may therefore show many kinds of surpluses, and in turn a modern corporation statute may declare some kinds of surplus ineligible for purposes of charging an asset distribution to shareholders.

a. Capital Surplus (Paid-in Surplus)

If a share of stock with a par value of $10 is issued for $25, and the existing stated capital is correspondingly increased by $10, as it normally would be, some kind of surplus has been created to the extent of the $15 difference. In older usage, this $15 difference was called a "capital surplus"; and the term persists in many statutes though accountants typically refer to it today as "paid-in surplus". Or if the corporation "buys in" a share of its outstanding stock for $10 and then later sells "that share" for $15, the $5

12. Del.Gen.Corp.Law §§ 242(b), 244(a); N.Y.Bus.Corp.L. § 516. See also former N.C.Gen.Stats. § 55–48, re- pealed effective July 1, 1990. See supra, note 4.

13. See discussion, infra, pp. 84–87.

difference may show up on the balance sheet as a paid-in surplus item. Paid-in surplus can be generated in other ways. When, for example, no par stock is issued, the directors are required by the statutes to designate all or some portion of the proceeds as stated capital; if they so designate less than the full amount received, the balance is entered on the balance sheet as paid-in surplus.[14]

Where a corporation has a paid-in surplus, and no other surplus, may it legally distribute assets to shareholders and charge the paid-in surplus account? On this key point, the statutes are divided, some specifically providing that paid-in surplus may be a basis for equity distributions, some providing that it may not, and some providing nothing. Where the statutes do not distinguish among surpluses, the courts have declined to read in a distinction.[15]

A few statutes provide that paid-in surplus may be used as a basis for distributions to preferred stock but not to common stock.[16] The argument in favor of permitting the paid-in surplus to be used as a basis for dividends to preferred shareholders is that it is a more serious threat to the corporation's general financial standing to build up arrearages on preferred stock dividends than to skip common stock dividends and that the restraints on payment of preferred dividends should therefore be more relaxed.

14. Some earlier statutes, for reasons that are unfathomable, required the directors in such a case to allocate a designated minimum fraction, such as one-quarter or one-third, of the proceeds as stated capital.

15. An argument is available that even in states that generally forbid the use of paid-in surplus as the basis for a dividend distribution, an exception to that prohibition should exist in the case of so-called "equalization surplus". Of insufficient substantive importance to merit even a footnote, a visit to that argument and its context will serve to illustrate how readily the wanderer on these paths can be led off into intellectual marshlands from which few ever return.

Assume the case of a corporation that has ten shares of $10 par stock outstanding, a stated capital of $100, an earned surplus account of $100, assets of $200 in cash, and no liabilities. The book value, liquidation value and (probably) market value of each share is $20. If now the corporation issues one addi-

tional share, the purchaser may be expected to have to pay $20 for it, and the entries on the corporate books will be $10 additional to stated capital and $10 to paid-in surplus. But in this case, $10 was paid above par because each of the other outstanding shares had a claim to $10 of prior earnings. Before the issuance of the new share, the corporation could have declared a $10 dividend on each share based on earned surplus; why should it not be in a position after the issuance of the new share to pay a dividend of $10 on each of the eleven outstanding shares, even though $10 out of the total of $110 distributed would have to be charged against the $10 paid-in surplus created by the equalization payment made by the new shareholder? Neither statute nor court has thrown light in this corner, but some commentators have argued for recognition of the special situation of equalization surplus.

16. E.g., W.Va.Corp. Act § 31–1–100 (last par.) (any "capital surplus" may be so used).

b. *Reduction Surplus*

"Reducing capital" and "reduction surplus" are described earlier. May such reduction surplus, under a stated capital/surplus test statute, provide an appropriate basis for a dividend or other distribution of assets to shareholders? Some statutes say no, but most say yes.[17] If the statute countenances this usage, one can readily see the appeal that capital reduction has to a corporate management that is facing a negative surplus and that would have to skip a dividend payment unless something is done. Directors and managements do not like to skip dividend payments. Shareholders grow restive or even rebellious, unfavorable comment is aroused in the press, on the street and in the lunch clubs, and the management nearly always loses points on the scoreboard of managerial competition—the stock market. The reduction device has often been used to accommodate a dividend and the courts have not sought to prevent it.

c. *Appreciation Surplus and Unrealized Gain*

Is it permissible for a corporation's directors to revalue its assets upward, thereby increasing the surplus account, and then charge to the appreciated surplus a distribution of assets to shareholders? Surplus created through such a revaluation of assets is known as "appreciation surplus" or "revaluation surplus."

Almost all the statutes are silent on this question.[18] According to "generally accepted accounting principles", fixed assets are carried at historical cost less depreciation, and the usual accounting view is that no increment in market value should be recognized until the property is disposed of—until the gain is "realized." In general, the income tax laws proceed on a similar basis. Nonetheless, in some situations a failure to reflect an increased market value may be more dangerously misleading than the "conservative" practice of continuing to carry the purchase price.[19] And a day may yet come when new techniques for indexed accounting, or replacement cost accounting, will better cope with the reality of shifts in price levels and currency values.

But again, it is not inevitable that the attitude of the accounting profession is determinative for purposes of determining the legality of a shareholder distribution. If the board of directors of a corporation, or corporate counsel, decides that it would be misleading to the investing public to continue to carry assets on

17. Id., § 31–1–100.

18. An exception is the former North Carolina, Section 55–49(e), which recognized that there may be "surplus arising from a revaluation of assets made in good faith upon demonstrably adequate bases of revaluation." See supra, note 4.

19. Compare *Zahn v. Transamerica Corp.,* 162 F.2d 36 (3d Cir.1947).

the balance sheet at cost after they have radically increased in value, and instructs the company's bookkeeper to write the assets up to the market value as judged by the board, the mere fact that the company's outside auditors are unhappy about the entry or even qualify their audit certificate, does not necessarily force the conclusion that the surplus created by the write-up may not be legally used under the applicable corporation code as a basis for a dividend or other distribution of assets to shareholders.[20]

At the least, it may be expected that a present-day accountant would insist that the surplus created by a write up of assets be specially designated in the surplus accounts as "appreciation surplus" so that there is at least disclosure of the method by which the corporation put itself into compliance with the statutory legal capital scheme before making the distribution of assets to shareholders.

d. Earned Surplus

The next section includes discussion of legal capital statutes that prescribe earned surplus as the standard for determining the legality of shareholder distributions. Earned surplus as a concept is discussed there.

e. Other Surpluses

Many kinds of transactions involving changes in the capital structure of a corporation have an impact upon the stated capital and surplus accounts. Surpluses created by these transactions and adjustments may either be viewed generically as "surplus", or they may be fitted into the sub-categories of surplus just reviewed, or may be further sub-classified; or, increasingly it is observable that accounting usage on the balance sheet is simply to describe the way in which the surplus was created, without seeking to categorize it. Accounting refinements have today moved far beyond the gross and clumsy conceptual tools of the legal capital statutes. The legal capital provisions are attempting to work on a watch movement with a one-inch wide screwdriver. Eventually the question must be asked whether either to make a large investment in a set of watchmaker's tools—a dubious investment for a dubious purpose—or give up the job. As appears in the

---

20. In *Randall v. Bailey*, 288 N.Y. 280, 43 N.E.2d 43 (1942), which arose under an earlier New York statute, the New York Court of Appeals upheld the legality of a shareholder distribution charged to an undivided surplus account that was attributable in part to a write-up of appreciated corporate assets. Both the lower court and appellate court opinions are less than satisfactory, however, and the statute involved was unusual in that it explicitly referred to the "value" of the corporate assets as a factor in determining the propriety of a distribution.

discussion in the Second Part, increasingly the answer is to give up the job.

D. STATED CAPITAL STATUTES—TYPES

1. Stated Capital/Surplus Statutes

The discussion in Chapter II developed the general history and concept of stated capital. The simple model transactions reviewed there illustrate the way in which the concept of stated capital could be used as a device for inhibiting distributions to equity holders. The examples shown there illustrate the working of a stated capital/surplus test. Under that test, one deducts the liabilities shown on the balance sheet from the assets shown on the balance sheet, and then deducts from that difference the amount of the stated capital; if the result of that operation produces a positive dollar figure, then distributions may to that extent be legally made to shareholders. A number of state corporation laws have long used the balance sheet-stated capital/surplus test.

New York is a typical stated capital/surplus jurisdiction. Under the New York Business Corporation Law, the substantive restraint on equity distributions reads as follows:

> Dividends may be declared or paid and other distributions may be made out of surplus only, so that the net assets of the corporation remaining after such declaration, payment or distribution shall at least equal the amount of its stated capital.[21]

The New York Business Corporation Law then provides the following statutory definition of stated capital as

> the sum of (A) the par value of all shares with par value that have been issued, (B) the amount of the consideration received for all shares without par value that have been issued, except such part of the consideration therefor as may have been allocated to surplus in a manner permitted by law, and (C) such amounts not included in clauses (A) and (B) as have been transferred to stated capital, whether upon the distribution of shares or otherwise, minus all reductions from such sums as have been effected in a manner permitted by law.[22]

Stated capital/surplus statutes are subject to the difficulties inherent in any balance sheet-based test. In the effort to carve out from the net worth section of the balance sheet a special protective cushion called "stated capital", such statutes introduce additional difficulties, as reviewed above. But as compared to other types of stated capital statutes, these are the simplest to

---

21. N.Y. Bus.Corp.Law § 510(b).   **22.** Id., § 102(a)(12).

operate, since their regulatory system does not demand more refined analytic subdivision of the aggregate "surplus".

2. Stated Capital/Earned Surplus Statutes

As accountants and other analysts have brought closer focus to bear upon the concept of balance sheet surplus, and have further asked themselves what kinds of transactions should provide a basis for distributing corporate dividends, the general majority view has emerged increasingly that, in general, corporate dividends should be the product of enterprise earnings. Development of this viewpoint is in part attributable to a perception of the analytic limitations of the stated capital/surplus test. In part the argument in favor of a stated capital/earned surplus test has arisen out of an increasing awareness that there are interests at stake other than those of the creditors, mainly the interest of one class of shareholders against another and the general interest of all shareholders and the market place to be more specifically informed about the business activities and condition of the enterprise. And finally, the turn of focus from the general concept of surplus to the more restricted conception of earned surplus coincides with and is associated with a major change in perspective in the world of finance that has taken place during this century; affecting lawyers, accountants and bankers alike, earlier concentration upon static, balance sheet, asset accounting has been overtaken by a more sophisticated concern with the dynamic, ongoing, profit and loss statement, earnings flow of an enterprise and, in recent years, cash flow.

Balance sheet analysis is important, particularly when liquidity is a major concern. But sad experience with gilt edge bonds in the 1920's and 1930's drove home the point that ultimately enterprise debt will be paid off, if it is paid off, out of enterprise earnings. What good does it do bond holders to foreclose on several hundred miles of unprofitable rusting railroad track?

With the emergence of these newer attitudes, state corporation codes tended to move away from the general stated capital/ surplus test and adopted a new approach restricting distributions to shareholders based upon earnings. In general, such statutes permit shareholder distributions only to the extent of available earned surplus and only in the absence of insolvency.

An illustration of legal capital provisions of the stated capital/ earned surplus statutes was contained in the Model Business Corporation Act as it was in 1979. The Model Act has since been radically altered in these respects by amendments in 1980, 1984 and 1987, as discussed in Second Part, Subpart One, infra. But the Model Act as it existed in 1979, immediately prior to the

Manning Leg.Capital 3rd Ed. UTB—4

amendments in 1980, continues to warrant review here. One reason is that it is generally representative of other stated capital/earned surplus statutes in states that have not adopted the 1980 amendments or the subsequent Revised Model Act, though considerably better worked out than most. The second reason is that most Model Act states have not yet legislatively adopted, and some may never adopt, the sweeping doctrinal revisions that have been made by the Revised Model Act's new legal capital provisions. (The Model Act as it existed in 1979 is hereafter referred to as the "1979 Model Act" or the "Model Act (1979)".)

The 1979 Model Act purports to be a stated capital/earned surplus statute as Section 45 appears to limit dividends to unreserved and unrestricted earned surplus of the corporation. In fact, however, the restraints imposed by the 1979 Model Act are weaker than that term would imply since the exceptions are nearly as large as the rule.[23]

Absent insolvency, corporations engaged in exploiting natural resources and holding wasting assets are permitted by the 1979 Model Act to make dividend distributions regardless of the absence of earned surplus as they turn their natural resources into liquid assets.[24]

The 1979 Model Act's stated capital/earned surplus test is more fundamentally undermined by the provision authorizing "distributions from capital surplus."[25] This is a procedure for capital contraction—a reality more explicitly recognized in the earlier version of the Model Act describing the analogous procedure as a "distribution in partial liquidation." Distributions of corporate assets may, under the 1979 Model Act, be charged against a capital surplus account, if the company will not thereby be made insolvent, if it is current on its dividends on any cumulative preferred stock outstanding, if there is enough surplus (of some kind) remaining to cover the liquidating preference of the preferred stock, and if the recipients are informed that the distribution is being charged against a capital surplus account. In addition, a shareholder vote is needed unless the certificate of incorporation grants to the board of directors the authority to make such payments. There is no requirement that the corporation exhaust its earned surplus before turning to the device of charging capital surplus; as a result, the board can, while reducing the creditors' cushion through pay-outs to shareholders, hoard a favorable earned surplus balance against the day when it might

---

23. See Hackney, *The Financial Provisions of the Model Business Corporation Act*, 70 Harv.L.Rev. 1357, 1358–59 (1957).

24. Model Act (1979) § 45(b).

25. Model Act (1979) § 46.

have a special use for it. There is no requirement of notice to creditors; in fact, creditors, those for whom the whole statutory legal capital scheme was built, are completely forgotten.

Further, all companies subject to the 1979 Model Act may use capital surplus to support dividend payments on cumulative preferred stock if they have no earned surplus, assuming again that the distribution does not precipitate insolvency.[26]

Then, the 1979 Model Act explicitly makes place for the so-called "quasi-reorganization." This strange term requires a little explanation. If the only permissible statutory basis for dividend payments is earned surplus, the management has a considerable incentive to "hoard" earned surplus by avoiding making other kinds of charge against "earned surplus" and, if some charge against some surplus must be made, to try to arrange for a charge against some subcategory of "capital surplus". It would be nice, for example, if an uninsured fire loss could be charged against a capital surplus account, leaving the earned surplus account intact. That particular manoeuvre is, however, denied by generally accepted accounting principles and also by the 1979 Model Act. But after having taken that step, Section 70 of the Act provides:

> A corporation may, by resolution of its board of directors, apply any part or all of its capital surplus to the reduction or elimination of any deficit arising from losses, however incurred, but only after first eliminating the earned surplus, if any, of the corporation by applying such losses against earned surplus and only to the extent that such losses exceed the earned surplus, if any. Each such application of capital surplus shall, to the extent thereof, effect a reduction of capital surplus.[27]

What does that mean? What it means is that a corporation that has distributed assets to shareholders to the full extent of its earned surplus and later develops a negative earned surplus may then apply a portion of its capital surplus to the deficit to bring the deficit up to zero and thereafter pay out additional assets to its shareholders as soon as there are any earnings. As has been described earlier, capital surplus is not difficult to generate; a simple reduction of par or other reduction of stated capital will do it.[28] The net result of these provisions of the 1979 Model Act, therefore, is that in addition to permitting direct distribution of capital surplus a corporation may, through use of capital surplus as an offset to deficit, pay out all current earnings to its shareholders despite a deficit in the earned surplus account prior to the

26. Id. (last par.).

27. Id. § 70 (third par.).

28. Id. (first par.).

offset. Thus, by going through the right moves, capital surplus, *or even stated capital,* can be set off against a corporate deficit. That is a so called "quasi-reorganization". The consequence is precisely antithetical to the creditor protection purposes of the stated capital scheme in general—and to the earned surplus standard in particular.

Finally, see the discussion below of reacquisition of shares.[29]

3. Other Stated Capital Statutes

Other mutations or sports of stated capital statutes exist. Two of them in important corporation law states merit attention.

a. Stated Capital/Surplus or Net Profits Statutes

A corporation law provision adopted in New Jersey in 1904 provided that "the directors of a corporation shall not make dividends except from its surplus, or from the net profits arising from the business, nor shall it divide, withdraw, or in any way pay to the stockholders, or any of them, any part of the capital stock of such corporation, or reduce its capital stock except as authorized by law." [30] To the extent that this language is comprehensible at all, it appears to draw a distinction between surplus and net profits arising from the business. The New Jersey court accepted the distinction and sought to provide meaning for both.[31] Statutory variants in other states have included "surplus profits . . . [nor] . . . divide capital stock"; "surplus or net profits . . . nor divide . . . capital stock".

It is very difficult to tell what statutes like New Jersey's may mean and very little judicial gloss has been put upon them. On the whole, these statutes bear with them all the problems of the surplus statutes, compounded by their own special verbal obscurity.

b. Stated Capital/Surplus or Current Net Profits Statutes: "Nimble Dividends"

The law of stated capital and pay-out restriction is the product of a continuing conflict between an urge to protect creditors by a simplistic mechanical rule, on the one hand, and on the other, the

---

29. See discussion, infra, pp. 84–86.

30. Note here again the classical use of "capital stock" to mean "assets" in the phrase "to pay to the stockholders . . . the capital stock." Is the meaning the same in the following line of the statute? For another example, see Treas.Reg. § 1.6043–1(a) ("liquidation of . . . capital stock").

31. *Goodnow v. American Writing Paper Co.,* 73 N.J.Eq. 692, 69 A. 1014 (1908). The revisers of the New Jersey corporation law intended to eliminate the possibility of declaring dividends from "historical" net earnings while there is a capital deficit. Comment to N.J.Bus.Corp. Act § 14A:7–14, noting that such a practice was possible under the old statute, N.J.Rev.Stat. § 14:8–19.

pressures of business reality. Business reality won a big round in the development of the concept of so-called "nimble dividends".

As a practical business matter, a corporation that has accumulated large deficits and has a heavy burden of unpaid debt has no prospect of obtaining further credit unless new equity capital can be attracted to the enterprise. In turn, there is no hope of attracting additional equity capital unless there is some prospect that dividends will be paid. The old deficits must not, therefore, be allowed to block future dividends. The obvious—perhaps the only—way out is to arrange matters so that dividends can be paid if the enterprise earns a current profit from its operations, even through the deficits piled up in previous years have not yet been eliminated.

The Delaware corporation statute in 1927 took the lead in sanctioning that result. The Delaware statute is basically a stated capital/surplus statute; but it also permits dividends to be paid out to the extent of the "net profits" for the current or preceding year in spite of the fact that the corporation's balance sheet has no surplus—*i.e.,* its stated capital account is in deficit. Such dividends are aptly nicknamed "nimble dividends".

The Delaware act makes it possible for a deficit corporation, deeply under water, to distribute its earnings to equity holders with respect to the fiscal year in which they are earned (or the year after) and thereby to continue indefinitely the deficit condition of the balance sheet. The statutory authorization of nimble dividends makes overt and explicit the usually unadmitted reality—the abandonment of all effort to protect creditors through stated capital machinery. The Delaware provision does, however, nod in the direction of protecting the preferred shareholder by forbidding distribution of current earnings to common shareholders if the value of the corporation's net assets is not at least equal to the stated capital of the outstanding preferred shares.[32]

Given the importance of Delaware as a leading state of incorporation, it might be thought that its legal capital provisions would be elegantly sophisticated in their drafting. Regrettably, the situation is otherwise.

The statutory language of Delaware's nimble dividend provision summarized above states that the corporation "may declare and pay dividends upon the shares of its capital stock either (1) out of its surplus, as defined in and computed in accordance with Sections 154 and 244 of this title, or (2) in case there shall be no

---

32. Del.Gen.Corp.Law § 170. Why not the liquidation preference instead of the stated capital?

such surplus, out of its net profits for the fiscal year in which the dividend is declared and/or the preceding fiscal year." [33]

The reader with a taste for textual exegesis might wish to consider the interpretational questions set out below; they are representative of the spray of issues that spume out of Delaware's delphic provision on "nimble dividends." [34]

E. SHARE REACQUISITION BY THE ISSUER— "TREASURY SHARES"

As was earlier stressed, the corporate creditor's desire to restrict asset distributions to shareholders is much broader than keeping down dividend payments. *Any* transfer of corporate assets to equity holders, if not accompanied by an equivalent or greater pay-in of other assets, has the effect of reducing the total corporate asset pool available for the payment of creditors. Therefore a redemption or purchase by the corporation of its outstanding stock, or a retirement of preferred stock, or a bargain sale of corporate assets to shareholders, or a cancellation of indebtedness owing by shareholders, or a payment of assets to shareholders as compensation are all equally objectionable from the creditor's standpoint. See Chapter VI for discussion of creditor protection against such asset leakages.

Earlier discussion dealt with the appropriate way to handle entries to stated capital and surplus accounts to reflect share reacquisitions and "treasury share" transactions. Still to be considered is whether, under the applicable statute, the acquisition by

---

33. Id.

34. For example: *Accounting questions:* What is intended by "net profits"? Same as "earnings"? Why "net"? Assuming that the imprecise term "out of surplus" means "charged against surplus", what does it mean as an accounting matter to have dividends "charged against net profits"? *Substantive questions:* The provision purports to make the "net profits" avenue available as an option if but only if there is no surplus. But suppose the corporation has a $1 surplus and net profits of $20? How much can be distributed? Is it permissible to distribute $1 first and then, since no surplus is left, pay out the $20 in a second distribution? Or $19? To require two steps is formalistic; whether in one step or two the economic result is that the options are summed, not alternative. *Timing questions:* Is the reference to the fiscal year to be taken literally (*i.e.,* as meaning a full year), so that the

corporation may not, at six months into the year, pay dividends "out of" the "net profits" of the first six months? On the other hand, if the corporation has its income statement for Year N, it also has the balance sheet for Year N, so the earnings in Year N are already reflected on the balance sheet; if both surplus *and* earnings for that year can be used, does that not double count? And what is the "preceding year"? Preceding what? And if (i) at the end of Year N there is no surplus, (ii) during Year N there were net profits of $10, (iii) a dividend of $10 was paid out, and (iv) during Year N + 1 there were no net profits so the surplus is still 0—may a dividend of $10 be paid "out of" the net profits of the "preceding year"? And what is the timing relationship implied in the reference to the separate dates of declaration and payment? *Miscellaneous question:* What could be intended by the inviting but puzzling "and/or" in the statutory text?

the issuing company of its own outstanding shares, and corresponding distribution of corporate assets to a shareholder, is itself restricted by the statutory restraints on dividends, and with what results.

The entire topic of share reacquisition, treasury shares, resale, retirement and the like is technical and sorely vexed under the legal capital statutes and under accounting practice, and generalization is not reliable. But it is important that the nature of the problems be recognized.

Some older statutes do not cover the matter at all, and seem to restrict "dividends" only. More modern statutes, such as the 1979 Model Act, are at least clear in requiring that the pay-out to the shareholder to buy in his shares is a "distribution" and can only be made if there is an appropriate surplus account available to be charged. But then what happens?

Suppose a corporation has assets of $2,000 in cash, $500 in liabilities, ten shares outstanding with a par value of $100 each, a stated capital of $1,000 and a surplus account (let us say earned, to make it easy) of $500. It now "buys in" one share for $100 and pays $100 out to the selling shareholder, the board of directors directing that the share be carried as a "treasury share." The company's cash is reduced to $1,900; stated capital is unaffected; an accounting entry "restricts" the surplus account by $100, but leaves its total at $500; and a separate line item reading "Less shares held in the treasury $100" is deducted from the shareholders' equity part of the balance sheet.

Then, at a later time, the board by resolution "retires" the share to the status of authorized but unissued stock, or "cancels" it. Upon the retirement or cancellation, the share is obviously no longer "outstanding" (though traditionally it remains "issued"), and the stated capital is reduced by (in this case) the stated capital attributable to it, $100; the restriction of $100 on the surplus account is now removed, the total remaining at $500; and the line item on treasury shares disappears. The end consequence of these steps is that $100 has been paid out to a shareholder, yet the company's surplus account is just where it was at the beginning—available to be charged as assets are paid out to buy in other shares or pay out dividends. Expressed another way, stated capital has been reduced concomitantly with a direct payment of assets to shareholders—precisely the result the stated capital engine was supposed to avoid as a protection to creditors—and this reduction has been effectuated without even the shareholder vote or notice to shareholders usually prescribed by the statutes for reducing capital. Insolvency, of course, always remains as a legal barrier to further pay-out to shareholders.

The share acquisition transaction just outlined is greatly simplified. As an exercise, it is worth considering under various kinds of statutes the effects of the introduction of elements such as these: The aggregate stated capital is greater than par times the number of shares outstanding; the price paid for the share is less (or greater) than the par (or the stated capital attributable to it); the company has other surpluses besides earned surplus; the company later "reissues" the treasury share at a price less (or greater) than the par (or than the stated capital attributed to it) (or than the price at which it was purchased); the company has several classes of shares outstanding with (without) separate stated capital and surplus accounts; etc., etc.

From a technical standpoint, the legal capital statutes are a shambles in their treatment of share reacquisitions. From a substantive standpoint, the transaction called "share reacquisition" pokes another major perforation in the protective wall supposedly built for the creditor by the legal capital statutes.

Legal capital provisions governing share "reacquisition" are in rapid motion, as appears in the Second Part. Intellectual command of such provisions is of frequent practical importance to the practicing corporation lawyer in dealing with closely-held corporations where it is common for shareholders to enter into share repurchase agreements effective upon the death or retirement of a major shareholder.[35]

F. THE CLASS STRUGGLE: CLASSES OF SHARES

Several times reference has been made here to the special problems raised by legal capital statutes where a corporation has two or more classes of shares outstanding. As a simple illustration of the problem, consider the case under a stated capital/ surplus statute of a corporation that, having a zero surplus, issues 100 shares of $10 par preferred stock for $15 per share, thus creating a stated capital attributable to the preferred of $1,000 and a paid-in surplus of $500. If the board of directors now undertakes to pay out a $500 dividend to the common shareholders, based on a charge against the newly-created paid-in surplus, it can be readily seen that the preferred shareholder will not be happy to see the money he has just paid in go out to the common shareholders. The same kind of problem would also arise if the par value of one class of shares were reduced, thus creating a reduction surplus, and the board then charged that reduction surplus as the basis for a dividend payment to another class of shares.

35. See First Part, Subpart Two, Transactions 13, 14, 15 and 16.

In point of fact, a little reflection will reveal that separate classes of shares can be put at loggerheads by almost any transaction that involves adjustments of stated capital accounts and surplus accounts. An interesting aspect of the evolution of stated capital machinery is that the modern statutes have gradually come to recognize this conflict of interests among classes of shares. For example, some statutes require, in a vote to reduce capital, that the shareholders vote by class. A New York court has held that a reduction of stated capital attributable to common shares was such a serious event that it gave rise to an appraisal remedy in favor of an objecting preferred shareholder under a statute that provided appraisal rights to preferred shareholders whose rights are altered" by an amendment to the certificate of incorporation.[36] Delaware, as mentioned earlier, restricts the availability of nimble dividends to situations where the corporation's net assets are at least equal to the stated capital of the preferred. The 1979 Model Act permits asset distributions to common shareholders only so long as the company's net assets exceed the aggregate liquidating preference of the preferred—which, while rational, drops entirely the facade that par has any real significance or is aimed at protection of creditors.

Still, even the most modern legal capital statutes have only started to enter upon the problem of interclass conflict and have not gone far in specifying the accounting procedures to be followed in multi-class capital structures. Balance sheets carry separate stated capital accounts for separate classes, but treatment of surplus accounts is varied and uncertain. If a stated capital scheme were to be rigorously worked out so as to be coherent intellectually (whatever its substantive desirability), it would maintain a careful separation in the capital and surplus accounting for each class of shares. The point is faintly recognized in a few statutes, such as those of Maryland and Ohio, but no statutory draftsman has carried the analysis through with determination and consistency—so complex does it become, and so inconsequential are the marginal returns. But it may be hazarded that litigation under legal capital statutes today is more likely to arise at the instance of a discomfitted shareholder of a multi-class corporation than at the instance of a creditor.

36. *In re Kinney,* 279 N.Y. 423, 18 N.E.2d 645 (1939).

G. LIABILITY FOR SHAREHOLDER DISTRIBUTIONS VIOLATING THE APPLICABLE STATUTE

What are the consequences if an asset distribution of some kind, whether by dividend or other technique, is made to shareholders in violation of the applicable statutory restriction? [37]

As a generalization, the statutes now specifically impose liability upon directors who vote for or assent to a dividend or other distribution, or stock repurchase, if the action violates the statute or restrictions in the articles of incorporation. In the prototype to the Revised Model Business Corporation Act, promulgated in 1984 (the "Revised Model Act"), the liability runs to the corporation. In some jurisdictions, statutory or case law may identify other possible plaintiffs. There are few reported cases, however, and the statutes generally provide little or no guidance on questions of remedial procedure.

Also, the statutes usually contain significant limitations on the directors' liability for making an improper distribution. Generally, a director's reliance upon the corporate financial statements, figures provided by an accountant, or reports of the chief executive or the financial officers of the corporation exonerates him from liability.[38] Directors who are required to make payment to the corporation ordinarily have a statutory right of subrogation against shareholders who received the distributions knowing of their illegality; such directors also have rights of contribution from their guilty confreres.[39]

What of the measure of liability? Older statutes sometimes provided that the directors should be liable for all debts to creditors of the corporation if improper distributions were made to shareholders.[40] But modern statutes typically narrow the liability to the amount of the illegal distribution, or to the amount of the unpaid debt, whichever is lower.[41]

The question of who, if anyone, has a remedy against the directors raises another cluster of questions unsatisfactorily handled by the statutes. Is the remedy limited to creditors? If so, to what kinds of creditors? That is, must the creditor's claim be liquidated and matured, must he be a judgment creditor whose

37. No doubt, absent statute, a director's general duty of care includes a duty not to declare unlawful dividends. However, the Model Act some years ago codified the director's duty in this area. Model Bus.Corp. Act § 48(a) (1979).

38. E.g., Rev. Model Business Corp. Act § 8.30(b).

39. Id. § 8.33(b).

40. See, e.g., former Del.Gen.Corp. Law § 172.

41. See, e.g., Tex.Bus.Corp.Act § 2.02(A)(8); Wyo.Bus.Corp.Act § 17-1-105(a).

execution against the corporation has been returned *nulla bona,* must he have been a creditor at a time prior to the illegal distribution to shareholders, etc. May the complainant bring an action to enforce the full liability of the director (whatever it may be) or may he sue only for the amount of his personal debt claim? May a trustee in bankruptcy of the corporation enforce the remedy, and if so, is he acting on behalf of all the creditors or in his capacity as successor to the rights of the corporation? What kinds of releases or waivers from whom would constitute a defense to the director? May a shareholder, or a shareholder of a particular class, pursue the director, either directly or on the theory that the director's action has placed the shareholder in jeopardy of having to respond to creditors? And if a shareholder may bring such a suit does he do so in derivative form on behalf of the corporation, or is the action a personal action of the shareholder? Most of these questions have never been answered, nor indeed even publicly asked.[42]

Apart from the director's liability, what about the liability of the shareholder who receives the illegal distribution? Most of the remedial questions just raised in connection with enforcement of the director's liability reappear—and in a more complex form—in the case of an effort to enforce liabilities against shareholders. How, for example, does a qualified plaintiff, whoever that may be, obtain a judgment of liability against shareholders that is binding upon all shareholders of the company or, at least, provides a basis for collateral estoppel in subsequent lawsuits against other shareholders? What now of the question of contribution as among shareholders? May the corporation sue the shareholders to recover the assets improperly distributed? Does the liability for the illegal distribution run with the stock or remain attached to the person who received the dividend? And his estate? Typically, of course, the recipient shareholder has no way to know at the time he receives the dividend check whether the dividend was properly declared or not. Does that make any difference to his liability? It is an interesting line of speculation to contemplate what would be involved in unwinding the tax consequences of an illegal dividend payment to thousands of shareholders in a large publicly-held company.[43]

Viewed as a whole, one is forced to conclude that the enormously complex and technical machine of legal capital goes through an extraordinary amount of grinding and clanking to

---

42. Many—but not all—state director liability limitation statutes specifically exclude liability for unlawful dividends. See generally Hanks, *Evaluating Recent State Legislation on Director and Officer Liability Limita-* *tion and Indemnification,* 43 Bus.Law. 1207 (1988).

43. And recapturing from the government the portion of the distribution it collected as tax.

produce, at the end, very little. It is difficult not to be reminded of the popular Black Box toy that features a switch that when turned on, activates a motor, that activates a small mechanical hand that emerges from the Box, and turns off the switch.

Nonetheless, the almost complete absence of cases imposing liability on directors or shareholders does not mean that the question of possible liability is a dead issue. Boards of directors do not wish to undertake personal risks needlessly and it is normal therefore for them to look to the corporation's legal counsel and chief financial officer to design a distribution transaction in a way that removes all doubt of its legality. Despite the absence of litigation attesting to the reality of the risk, the lawyer who does corporate work must continue to have a working knowledge of the way in which the statutory scheme operates—and how to thread his way through the maze to the desired result. As a practical matter, virtually any distribution to shareholders can be done legally by the experienced practitioner so long as the company is not insolvent. But it may not be legally possible without an expensive formal shareholders' meeting, a delaying notice procedure, or a sometimes risky exposure to the blackmailing propensities of a cranky shareholder who has a statutory right to demand a vote by class.

————

This chapter will be considerably clearer to the reader when he has worked his way through Subpart Two of this First Part. Set out there is a sequence of illustrative corporate financial transactions, a discussion of accounting entries and a review of the permissibility of shareholder distributions under different types of statutes.

Chapter V

A PRELIMINARY EVALUATION OF LEGAL CAPITAL STATUTES

What has preceded has been largely descriptive of the legal capital scheme as it existed in many states until relatively recently and as it continues to exist in most states today. It is now both possible and in order to ask how well it works.

First, the legal capital machinery makes only the most marginal effort to protect groups or classes of shareholders from each other despite their often conflicting interests.

As for creditors, the system makes no attempt to ward off three of their main worries—erosion of the corporation's cash flow out of which debt will be repaid, incurrence by the corporation of additional debt liabilities and creation of secured or senior debt claims.

All the system ever purports to do is to assure that shareholders have put something into the corporate pot and that they will not redistribute corporate assets to themselves without first protecting the corporate creditors. Does it work at all?

We have no systematic empiric studies. It is a safe generalization, however, that the statutory legal capital machinery provides little or no significant protection to creditors of corporations. The legal capital schemes embedded in the nation's state corporation acts are inherently doomed to a low level of effectiveness (perhaps even zero). Some of the reasons are:

1. The system is analytically incomplete in the same sense that an encircling wall is useless for containment if not closed throughout its perimeter. A stated capital/surplus figure, and even a stated capital/earned surplus figure, is the product of dozens of judgmental accounting decisions. If one were seriously interested in using surplus accounts as an on-off switch for certain transactions, he would inevitably find himself involved in full-scale regulation of corporate accounting systems, just as state utility and insurance commissions have found that pursuit of the goal of fair rate regulation has inexorably transformed them into legislatures of accountancy and tribunals of bookkeeping. Without the development of a jurisprudence of accounting to support the statutory legal capital scheme, the system is inherently incomplete and haphazard in its operation.

91

2.   To the extent that the purpose of the legal capital scheme is to protect creditors from transactions that benefit shareholders but prejudice creditors, it is at least odd that the statutes should hand over all the control switches and levers to the shareholders and those whom the shareholders elect, the board of directors. The statutes are detailed and explicit about the procedures and steps to be taken in order to effect changes in the capital structure of a corporation, but the decision-making power is always vested in the board or the shareholders, or the two together; in no case do the statutes provide for participation by the creditors, consultation with the creditors, or even notice to the creditors.

3.   A corporation's "legal capital" is a wholly arbitrary number, unrelated in any way to any economic facts that are relevant to a creditor. No one who is considering whether to lend money today to General Motors Corporation is interested in knowing what, or whether, a shareholder paid for his shares 50 years ago, or what was the par value that was stamped on the stock certificate that he received at that time. Given the existence of the legal capital system, the creditor would prefer to see a high stated capital figure rather than a low one, but from his standpoint the stated capital is simply a fortuitously-derived number that could as well have been taken from a telephone directory as from a series of unconnected and irrelevant historical events.

4.   Similar to the next preceding point is the fact that the entire system has no fundamental "why" to it. There is no reason why a reasonable man would take the number called stated capital and use it as a measure for limiting distributions to equity investors. At the same time, the kinds of things the creditor is interested to know and does want to police—some of which are mentioned in the next chapter—are left unasked and unattended by the legal capital system.

5.   The statutory legal system is inherently deficient for want of a time dimension. Ancient, present and future economic events are all scrambled together without regard to their differing current economic significance. In computing the availability of "surplus", a debt due in 20 years is treated no differently from a debt due next week; to a lender it makes a lot of difference. For purposes of the statute, cash and other quick assets are treated exactly the same as assets that would take years to liquidate for purposes of paying debts; a prospective creditor sees it

differently. It is assumed by the statute that creditors of today and tomorrow care about sales of stock made years before. They don't. And so forth.

6. Efforts to apply the system in the context of sophisticated modern corporate finance produce appalling, even revolting, conceptualistic debate. In the manner of medieval theologians at their worst, lawyers and accountants hold up (and are forced to hold up) sensible economic transactions while they wrangle over the appropriate stated capital treatment for stock subscriptions, agreements to purchase stock, mergers, treasury share cancellation, retirement conversions, stock warrant purchases, option exercises, stock discounts, liquidation preferences, allocation of "capital" among classes, series, and individual shares, etc., etc., endlessly. No one is to be faulted for this pointless expenditure of the energies of intelligent men and women; it is the inevitable, and unresolvable, by-product of the primitiveness and essential irrelevance of the legal capital system.

7. Whether one views it as a blessing or a deficiency of the existing statutory systems, it is at least a fact that the corporation acts do not pursue the implementation of their own scheme with any real seriousness.

- Statutes that provide for nimble dividends admit overtly that companies with heavily-impaired legal capital may still make payments to shareholders. Other statutes go almost as far when they permit deficits to be written off against capital surplus.

- Where dividend payments may be made to shareholders and charged to capital surplus, the statute offers a direct invitation to the lawyer architect to design a capital structure using low par stock and creating large capital surplus accounts—an invitation that is usually accepted.

- Many of the statutes permit payments to shareholders to be charged against reduction surplus, a form of surplus that is usually easy for the board to generate. Other statutes, through provisions allowing shareholder distributions to be charged against capital surplus, explicitly direct attention to this device.

- Some statutes leave an open trap door for corporate assets to go out to shareholders to buy in their stock.

- Legal capital statutes vest in the fox control of the machinery for protecting the chickens.

- The statutes display no interest in providing serious remedies and they are a procedural wasteland. Almost no instances can be found where liability was in fact imposed either on directors or on shareholders for violations of the legal capital scheme.

- When a certificate of dissolution is filed with respect to a corporation, the entire stated capital machinery is instantaneously suspended. Of course, it is true that the corporation acts call for payment of creditors during the process of corporate liquidation and impose liability on the directors if that mandate is disregarded. But once the dissolution certificate has been filed, following a dissolution vote by shareholders under the state corporation statute's procedure, asset distributions may be made to the corporation's shareholders with no further regard for the statutory stated capital provisions. It is at least peculiar that a system designed to create a protective cushion to protect creditors against distributions to shareholders should automatically cut out of operation in precisely the situation where massive distributions to shareholders are most likely to occur—in precisely the situation, indeed, of *Wood v. Dummer,* the progenitor of the entire system.

- The most persuasive evidence of the quintessential triviality of the system, however, lies in the fact that any corporation lawyer of moderate skill can nearly always arrange things (perhaps at some expense and after some procedural dance figures) so as to make a shareholder distribution lawful so long as insolvency is not the immediate consequence. Advance planning and precautionary steps by the lawyer can also go very far to prevent the legal capital question from ever arising for his corporate client.

8. It may be, though it would be difficult to prove, that the legal capital system has some unfortunate side effects. It can operate as a trap. Many lawyers are not sufficiently familiar with the arcana of legal capital to recognize a related problem when it does arise, and warn their clients accordingly. Other practitioners, more sensitized but without the experience or ingenuity to design around the system, sometimes feel compelled to advise their clients that a transaction that is economically sensible cannot be lawfully consummated even though no genuine economic risk to creditors exists. In particular, the legal capital system may operate to prevent the performance of stock

buy-out agreements in close corporations when one of the partners of the enterprise has died or withdrawn; in such cases the economic consequences upon the estate, upon the surviving widow, upon the withdrawing partner, and upon those remaining in the enterprise can be severe. Finally, while class voting has its merits, it is also true that a skillful corporate lawyer representing a special stock class in a multiclass corporation can use the legal capital class voting requirement as a stick-up gun at the head of the board of directors and majority holders who are seeking to restructure the corporation's capital accounts to the advantage of the enterprise, its creditors and its community. Stated capital procedures should not facilitate extortion of one class of shares by another but they can.

Altogether, it must be recognized that the machinery of legal capital established by our corporation acts suffers from a number of deficiencies. Is there nothing to be said for it? Do creditors receive from the system some degree of practical protection despite its analytic frailty? To make such a case persuasive is impossible but perhaps something can be put together.

The best argument suggesting that the system has some protective consequence for creditors is the argument historical, cultural, and psychological. For nearly 150 years, it has been thought important that an enterprise have something called its "capital" and the concept has acquired its own independent aura of respectability, whatever its actual significance to real creditors in real business situations. Bankers and other businessmen occasionally view a "thin" stated capital with suspicion, and it is—in some sense—considered to be a mark of fiscal probity to have a substantial stated capital on the right-hand side of the corporate balance sheet.[1] Deep in the consciousness of the American businessman, lawyer, accountant and banker is the general principle that distributions to shareholders are not supposed to be made "out of" capital. Everybody knows that ways are available to design around statutory restrictions; but the restrictions themselves are a reflection of that general principle. The statutory provisions on stated capital and distributions to equity investors are expressions of a general norm of behavior to which the business community has accustomed itself if only because of their essential irrelevance to anything the business community cares

---

1. This point is wholly different from the wise creditor's insistence that there be a substantial investment of equity assets in the enterprise; that exposure arises out of the entire equity account, not how it is divided among stated capital and various kinds of surpluses.

about. For this reason, among others, changes to the legal capital system [2] have not originated with the business community.

Perhaps it may be argued artfully that the statutes hang in just the right balance. They announce a general and salutary principle which commands wide assent; but they are so feebly constructed and loosely enforced that a corporation's financial managers, lawyers, and accountants can move as they wish when it is necessary to do so, as everyone agrees one should be able to do. If this line of thought is valid, creditors do, in some general sense, benefit from the statutory scheme to the extent that the stated capital provisions contribute to an atmosphere in which corporate managements psychologically feel themselves inhibited from distributing assets to shareholders indiscriminately.[3]

A second line of speculation, unprovable, is that the statutory provisions may have a degree of actual operating impact upon corporations of the medium-size range. Those in control of the incorporated small enterprise typically manage its, and their, economic lives with little or no awareness of or regard for the niceties of procedure spelled out in legal capital provisions. Large public enterprises on the other hand, can draw on lawyers and other professionals who see to it that wide flexibility of corporate financial action and decisions is maintained while scrupulously observing the statutory mandates. But it may also be that the managers of a medium-sized incorporated enterprise may be sufficiently conscious of statutory and regulatory requirements to be affected in their behavior, and yet not served with sufficient continuity or professionality of advice to enable them to control their own destinies in the legal capital thicket. And perhaps the medium-sized corporation is the one that offers the greatest problem for the creditor; there he has not the close personal contact that grounds his extension of credit to the incorporated barbershop nor has he the institutional protections that back up a credit to General Motors.

But whatever may be argued at these general and abstract levels, one basic bit of evidence almost compels the conclusion that creditors do not gain very much from the system. That evidence is the almost total lack of interest that creditors show in this subject. Creditors' groups do not try to lobby changes into the corporation acts to tighten up the obvious loopholes. They do not clamor for participation in the procedures by which corporations

2. See Second Part, infra.

3. But at best the argument is terribly thin. Salary payments and other fringe benefit pay-outs to executive shareholders are not affected by the legal capital statutes at all. And the real determinants of dividend payment levels are tax considerations, the board's perception of the corporation's working capital needs, and the estimate of the stock by the market.

shuffle about their capital accounts. And, on the affirmative side, creditors have, where they have cared to, gone ahead to develop, negotiate for, and put into practice genuinely effective techniques for achieving the purposes that the statutory legal capital provisions purport to address. The next chapter takes a look at these privately-ordered techniques, not only to see how the job is done, but also because they provide light on the question of the efficacy of the statutory machinery. The next chapter shows the kind of control structure that must be constructed if one wishes to pursue seriously the objective of the statutory schemes. It throws into contrasting and visible relief the seismic faults that inhere in the statutory legal capital scheme.

Chapter VI

CREDITOR PROTECTION OUTSIDE THE LEGAL CAPITAL STATUTES

How does the modern creditor of a corporation actually go about protecting himself against the risks outlined in Chapter I?

A. THE GENERAL TRADE CREDITOR

The typical incorporated enterprise, unlike an individual end consumer, does not become an installment debtor. If the enterprise owes money, it is normally either to a trade creditor who has provided trade goods or services to the corporation, or to an institutional or finance creditor, such as a bank. Leaving the institutional or finance creditor for later discussion, what does the general trade creditor do to try to maximize the chances that his billings will be paid?

The main answer is that he stays alert. Like the price of freedom (and the price of tyranny), the price of successful credit management is eternal vigilance. The credit manager's main protection is to stay close to the situation, to know his debtor, to spot the slow-downs in payment, the main telltale sign of drying up of working capital, to put prudent limits on the amount of credit extended to each trade purchaser, to clear checks immediately, to take instantaneous action, perhaps legal action, when a delinquency is spotted, to badger and cajole the delinquent debtor tirelessly, to see to it that when the next payment is made it does not go to other creditors, etc.

The credit manager has a number of things going for him, and a number of tools available to him, that upgrade his assignment from the impossible to the very difficult.

National professional credit agencies, such as Dun & Bradstreet, can provide him much information rapidly and at relatively small cost about a customer's liquidity and record of timely payment. Modern telecommunications and the computer afford the credit manager today almost instantaneous information on check clearances, bank balances, and the like, whether in or out of his own local area. Regionalization, including regionalization of economic interests, was characteristic of nineteenth century America. Much of the development of commercial law, and some of the development of corporation law, in the last century were attributable to regional differentiations. In a rapidly-developing, erratic and wide open entrepreneurial economy, shareholder investors, and particularly bank investors, tended to be urban and tended to be Eastern. The inevitable division of interest between the long-term player and the short-term player—between shareholders and bondholders on one hand and trade creditors on the other—often tended to be a division as well between outsiders and locals.

In the nineteenth century, the economic conflict between outside interests and local interests was a major theme in the evolution of American law appearing on stage in many guises and contexts, including the long contest over federal diversity jurisdiction, the concept of federal common law and *Swift v. Tyson*,[1] state legislation providing liberal homestead exemptions for local debtors, struggles over the rights of *bona fide* purchasers of goods and holders in due course of financial paper, the rejection of the English doctrine of the floating charge on inventory and receivables, the federal doctrine of irrebuttable recitations in municipal bonds, and the like.

In the twentieth century, by contrast, relative homogenization of the national economy, the development of major financial and industrial centers scattered throughout the nation, physical and cultural mobility and the emergence of instantaneous communications, have virtually eliminated the legal-economic regionalism of America's past. A supplier can do business anywhere in the country and draw upon a nationwide juridical system, a relatively uniform set of state laws and a national intelligence network to help him assess whether to extend credit to the prospective purchaser.

The relative stability of modern patterns of business and of business enterprises is also of immeasurable help to the credit manager. Except for businesses that do deal primarily with the transient consumer public passing by their doors, most enterprises build up a central core of regular customers with whom they have had experience and about whom they usually know a great deal. In turn, to a regular customer his regular supplier is an important person; the customer is generally satisfied with the supplier's goods or services and with his prices; the customer has some bargaining position with his supplier and can from time to time ask for and be confident of receiving special favors; and the customer knows that if he does not pay his bills to his supplier a valuable resource will be converted into a hostile voice that will pass the word through the commercial intelligence network that the customer is in economic trouble—a report that will almost instantly dry up other sources of credit. The credit manager who

1. 16 Pet. (41 U.S.) 1, 10 L.Ed. 865 (1842).

is dealing with a newly-formed enterprise often does not have this confidence of experience; a new enterprise may therefore find trade credit less readily available to it.

Other institutional arrangements also serve to protect the trade creditor. For example, the creditor may send out bills that are due 30 days after the billing date, but on which a discount will be given if paid within 10 days. In effect, the trade creditor becomes a banker after 10 days and charges interest on his advance to his customer. That interest charge will not make the creditor's fortune; but if the customer is any kind of a businessman, and adequately liquid, he will be moved by the discount incentive to avoid the interest charge by paying his bills promptly. If he does not, the trade creditor has at least passed along to his customer a portion of the creditor's cost of having his capital tied up in the account receivable plus the administrative costs of paying his credit manager to hound the debtor. The discounted bill system also provides the credit manager with a built-in early warning system. Since no rational businessman who has sufficient funds at his disposal will forego the opportunity to take the discount, as soon as the credit manager spots a customer who is not taking his discounts he will smell trouble and start enquiry.

Then there are the tax laws. Business enterprises know that from time to time they will wind up with a sour account and have to absorb the loss for an unpaid bill; their accountants allow for this through the creation of "reserves" for bad debt losses. When a loss is actually sustained, the United States Treasury, and any local jurisdiction that has an income tax law applicable to the creditor, share the loss with him by allowing him to deduct it as a business expense.

As may be seen even from this brief sketch, the real world of the trade creditor and his credit manager stands in remarkable contrast to the overall concept and set of assumptions that underlie the legal capital provisions of corporation acts. The small creditor's real concerns are at very close range and in an immediate time frame. They have nothing to do with stated capital accounts. The trade creditor measures his world in days and hours; his concern with ancient business history is minimal; his regard for subtleties of balance sheet accounting is almost nonexistent. He wants cash, he wants it promptly, he cares little where else the debtor's earlier-held cash may have gone, and he will act immediately in one institutional way or another if he is not paid. Of course the creditor would be pleased if he should be told by a lawyer that he may be able to sue a shareholder of a bankrupt debtor corporation on the ground that the shareholder had, at an earlier time, received an asset distribution that did not conform with the stated capital provisions of the local corporation act: any port in a storm, and any remedy is better than no remedy. But the trade creditor is certainly not looking to that resort in his daily business. Often, too, the creditor would prefer simply to write off the bad debt rather than spend time and money pursuing a "no good" account.

It is relevant to recall again that there are virtually no modern cases reported where creditors, or bankruptcy trustees, have successfully pursued the avenue of forcing shareholders to disgorge distributions. Perhaps this is because corporate shareholders and their lawyers are able, almost at will, to design distributions to equity holders in a legal way. Or perhaps the remedy of litigation is usually too complex or expensive for the gains to be achieved. Whatever the facts may be (and we do not really know), it is clear that the stated capital machinery is not in fact a significant part of the trade creditor's armory.

B. THE FINANCE OR INSTITUTIONAL CREDITOR

Finance creditors of incorporated enterprises may for convenience be considered to fall into two categories: commercial (or short-term) creditors and investment (or long-term) creditors. Typical of the former are banks, factors, and other institutional lenders that extend revolving lines of short term credit to commercial enterprises. Typical of the latter are holders of bond and debenture issues. Under modern practice, a bank might appear in either role, since some long-term bank loans and bank loan agreements are functionally almost indistinguishable from short-duration bond and debenture issues. The long-term finance creditor— or investment creditor—is considered later in these pages.

1. The Commercial Creditor

How does the short-term commercial lender go about the business of protecting himself against the risks of non-payment by his debtor?

Anyone who has ever borrowed money from a bank knows the two major answers. First, the bank insists upon full disclosure of the economic situation of the borrower and conducts an investigation of his economic resources. Unless the bank is satisfied that the borrower has both the resources for repayment and the reputation for repayment, the loan is simply refused, giving rise to the canard that the only people who can borrow money from a bank are those who do not need it. Second, unlike the trade creditor, the bank will often insist upon collateral of some kind. The collateral may take the form of a mortgage of real estate or a security interest in investment securities, readily saleable chattels or accounts receivable, the classic collateral of the lending factor.

Unsecured open lines of credit are of course provided by banks too, but the lender reserves these for the well-established and well-known enterprise, and to limit the bank's exposure (while shading the interest rate upward), the bank will usually require that the borrowing enterprise maintain substantial "compensating" balances in its account with the bank—balances that add to the bank's deposits and are at all times available to be set-off by the bank against the borrower's indebtedness (thus increasing the rate of interest by reducing the amount of dollars loaned without reducing the amount on which interest is charged.)

Where the incorporated enterprise is not yet well-established, is lightly-funded, or is closely-held, the bank will usually insist upon another form of collateral that, in effect, eliminates much of the significance of the corporate form. The bank will insist that the directors, shareholders, or other persons in interest, become co-makers or endorsers or guarantors of the corporation's note so that their individual assets become liable for payment of the corporation's debt to the bank.

With increase in the amount of the loan, or lengthening of the time for payment, the bank or other commercial lender begins to think of additional commitments it would like to extract from the debtor corporation. As this occurs, the commercial lender begins to act more and more like the long-term investor creditor, and a bank loan agreement comes increasingly to resemble an indenture of the kind discussed below.

When to these protective measures taken by the commercial lender there are added the techniques of surveillance used by the trade creditor, the availability of the national credit intelligence network, and the usual strong desire of the borrower to preserve its credit standing, formidable arrays of defensive arrangements can be constructed by the lender, and usually are.

They do not always work. Like everyone else, banks and other commercial lenders sometimes get stuck on a bad credit. But certainly their protections against bad deals do not lie in the legal capital machinery of the corporation acts, nor do they rely upon those provisions, nor do they seek to enforce them. To the eye of the current lender, it is wholly irrelevant whether shareholders in years past did or did not pay par value for their stock, as is the entire question of the structure of the company's legal capital accounts. And if the commercial lender is worried about the risk of corporate asset distributions to equity investors, it does not look to the corporation statutes for protection but attacks the problem directly and effectively, as discussed below.

2. The Investment Creditor and His Contract—The Corporate Indenture

The investment creditor—one who extends a large amount of credit for a substantial period of time to an incorporated enterprise—wheels into place for his protection the Long Tom of corporate finance, the bond or debenture indenture, or a loan agreement that is substantially equivalent to it. A century of experience has gone into the development of this awesome engine, and though in the process it has become a Leviathan and slow-footed, its design is subtle, its range is great, its fire power is devastating, and its boiler plate armor is impenetrable.

No attempt can be made here to conduct a full tour through a modern indenture dreadnaught or its more compact or pocket version—the triple-riveted bank loan agreement. But it is worth pausing to note what kinds of things are in it and, in particular, to see how it handles the problem of regulating distributions to shareholders.

a. Structure

A corporate indenture is a contract entered into between the corporate borrower and the lender (or many coequal lenders) through their representative, the "indenture trustee". The loan may be a secured loan in which case the indenture will contain elaborate provisions concerning the management and handling of the properties being secured or mortgaged. If the security is real property, the pieces of credit paper issued "under" the indenture are called "bonds"; if there is no security pledged, or chattels are pledged, the instruments are called "debentures"; both bonds and debentures are in essence simply promissory notes, but all gussied up.

An indenture has two major parts, divided by a great hinge. The first part spells out all the things that, after much negotiation, the borrowing company has obligated itself to do, and many things it has obligated itself not to do; this part imposes the will of the lender upon many aspects of the conduct of the enterprise. Any substantial breach of any of these affirmative or negative covenants by the debtor corporation constitutes, by the terms of the indenture, an "event of default". Upon the occurrence of such an event of default, the lender, or trustee, may, according to the terms of the indenture, accelerate the entire debt, step into control of the enterprise and take all sorts of drastic action to see to its own payment.[2]

---

2. In fact, of course, typically creditors do not actually institute litigation to enforce their remedies. The wide array of remedial options provided to them by the indenture gives them sufficient negotiating ability with the debtor (and, more important, with the other creditors) to achieve all, or most, of

The section of the indenture specifying the events of default, are the hinges of the document.

The balance of the contract relates to the time period following an event of default. The functions of this latter part of the indenture are two. It does what it can to provide the lender as favorable a position as possible vis-à-vis other creditors of the corporation; if there is an event of default and the lender has to step in to protect its loan, it is certain that swarms of other creditors will appear on the scene in a hurry, all clamoring to be paid out of the limited assets and enterprise earnings of the corporate debtor. Following the precise prescriptions of the federal Trust Indenture Act of 1939, this part of the indenture also delineates the relationships between the body of bond holders or debenture holders and their representative, the indenture trustee, and the procedures that the trustee must follow in fulfillment of his fiduciary obligations to them.

The indenture provisions that detail what will happen after an event of default are of little interest to the management and shareholders of the borrowing corporation; if the disaster of default and takeover should occur, the game will probably be over for the shareholders (though the management may survive), and the creditors of various types and kinds will be left to fight among themselves over the remains. By contrast, the management and shareholders will be intensely interested in the first part of the indenture, and negotiations between them and the lender over the restrictive covenants will be hard fought.

b. *Key Covenants*

Chapter I of this book begins with a recitation of the main concerns that a lender will continue to have after he has satisfied himself that the general economic position, character, cash-generating and income-producing capacity of the prospective borrower is sufficient to induce the lender to go ahead with the transaction. He wishes to be sure that there are equity investors exposed to risk in the enterprise ranking junior to him; he wants assets to stay in the enterprise and not be distributed to junior security holders; he is concerned to keep down the number of other creditor claimants in his own class; and he is even more concerned to keep down the claims of creditors who would rank senior to him. The indenture may contain restrictive covenants on many

what could be achieved through litigation—and a lot cheaper. In any event, launching of this massive remedial onslaught will likely trigger counter-action by other creditors or the corporate debtor and precipitate action by all parties into a corporate reorganization proceeding under Chapter 11 of the Bankruptcy Act. But the indenture seeks to do all it can by way of providing the widest possible array of options to the holder of obligations issued under the indenture.

other aspects of the conduct of the business enterprise, but it will always contain provisions carefully tailored to assuage these particular concerns of the lender.

(i) Covenant on Secured or Prior Debt

The indenture normally includes a covenant either flatly prohibiting the borrowing company and its subsidiaries from incurring secured or prior debt, or at least narrowly restricting the freedom of the company to do so (often with exceptions for purchase money mortgages and security interests on raw materials or other goods used or consumed in the ordinary course of the borrower's business.) Against this risk, it will be recalled, the corporation acts provide the lender no help at all.

(ii) Covenant on Unsecured or Funded Debt

Covenants forbidding the company to incur further long-term unsecured debt are sometimes seen in indentures and bank loan agreements but absolute prohibitions against such debt are not usual. More often the borrower agrees that it will not incur further debt unless a particular financial formula of some kind can be met. Various approaches to this formula, or combinations of them, are used: The company may be forbidden to incur further debt unless its cash and other readily liquidatable assets bear a designated relationship to its liabilities due and payable within a set time, such as a year; additional debt may be prohibited unless the company's average earnings over a period of years have been a multiple of the amount required to meet carrying charges and installment principal payments of all existing debt, including the debt of the indenture; or, new debt may be permitted but only if certain other steps are taken, such as retirement of existing debt, the sale of stock that produces junior equity proceeds in a certain amount, or subordination of the new debt to the debt of the indenture. (By a provision of this sort, the indenture can exert significant pressure on the borrower to maintain a high proportion of equity or junior debt investment.) The indenture will also typically be especially strict in limiting the freedom of subsidiaries of the borrower to incur debt, however junior that debt may be, since the claim of any creditor of the subsidiary against the assets of the subsidiary stands higher in rank than the parent's equity claim to those assets and therefore higher than the claim of the parent's creditor.

(iii) Covenant on Distributions to Shareholders

The indenture invariably carries special provisions designed to carry out the investment creditors' desire to hold down the distribution of corporate assets to shareholders. Set out below is the text of a dividend restriction covenant taken from a modern bond indenture of a public utility. It is somewhat more detailed than many such provisions, but it is quite standard in its structure and technique. A fairly elaborate specimen has been selected to illustrate the subtlety and the range of matters that must be addressed if such a contractual control mechanism is to be effective. Following the quoted excerpt appears some explanatory comment about it. The following indenture text itself, however, should be read before the commentary.

Under the indenture agreement, the borrowing corporation (the "Company") agrees, in addition to many other things—

Section 7.12. That, so long as any of the bonds of any of the present series are outstanding, the Company will not

(a) declare or pay any dividends or make any other distribution on any of its capital stock of any class (other than cash dividends on shares of any class of such stock ranking prior to the Common Stock in respect of dividends or assets at the rate applicable to such shares under the Certificate of Incorporation of the Company, as amended, and other than dividends on Common Stock paid solely in shares of Common Stock of the Company), or

(b) purchase, redeem or otherwise retire for a consideration any shares of its capital stock of any class (otherwise than in a transaction involving the purchase, redemption or retirement of shares of capital stock of the Company, other than its Common Stock, in exchange for or from the proceeds of the substantially simultaneous sale of other shares of capital stock of the Company), except any shares of any class of stock ranking prior to the Common Stock, in respect of dividends or assets, which may be purchased, redeemed or otherwise retired to the extent required to comply with the provisions of any sinking fund applicable to such shares under the Certificate of Incorporation of the Company, as amended, if

(i) any such dividend is declared to be payable more than 75 days after the date of declaration; or

(ii) after giving effect to such proposed dividend, distribution, purchase or retirement, the aggregate amount so declared or distributed for all such dividends or distributions or expended for all such purchases or retirements after December 31, 1990, plus the amount of any cash dividends paid on any shares of its capital stock of any class ranking prior to its Common Stock (other than amounts so paid which represent the disbursement of sums received by the Company as accrued dividends as a part of the selling price of any such shares) after December 31, 1989 to and including the date of declaration, in the case of a dividend, or the date of payment, in any other case, would exceed the aggregate net earnings of the Company, computed as hereinafter in this Section provided, for said period from December 31, 1989 to and including such date of declaration or date of payment, as the case may be, plus the sum of $30,000,000, less the amount of expenditures for the retirement for sinking fund purposes of any shares of any class of stock of the Company ranking prior to the Common Stock in respect of dividends or assets in any year subsequent to December 31, 1995 in which as of the close of any calendar quarter the Common Stock equity of the Company is less than 25% of the total capitalization of the Company.

The term 'Common Stock equity of the Company' shall mean, at any date as of which the amount thereof is to be determined, the aggregate of the amount of the Common Stock liability of the Company, plus (or minus in the case of a deficit) the capital surplus applicable to the Common Stock and earned surplus of the Company, plus any premium on Common Stock of the Company, all as determined in accordance with sound accounting practice.

The term 'total capitalization of the Company' shall mean, at any date as of which the amount thereof is to be determined, the aggregate of (a) the amount of the capital stock liability of the Company, plus (or minus in the case of a deficit) the capital surplus and earned surplus of the Company, plus any premium on capital stock of the Company of any class, all as determined in accordance with sound accounting practice and (b) the aggregate principal amount of all funded debt of the Company outstanding at such date. The term 'funded debt' shall mean all indebtedness of the Company which matures by its terms, or is renewable at the option of the obligor at a date, more than one year after the date of its creation or incurring by the Company.[3]

[So long as any of the bonds of any of the present series are outstanding, the Company will not at any time after October 1, 1990 issue any shares of any class of stock of the Company ranking prior to the Common Stock in respect of dividends or assets the terms of which shall require the

---

3. Note that long-term (more than one-year) debt is being treated as part of "capitalization". This is an example of the gray continuum along which debts and equity exist and, at points, blend.

redemption of said stock by the operation of a sinking fund at a rate more rapid than that applicable to any of the Company's Preferred Stock outstanding on October 1, 1990.] [4]

For the purposes of this Section, the amount of any dividend declared or distribution or payment made in property of the Company shall be deemed to be the book value of such property at the time of declaration in the case of dividends, or at the date of distribution or payment in any other case.

[The Company will not permit any subsidiary or any controlled corporation to purchase any shares of any class of stock of the Company from any person other than the Company.]

For purposes of this Section, the term 'net earnings of the Company' shall mean the sum of the operating revenues and other income of the Company, less all proper deductions for operating expenses, taxes (including income taxes or other taxes based upon or measured by or in respect of net earnings or income or based upon or measured by or in respect of undistributed net earnings or income) and interest charges (exclusive of interest or taxes properly capitalized as interest or taxes during construction), appropriations to retirement or depreciation reserves for properties other than gas or oil production properties and provisions for depreciation and depletion of gas and oil production properties (which appropriations to retirement or depreciation reserves with respect to properties referred to in the first paragraph of Section 7.11 and which provisions for depreciation and depletion with respect to gas production properties shall be in amounts not less than those required by the provisions of Section 7.11 as in effect from time to time) and other appropriate items, all determined in accordance with sound accounting practice; provided, however, that in computing the amount of the net earnings of the Company as aforesaid (A) any interest received by the Company on obligations or indebtedness of any subsidiary or controlled corporation may be included in other income of the Company only to the extent that (i) such interest is not in excess of the net earnings available for interest of such subsidiary or controlled corporation, computed in accordance with sound accounting practice, for the period in respect of which such interest was paid (after first deducting from such net earnings available for interest an amount equal to all interest, if any, accrued for such period on obligations or indebtedness of such subsidiary or controlled

---

4. See comment at pp. 110–11, infra.

corporation held by others than the Company and ranking prior to or on a parity with the obligations or indebtedness of such subsidiary or controlled corporation held by the Company in respect of which such interest was received) or (ii) such interest is properly capitalized by such subsidiary or controlled corporation as interest during construction in accordance with sound accounting practice; and any dividends received by the Company on stock of any subsidiaries or controlled corporations may be included in other income of the Company only to the extent that the aggregate amount of such dividends is not in excess of the combined net earnings of all subsidiaries and controlled corporations applicable to the stock interest of the Company in such subsidiaries and controlled corporations, computed as to each subsidiary or controlled corporation, in accordance with sound accounting practice, from the date on which such subsidiary or controlled corporation became a subsidiary or controlled corporation to the date of the most recent payment of a dividend to the Company by any subsidiary or controlled corporation, and (B) no deduction or adjustment shall be made for or on account of (i) any charges for redemption or prepayment premiums or other expenses in connection with the retirement by the Company, by redemption, payment or otherwise, of any of its bonds, debentures, promissory notes or preferred stocks or any charges for the write-off of the unamortized portion of any debt discount and expense applicable to any such retired bonds, debentures, notes or preferred stocks remaining at the time of the retirement thereof, or any expenses in connection with the creation, issuance or sale by the Company of any of its bonds, debentures, promissory notes, preferred stocks or Common Stock, (ii) interest, taxes or other overhead charges during construction to the extent chargeable to fixed property accounts of the Company in accordance with sound accounting practice and so charged, (iii) any profits realized or losses sustained in the sale of fixed properties or securities by the Company, (iv) any earned surplus adjustments properly applicable to any period or periods prior to January 1, 1990, other than adjustments required to give effect to assessments of additional income taxes paid by the Company or refunds of income taxes received by the Company applicable to any fiscal period or periods prior to January 1, 1990, or (v) any charges for amortization or elimination of gas plant adjustment accounts or acquisition adjustment accounts or other intangibles.

Beneath the stifling verbiage and detail of this indenture covenant restricting shareholder distributions, its underlying skeletal structure can be readily (well—more or less readily) seen. It is quite typical. In general, it sets up a formula restricting asset distributions to the effect that the debtor company may not make any payments specified in subparagraph (a) or any payments specified in sub-paragraph (b) if the conditions specified in sub-paragraph (i) exist or if the conditions specified in sub-paragraph (ii) exist. The balance of the Section 7.12 is largely made up of finely honed definitions of the terms, and specifications of circumstances that are referred to in the restriction formula.

Sub-paragraph (a): This sub-paragraph includes within the range of its prohibitions any payment of dividends or any other asset distribution on common stock. So-called "stock dividends" on common stock are permitted since a stock dividend entails no more than a splitting up of pieces of paper and does not involve the pay-out of assets from the corporate treasury. The provision also excludes from its reach dividends paid on the company's preferred stock; this exclusion is usual, since neither the management nor the lender is anxious to create the unfavorable aura that attaches to a company that has fallen into arrears on its preferred stock dividend payments and has perhaps thereby become subject to remedial resorts open to holders of the preferred.

Sub-paragraph (b): This sub-paragraph reaches out beyond dividend payments and similar distributions, to limit purchases, redemptions and retirements by the debtor company of its own shares. The lender forbids the Company to buy in its own stock because such a purchase is a form of distribution of assets to a shareholder. There are two exceptions. The Company is permitted to comply with the sinking fund provisions of its outstanding preferred stock and in so doing to distribute assets to the preferred shareholders in accordance with the requirements of the preferred stock provisions contained in the Company's certificate of incorporation. Sub-paragraph (b) also excludes from its prohibition a refunding or refinancing of the existing preferred stock; this leaves open to the Company, so far as the lenders are concerned, the option of calling in its existing preferred in favor of a new preferred issued on more favorable terms if the general price of the money market should drop. (Incidentally, the terms of the outstanding preferred stock may not be so permissive to the issuer.)

The drafting of sub-paragraph (b) is somewhat wanting in elegance since it contains, buried within the mass of definitional material, two other independent covenants. The brackets that set off these provisions have been added by the present author. In the first bracketed covenant, the Company agrees that so long as the bonds are outstanding it will not issue any preferred stock that has a sinking fund that works at a rate more rapid than the existing preferred stock; the lender is willing to see assets go to the preferred shareholders at the rate prescribed at the time of the loan, but no faster. The second bracketed provision forbids a subsidiary to buy in the Company's stock. As a matter of style— and for ease in locating them—these two provisions should be separately numbered as independent covenants in the indenture.

Sub-paragraph (i): This sub-paragraph requires the Company to pay a dividend promptly after its date of declaration, the lender's fear being that the Company could otherwise declare dividends whenever it is in a fiscal position to meet the formula contained in sub-paragraph (ii) and then later pay the money out to the shareholders at a time when the company is in a weakened condition and the lender's position is threatened.

Sub-paragraph (ii): This sub-paragraph contains the financial conditions that must exist whenever the Company declares or pays a dividend or makes any other distribution to shareholders pro-scribed by section 7.12. The formula begins with the figure $30,000,000—a sum arrived at by negotiation between the borrow-er and the lender. To this $30,000,000 the formula adds the net earnings of the Company since December 31, 1989—a date roughly coinciding with the issue of the bonds. The formula then provides, in substance, that no restricted distribution may be made unless at the time the sum of the $30,000,000 plus such net earnings is greater than all restricted distributions theretofore paid out, plus all cash dividends paid on the preferred stock since that date, plus the proposed dividend or distribution. Although, as noted, cash dividends on the preferred are not a restricted distribution under sub-paragraph (a), and may therefore be paid whether the formula is met or not, such cash dividends on preferred *do* count against the Company in computations under sub-paragraph (ii) so that they have the subsequent effect of making it more difficult for the Company to pay dividends on the common stock.

The restriction formula in sub-paragraph (ii) has a somewhat unusual twist regarding sinking fund requirements of the pre-ferred. Such sinking fund requirements are not restricted distri-butions under sub-paragraph (b), nor do they normally enter into the financial formula of sub-paragraph (ii), but they do count against the Company in the formula after 1995 if they are paid out at a time when the equity of the common stock in the company has become so thin as to drop below 25% of the Company's total capitalization. This special provision says, in effect, that the Company may proceed with its sinking fund retirement on the outstanding preferred, but if in the future the common stock equity exposure in the enterprise drops too low (below 25%), then the sinking fund retirement payments on the preferred stock will be counted against the Company in its formula with the result of further restricting the ability of the Company to pay dividends or make distributions on its common stock. Every dividend restriction like this representative section is individually negotiated by the corporate debtor and the lender in the context of the particular circumstances, and it is quite normal to find special hand-crafted features of this kind.

The lengthy definitional provisions do not require special comment, but they should be read over, for they illustrate what is actually involved in making a real dividend restriction formula work. The whole formula restricting shareholder distributions is based fundamentally on the earnings rate of the borrowing enterprise. The definition of "net earnings of the Company" is thus absolutely critical to its administration and the draftsmen of the indenture have consequently elaborated it in considerable detail. Even so, a careful reading of the definition will reveal that it contains many terms and references that are themselves hardly self-executing and that could in turn have been further refined in the covenant. The question of where the lawyer should stop in the process of specification in the document is a matter for negotiating and drafting judgment in each situation, line-by-line and term-by-term; there are no automatic stopping places; and no matter where one stops, the provision will contain open-ended, unresolved questions, breeding pools for later dispute.[5]

So much for indenture Section 7.12.

(iv) Covenant on Informing the Trustee

Once a long-term loan has been made to the corporate borrower, all the indenture covenants and provisions will be of little help to the lenders (trustee) unless they know what is going on at the borrowing company, and particularly whether the company has violated a covenant and precipitated an event of default. The lenders (trustee) must arrange to have current business information about the company—lots of it. Key provisions in the indenture will therefore require the company to provide the lenders (trustee) with a stream of reports about the company's operations and fiscal condition and grant the trustee freedom to inspect company records and interview executives. Without such an information flow, the lenders will have little hope of realizing full protection from the covenants they negotiated so hard to extract from the borrower.

Of course, any of these covenants may be waived, in whole or in part, by the lender (trustee). Their existence, however, puts the

---

5. Regarding Manning's Law of Conservation of Ambiguity, see Manning, *Hyperlexis and the Law of Conservation* *of Ambiguity: Thoughts on Section 385,* 36 Tax Law. 9 (1982).

lender (trustee) in a position to decide whether to enforce compliance by the borrower or to waive it, perhaps in return for other concessions by the borrower, such as accelerated payment or a higher interest rate.

c. *Contract and Statute Compared*

It is now possible, and fruitful, to compare the approach of the statutory legal capital machinery with that of the negotiated corporate indenture.

- The indenture hits squarely and effectively against the borrowers' incurring additional debt, and especially secured debt, both of which would be to the detriment of the present lender. Corporation acts make no effort to deal with that problem at all.

- The lender will not enter into the transaction at all without a close examination of the asset structure, cash flow and earnings potential, and general economic health of the enterprise. That perspective and attitude is reflected throughout the covenants of the indenture. By contrast, the stated capital machinery assumes—or rather simply asserts—that the key premise of concern to the lender has something to do with payments that shareholders did or did not make into the corporate treasury at an earlier day in payment for their stock.

- In the indenture's provisions restricting distributions to shareholders, the emphasis is placed upon a particular negotiated figure based upon the economic strength of the enterprise at the time of the borrowing, plus the earnings of the company. Attention is therefore focused on the enterprise's earnings track record, its potential to make a profit, and its capacity to throw off sufficient earnings to cover carrying charges on its debt, plus distributions to shareholders. Under the statutory scheme, in states having the stated capital/surplus test, there is no focus at all on the enterprise's earning ability and even in states that putatively use the earned surplus standard, earnings have only a limited role.

- The contractual indenture approach permits the lender and borrower to negotiate a platform figure on which to build the restriction formula (in the quoted case $30,000,000)[6] instead of seeking to find a universal answer. In the same way, the process of negotiation in the

---

6. The dollar figure is usually the regular quarterly dividend multiplied by an agreed upon number of quarters, typically four, thus providing the borrower one year's leeway in his dividend payments.

indenture permits the lender to protect himself against particular hazards or possibilities that he sees in his capital situation, as in the cited instance of the preferred stock sinking fund. By contrast, the legal capital statutes place the entire control over equity distributions in the hands of the board of directors and shareholders—those who are supposedly to be regulated. The indenture binds the borrower (i.e., its board and shareholders) by contract to the lender, gives the lender an elaborate machinery to protect his position, puts the lender's representative, the trustee, in control of that machinery and assures a flow of information that will enable the lender to proceed intelligently if trouble develops.

- Most important of all—and perhaps simply generalizing all of the points just made—however much the prose of the indenture may reek of legalese, it is at heart a businessman's document. In it are reflected the real needs, priorities, interests and worries of a lender who has put large quantities of its capital at risk in an enterprise that is controlled by others. By contrast, the statutory scheme of legal capital is a conceptual structure based mainly upon legalistic doctrines of the nineteenth century.

Chapter VII

END QUESTION

If the stated capital statutory machinery is as rickety and jumbled as appears from the preceding pages, is it not time to replace it?

Apparently so. And that is the topic of the Second Part. But before turning to the Second Part, the reader should look at the traditional machinery in operation. It is on exhibit in Subpart Two of the First Part, following.

Subpart Two

LEGAL CAPITAL DOCTRINE—
ILLUSTRATIONS

Before commencing this Subpart Two, let it be emphasized that some of the material in Subpart Two has in some states in some degree been superseded in the course of the 1980s. The Second and Third Parts scan some of the major changes and outline the state of affairs as we enter the last decade of this millennium. It is not the function of Subpart Two to depict the current law (though in large measure it does so). The mission of Subpart Two is to make Subpart One more comprehensible to the reader by demonstrating the traditional statutory legal capital scheme at work. Subpart Two surveys the balance sheets—particularly the owners' equity sections—arising from a series of common corporate transactions and reviews the legality of asset distributions to shareholders under different types of laws, given such balance sheets.

Seven initial observations:

1. Since the law in this field varies from state to state, and since more than one accounting option is often available, the shorthand legal and accounting entries set out here must be understood to be illustrative only. Thus, Subpart Two must also be read in context of the discussion in Subpart One.

2. As has been developed earlier, the experienced corporation lawyer, working with an experienced accountant, can almost always (absent existing or ensuing insolvency) find a lawful procedural way to design around legal capital restraints, to reconstruct the balance sheet so that a distribution to shareholders would be conformable to the applicable statutory scheme. This fact in no way implies fraud or sharp practice; it merely demonstrates the insubstantiality of the system of legal capital legislation.

Thus, for example, the pre–1980 Model Act, which purported to be a stated capital/earned surplus statute, made it very easy for shareholder distributions to be charged against capital surplus, and also very easy to create capital surplus.[1] Therefore, the reader must understand that any statement made here that, given a particular balance sheet, a shareholder distribution would be prohibited by a particular kind of legal capital statute must *not* be

1. Model Bus.Corp. Act §§ 46, 69 (1979).

116

taken to mean that no way can be found to arrange for a legal distribution to shareholders.

The real factors that determine corporate dividend policy in the absence of insolvency are, in the main, availability of cash, management's attitude toward profit reinvestment, availability of perceived investment opportunities, estimate of the effects of dividend policy on the market price of the stock, deference to shareholders' concerns about tax liability, and contractual restraints contained in loan agreements. As by now will have become apparent to the reader, the actual effect of legal capital restraints upon corporate distributions to shareholders is minimal.

Most corporate financial statements are prepared in accordance with and audited for compliance with generally accepted accounting principles (GAAP). The primary sources of GAAP have been the pronouncements of three successive accounting bodies: the American Institute of Accountants' Committee on Accounting Procedure (existing until September 1959), which promulgated principles in its Accounting Research Bulletins (ARB Nos. 43 to 51); the Accounting Principles Board of the American Institute of Certified Public Accountants (1959 until 1973), which promulgated accounting principles through their APB Opinions (Nos. 1 to 31); and the Financial Accounting Standards Board (since 1973), which promulgates accounting principles through Statements of Financial Accounting Standards. To the extent that the pronouncements of the Committee on Accounting Procedure and the Accounting Principles Board are not specifically amended or superseded by Statements of Financial Accounting Standards, the pronouncements of those predecessor bodies remain as authoritative pronouncements of GAAP.

3. Though some statutes irrationally use different tests for different forms of shareholder distributions, as used in the illustrations here, "shareholder distribution" means any form of distribution of corporate assets (in cash or in kind) to shareholders as such, such as dividends, stock repurchases, liquidating distributions, and the like. Correspondingly, the term "shareholder distribution" does not include payments made to persons who happen to be shareholders but who receive the payment in some capacity other than that of shareholders—for example, salary paid to an employee who is a shareholder or interest paid to a lender who is also a shareholder.

A statement here that a "shareholder distribution" is not legally allowable does not apply to a stock dividend or stock split since those transactions involve no distribution of corporate assets. This careful usage of "shareholder distribution" is not followed universally, however, and all too often one may hear persons who should (and do) know better, refer to stock dividends and splits as "distributions."

4. Most corporation laws, including the Revised Model Act, set *two* barriers before a proposed distribution to shareholders. Not only must the local form of balance sheet-based test be met, but directors are enjoined from making any distribution that will disable the corporation form paying its debts as they mature. This second barrier is the "equity insolvency test" discussed supra at pp. 63–65. *In each of the illustrative scenarios that follow, it is assumed that the proposed distribution would be in compliance with the local equity insolvency test.*

5. Virtually all discussion and application of the legal capital doctrines here occurs in the context of distributions to holders of common shares. But the legal restraints imposed on shareholder distributions are as applicable to preference shares as to common shares, except where otherwise provided (as, for example, in the last paragraph of Section 46 of the Model Act (1979)). Preference shares, for example, typically reserve to the corporation a so-called "right of redemption", under which the corporation may call outstanding shares of the preference shares—i.e., may require the holder to turn in his shares in exchange for cash or other consideration in an amount set forth in the certificate of incorporation. Such "redemptions" are merely one more form of share acquisition and shareholder distribution. For purposes of simplicity, in the examples that follow, it is assumed that no special statutory provisions apply to the preferred shares only.

6. The statutory term "earned surplus" is identical to the accountants' term "retained earnings". The statutory term "capital surplus" covers a number of different kinds of capital accounts in the language of accountants, such as "paid-in surplus", "reduction surplus" and "capital in excess of par".[2] The term "capital" is used in the illustrative balance sheets to refer to the statutory term "stated capital".

7. Each statement made at the end of each transaction as to the maximum shareholder distribution allowable in the circumstances speaks as of the date of the balance sheet and assumes that no corporate legal or accounting action has been taken other than as already described. In the real world, depending on the applicable state statute, it would often be possible for the corporation to take certain intermediate steps (such as a reduction of par) that would, once taken, change the maximum amount of distribution allowable.

2. See discussion pp. 74–78, supra.

TRANSACTIONS

The successive transactions considered below proceed from the balance sheet of Laminated Thumbscrew, Inc., appearing at p. 35, supra, immediately after its formation and the issuance at par for cash of 500 shares of common stock, with a par value of $100 per share—the simple high par model set out as the first illustration in Chapter II. The balance sheets shown are designed to reflect the particular transactions described and, except as indicated, are not year-end balance sheets.

Balance Sheet of Laminated Thumbscrew, Inc.,
Immediately Following Organization and Funding

ASSETS		LIABILITIES	
Cash	$50,000		–0–
		SHAREHOLDERS' EQUITY	
		Capital: $100 par	
		common, 500 sh.	$50,000
		Surplus	–0–
	$50,000		$50,000

Transaction 1 (Year 1): Loss

During its first year of active business operations, the corporation buys land, builds up inventory, develops some accounts receivable and payable, borrows $10,000 from the bank and incurs an operating loss of $20,000.

(a) *Balance sheet presentation:*

Laminated Thumbscrew, Inc.
Balance Sheet # 1 (giving effect to Transaction 1)
As at end of Year 1

ASSETS		LIABILITIES	
Cash	$20,000	Accounts payable	$ 2,000
Accounts receivable	6,000	Bank loan	10,000
Inventory	11,000	Liabilities	$12,000
Land	5,000	SHAREHOLDERS' EQUITY	
		Capital: $100 par	
		common, 500 sh.	$50,000
		Earned surplus	
		(deficit)	(20,000)
		Shareholders'	
		equity	$30,000
	$42,000		$42,000

(b) *Legal capital restraints:*

    (i) **Net worth jurisdiction:** shareholder distribution of $30,000 allowable since assets exceed liabilities by $30,000.

    (ii) **Stated capital/surplus jurisdiction:** no shareholder distribution allowable since there is a negative surplus of $20,000. That is, assets are $20,000 less than liabilities plus stated capital. The balance sheet is said to be "under water" and the capital "impaired".

    (iii) **Stated capital/earned surplus jurisdiction:** no shareholder distribution allowable since earned surplus is a deficit of $20,000.

    (iv) **Stated capital/surplus or current net profits jurisdiction:** no shareholder distribution allowable since there is no surplus and no current net profits.

Transaction 2 (Year 2): Small Profit

During the second year, the company has a small profit of $5,000, all of which is reflected in further build-up of inventory.

(a) *Balance Sheet presentation:*

Laminated Thumbscrew Inc.
Balance Sheet # 2 (giving effect to Transaction 2)
As at end of Year 2

ASSETS		LIABILITIES	
Cash	$20,000	Accounts payable	$ 2,000
Accounts receivable	6,000	Bank loan	10,000
Inventory	16,000	Liabilities	12,000
Land	5,000	SHAREHOLDERS' EQUITY	
		Capital: $100 par	
		common, 500 sh.	$50,000
		Earned surplus	
		(deficit)	(15,000)
		Shareholders'	
		equity	$35,000
	$47,000		$47,000

(b) *Legal capital restraints:*

    (i) **Net worth jurisdiction:** shareholder distribution of $35,000 allowable since assets exceed liabilities by $35,000.

    (ii) **Stated capital/surplus jurisdiction:** no shareholder distribution allowable since assets are $15,000 less than liabilities plus legal capital.

(iii) **Stated capital/earned surplus jurisdiction:** no shareholder distribution allowable since earned surplus is a deficit of $15,000.

(iv) **Stated capital/surplus or current net profits jurisdiction:** shareholder distribution of $5,000 allowable since current net profits equal $5,000. (These so-called "nimble dividends" are allowable despite the inability of the corporation to meet the applicable balance sheet standard for a shareholder distribution. See discussion pp. 82–84, supra.)

Transaction 3 (Year 3): Large Profit

In the third year of operations, the company has a large profit of $20,000.

(a) *Balance sheet presentation:*

Laminated Thumbscrew, Inc.
Balance Sheet # 3 (giving effect to Transaction 3)
As at end of Year 3

ASSETS		LIABILITIES	
Cash	$18,000	Accounts payable	$ 2,000
Accounts receivable	20,000	Bank loan	10,000
Inventory	24,000	Liabilities	$12,000
Land	5,000	SHAREHOLDERS' EQUITY	
		Capital: $100 par	
		common, 500 sh.	$50,000
		Earned surplus	5,000
		Shareholders'	
		equity	$55,000
	$67,000		$67,000

Accounting Note: Current usage among accountants is "Retained earnings" rather than "Earned surplus", but the older term is used here throughout because it is still the term generally used in the legal capital statutes and other legal materials.

(b) *Legal capital restraints:*

(i) **Net worth jurisdiction:** shareholder distribution of $55,000 allowable since assets exceed liabilities by $55,000.

(ii) **Stated capital/surplus jurisdiction:** shareholder distribution of $5,000 allowable since assets are $5,000 more than liabilities plus legal capital.

(iii) **Stated capital/earned surplus jurisdiction:** shareholder distribution of $5,000 allowable since earned surplus is $5,000.

(iv) **State capital/surplus or current net profits jurisdiction:** shareholder distribution of at least $5,000 allowable since surplus is $5,000. But is more allowable? See discussion pp. 82–84, supra.

Transaction 4 (Year 4): Asset Write-up—Appreciation Surplus

During the fourth year, the board of directors decides to apply for a bank loan to finance a proposed diversification into the production of laminated thumbtacks. The bank refuses to lend the company the money on the basis of Balance Sheet # 3. President Torquemada and the Thumbscrew board feel that this is unfair, and that the enterprise is worth more than its balance sheet shows. The land, for example, has appreciated in value to $10,000. The board decides (in contravention of generally accepted accounting principles) to show the land at its fair market value of $10,000, so land is "written up" by $5,000.

(a) *Balance sheet presentation:*

Laminated Thumbscrew, Inc.
Balance Sheet # 4 (giving effect to Transaction 4)

ASSETS		LIABILITIES	
Cash	$18,000	Accounts payable	$ 2,000
Accounts receivable	20,000	Bank loan	10,000
Inventory	24,000	Liabilities	$12,000
Land	10,000	SHAREHOLDERS' EQUITY	
		Capital: $100 par	
		common, 500 sh.	$50,000
		Appreciation surplus	5,000
		Earned surplus	5,000
		Shareholders'	
		equity	$60,000
	$72,000		$72,000

Accounting Note: By the tenets of today's generally accepted accounting principles, such a write-up would not be approved by an accountant.

(b) *Legal capital restraints:*

(i) **Net worth jurisdiction:** shareholder distribution of $60,000 allowable since assets exceed liabilities by $60,000.

(ii) **Stated capital/surplus jurisdiction:** a jurisdiction following *Randall v. Bailey,* 23 N.Y.S.2d 173 (1940), *aff'd without opin.,* 262 App.Div. 844, 29 N.Y.S.2d 512 (1st Dept.1941), *aff'd with opin.,* 288 N.Y. 280, 43 N.E.2d 43 (1942), would accept the written-up value for the land and allow a shareholder distribution of $10,000 since assets are then $10,000 more than liabilities plus legal capital. A jurisdiction not following the *Randall* case would, with the accountants, view the write-up of the land as improper, and, valuing the land at its $5,000 cost, allow a shareholder distribution of only $5,000.

(iii) **Stated capital/earned surplus jurisdiction:** shareholder distribution of $5,000 allowable since earned surplus is $5,000. The "appreciation surplus" is not considered as derived from a profit since it is not yet "realized."

(iv) **Stated capital/surplus or current net profits jurisdiction:** shareholder distribution of at least $5,000 allowable since surplus is $5,000. But is more allowable? See discussion pp. 82–84, supra. And, even in a jurisdiction following the *Randall* case, a court might (and an accountant surely would) balk at the idea that the write-up yields "current net profits".

Transaction 5 (Year 4): Elimination of Asset Write-up

During the same year (the fourth), the board of directors decides against expanding into laminated thumbtacks and negotiations for the bank loan are cancelled. At the end of the year, the board also decides it was a bit hasty in writing up the land and decides to write it down to its former book value, a decision no doubt influenced by the remonstrations of its auditors. There were no earnings during the fourth year.

(a) *Balance sheet presentation:*

Laminated Thumbscrew, Inc.
Balance Sheet # 5 (giving effect to Transaction 5)
As at end of Year 4

ASSETS		LIABILITIES	
Cash	$18,000	Accounts payable	$ 2,000
Accounts receivable	20,000	Bank loan	10,000
Inventory	24,000	Liabilities	$12,000
Land	5,000	SHAREHOLDERS' EQUITY	
		Capital: $100 par	
		common, 500 sh.	$50,000
		Earned surplus	5,000
		Shareholders'	
		equity	$55,000
	$67,000		$67,000

(b) *Legal capital restraints:*

   (i) **Net worth jurisdiction:** shareholder distribution of $55,000 allowable since assets exceed liabilities by $55,000.

   (ii) **Stated capital/surplus jurisdiction:** shareholder distribution of $5,000 allowable since assets are $5,000 more than liabilities plus legal capital.

   (iii) **Stated capital/earned surplus jurisdiction:** shareholder distribution of $5,000 allowable since earned surplus is $5,000.

   (iv) **Stated capital/surplus or current net profits jurisdiction:** shareholder distribution of at least $5,000 allowable since surplus is $5,000. But is more allowable? See discussion pp. 82–84, supra.

Note: The balance sheet presentation and the legal capital restraints after Transaction 5 are the same as after Transaction 3.

Transaction 6 (Year 5): Stock Issuance for Secret Process

During the fifth year of operations, Laminated Thumbscrew acquires a secret process for laminate adhesive that is valued by the board at $5,000; it issues 50 shares of $100 par stock to the inventor in payment for the process.

(a) *Balance sheet presentation:*

Laminated Thumbscrew, Inc.
Balance Sheet # 6 (giving effect to Transaction 6)

ASSETS		LIABILITIES	
Cash	$18,000	Accounts payable	$ 2,000
Accounts receivable	20,000	Bank loan	10,000
Inventory	24,000	Liabilities	$12,000
Land	5,000	SHAREHOLDERS' EQUITY	
Secret process	5,000	Capital: $100 par	
		common, 550 sh.	$55,000
		Earned surplus	5,000
		Shareholders'	
		equity	60,000
	$72,000		$72,000

(b) *Legal capital restraints:*

(i) **Net worth jurisdiction:** shareholder distribution of $60,000 allowable since assets exceed liabilities by $60,000.

(ii) **Stated capital/surplus jurisdiction:** shareholder distribution of $5,000 allowable since assets are $5,000 more than liabilities plus legal capital.

(iii) **Stated capital/earned surplus jurisdiction:** shareholder distribution of $5,000 allowable since earned surplus is $5,000.

(iv) **Stated capital/surplus or current net profits jurisdiction:** shareholder distribution of at least $5,000 allowable since surplus is $5,000. But is more allowable? See discussion pp. 82–84, supra.

Transaction 7 (Year 5): Write-down of Asset

At the end of year five, the corporation finds it has made a profit from operations of $6,000 during the year. Meanwhile, the accountant questions the valuation of the secret process for the laminate adhesive and suggests that it would be better practice to carry the secret process at a book value of $1. The board of directors grudgingly accepts this write-down.

(a) *Balance sheet presentation:*

Laminated Thumbscrew, Inc.
Balance Sheet # 7 (giving effect to Transaction 7)
As at end of Year 7

ASSETS		LIABILITIES	
Cash	$20,000	Accounts payable	$ 2,000
Accounts receivable	22,000	Bank loan	10,000
Inventory	26,000	Liabilities	$12,000
Land	5,000		
Secret process	1	**SHAREHOLDERS' EQUITY**	
		Capital: $100 par	
		common, 550 sh.	$55,000
		Earned surplus	6,001
		Shareholders'	
		equity	$61,001
	$73,001		$73,001

Accounting Note: The $6,000 profit for the fifth year passes through the company's income statement for that year to increase earned surplus at the end of the year to $11,000. Whether or not the secret process write-down of $4,999 was reflected on the current income statement, the $4,999 will be ultimately charged against the earned surplus account leaving a balance of $6,001.

(b) *Legal capital restraints:*

    (i) **Net worth jurisdiction:** shareholder distribution of $61,001 allowable since assets exceed liabilities by $61,001.

    (ii) **Stated capital/surplus jurisdiction:** shareholder distribution of $6,001 allowable since assets are $6,001 more than liabilities plus legal capital.

    (iii) **Stated capital/earned surplus jurisdiction:** shareholder distribution of at least $6,001 allowable.

Shareholder distribution of $11,000 may be allowable, depending on whether the $4,999 write-down of the secret process is considered a "loss" under the local statutory interpretation of earned surplus, which typically reads something like "balance of net profits, income, gains, and losses". In most earned surplus jurisdictions, it is unclear whether the write-down is to be treated as a "loss".

Here is a clear illustration of the point discussed supra at pp. 65–67, that the statutory question is one for a lawyer's decision. Corporate counsel may often have to go behind the accountant's treatment of a transaction on the balance sheet or income statement "in accordance with generally accepted accounting principles" to assess its legal effect on the permissibility of equity distributions.

Note further that the legal decision reached on a transaction like the write-down will have a forward impact into the indefinite future; if the allowable distribution to shareholders is $11,000 under the local stated capital/earned surplus statute while at the same time the accountants insist on passing the write-down through the income statement, future balance sheets will continue to carry an accountants' "earned surplus" that is $4,999 less than the legal "earned surplus" used to measure the legality of shareholder distributions.

(iv) **Stated capital/surplus or current net profits jurisdiction:** shareholder distribution of at least $6,001 allowable since surplus is $6,001. But is more allowable? See discussion pp. 82–84, supra.

Transaction 8 (Year 6): Stock Dividend

The company's cash position drops, as inventories and accounts receivable have risen, so during the sixth year the board of directors decides to skip a cash dividend and declare a ten percent "stock dividend". The shareholders are informed of the declaration of this "dividend" and shortly thereafter each shareholder is mailed a one-share stock certificate for each ten that he already has, a total of 55 new shares being thus added to the 550 shares theretofore outstanding.

(a) *Balance sheet presentation:*

Laminated Thumbscrew, Inc.
Balance Sheet # 8 (giving effect to Transaction 8)

ASSETS		LIABILITIES	
Cash	$ 1,000	Accounts payable	$ 2,000
Accounts receivable	37,000	Bank loan	10,000
Inventory	30,000	Liabilities	$12,000
Land	5,000	SHAREHOLDERS' EQUITY	
Secret process	1	Capital: $100 par	
		common, 605 sh.	$60,500
		Earned surplus	501
		Shareholders'	
		equity	61,001
	$73,001		$73,001

Accounting Note: A stock dividend is a paper transaction and an accounting transaction only; no assets leave the corporate treasury for distribution to the shareholders. In the case at hand, it merely leads to an accounting entry increasing the stated capital account by $5,500 (55 shares times $100 par) and reducing the earned surplus account by the same amount. This is sometimes called "capitalizing surplus".[3]

As a matter of rational analysis, the market price per share should respond to a stock dividend by a drop equal to the dividend percentage, in this case ten percent. If, however, the market does not drop the full ten percent (as it often does not), the recipient of the stock dividend may be put in a position to realize a gain "from" the stock dividend by selling some or all of his shares, of which he has a 10% greater number than he had before the dividend. Another real economic consequence of a stock dividend may arise in the future. If a company continues to pay out an annual cash dividend per share equal to that which it had been paying out before the stock dividend, the stock dividend will lead to a ten percent increase in the assets paid out annually to shareholders as dividends (and reduce correspondingly the cash in the corporate treasury).

Granting that the stock dividend will increase stated capital, and that a surplus account should be charged, *what* surplus account may be charged under the statutes? It appears that, regardless of the form of the local statute, any surplus account may be charged.[4]

But is it legally necessary that there be *any* surplus account available before the dividend? Why should there be? Notice that if the stock dividend is effected when there is no surplus to charge, the result of the increase in the stated capital will be to create a deficit surplus account. That looks bad and sounds worse if, in classical language, it is described as putting the stock "under water". But if the board of directors is willing to create such a deficit and thereby, without distributing corporate assets, further inhibit *future* distributions of assets to shareholders, why should creditors complain or the statute prevent it? Most lawyers would say, however, that, in the nature of things, a stock dividend may not be made if it creates a deficit surplus. Why not then reduce the par? Why not indeed. See Transaction 9.

A second accounting question has to do with the *amount* by which stated capital should be written up and a surplus account charged to reflect the stock dividend. Three answers are analytically possible: (i) Stated capital should be increased by the par value of the shares issued through

3. See, e.g., Md.Gen.Corp.Law § 2–203(c).

4. The current accounting rule is, however, that retained earnings be charged to support the increase in permanent capital. Accounting Research Bulletin 43, ch. 7B, ¶ 10.

the dividend; (ii) stated capital should be increased by the fair market value of the shares issued, so long as not less than par (after or before giving effect to the dividend itself?); (iii) stated capital should be increased for each share newly-issued through the dividend by an amount equal to the average stated capital per share as shown on the books before giving effect to the dividend, so long as it is not less than par. For reasons that may or may not be persuasive to others, accountants have chosen the second option. The statutes are silent as usual. The answer chosen will determine the size of the corresponding charge to be made against the surplus account and thereby the future availability or nonavailability of dividend payments. To simplify the balance sheet above, it has been assumed that the entry to be made in the stated capital account, and the charge to earned surplus, is the par value of the shares issued through the dividend.

A question for the Scaramouche reader with a sense that the world is mad: Is it not evident that all shares issued by way of stock dividend are illegal and void? On the face of it, these shares are not issued for "goods, services, or labor done", as all the statutes require that they be. May not then the shareholder who receives the stock dividend later be required by a creditor, or someone, to pay in to the corporation an amount of money or property equal to the par value of the shares he received? The only available counterargument to that contention must be that (i) corporate "surplus" is "goods", and that (ii) an accounting entry charging a surplus account and increasing a stated capital account constitutes a "payment" to the corporation that complies with the statutory sections requiring that stock be "paid" up to its par value. It is difficult to think that anyone could advance that two point argument with a straight face. But it is exactly the position that lawyers, accountants, courts and commentators take on the question. Those who work regularly with these materials have become so accustomed to talking about issuing stock "against surplus" that they are no longer sensitive to its manifest non-compliance with the principle that assets are supposed to come into the corporate till when shares of the company are issued. Or perhaps they simply never ask the question, in tacit recognition that the statutory legal capital structure is in such disrepair that it will inevitably produce answers that are inconsistent or palpably unsupportable.

(b) *Legal capital restraints:*

    (i) **Net worth jurisdiction:** shareholder distribution of $61,001 allowable since assets exceed liabilities by $61,001.

    (ii) **Stated capital/surplus jurisdiction:** shareholder distribution of $501 allowable since assets are $501 more than liabilities plus legal capital.

    (iii) **Stated capital/earned surplus jurisdiction:** shareholder distribution of $501 allowable since earned surplus is $501.

    (iv) **Stated capital/surplus or current net profits jurisdiction:** shareholder distribution of at least $501 allowable since surplus is $501. But is more allowable? See discussion pp. 82–84, supra.

Transaction 9 (Year 6): Stock Split

During year six, Laminated Thumbscrew's financial vice president, Mr. Rack, believing that the current market price of Thumbscrew stock ($120 per share) is too high to attract the small investor, proposes, and the board decides, that a stock split of two for one is called for. By vote of shareholders and directors, the certificate of incorporation is amended to reduce par value from $100 to $50 per share, and each shareholder receives, by one or another mechanical procedures, two shares of common stock with a par value of $50 per share in exchange for each share of $100 par stock he theretofore held. The market price per share promptly drops to $62.

(a) *Balance sheet presentation:*

Laminated Thumbscrew, Inc.
Balance Sheet # 9 (giving effect to Transaction 9)

ASSETS		LIABILITIES	
Cash	$ 1,000	Accounts payable	$ 2,000
Accounts receivable	37,000	Bank loan	10,000
Inventory	30,000	Liabilities	$12,000
Land	5,000		
Secret process	1	SHAREHOLDERS' EQUITY	
		Capital: $50 par common, 1,210 sh.	$60,500
		Earned surplus	501
		Shareholders' equity	61,001
	$73,001		$73,001

Accounting Note: Obviously, the transaction denominated a "stock dividend" in Transaction 8 could have been effected by reducing par rather than charging surplus, and the transaction denominated a stock split in Transaction 9 could have been effected by charging surplus (assuming there is enough surplus for the purpose) rather than by changing the par value per share. On the whole, lawyers and accountants tend to use the term "stock dividend" where the change in the number of outstanding shares is relatively small and "stock split" when it is relatively large. If par stock is involved and if the transaction is denominated a "split", the lawyer assumes that a reduction of par value per share will be made, since otherwise stated capital will be sharply increased and the company's freedom to declare dividends correspondingly reduced.

(b) *Legal capital restraints:*

No change from 8(b).

Transaction 10 (Year 6): Reduction of Stated Capital

(A) Near the end of year six, it appears to the Laminated Thumbscrew management that a loss of $7,000 will occur from operations that year. The loss, plus routine changes in cash and accounts receivable, would produce the following balance sheet:

Laminated Thumbscrew, Inc.
Trial Balance Sheet # 10A (giving effect to Transaction 10(A))

ASSETS		LIABILITIES	
Cash	$ 6,000	Accounts payable	$ 2,000
Accounts receivable	25,000	Bank loan	10,000
Inventory	30,000	Liabilities	$12,000
Land	5,000	SHAREHOLDERS' EQUITY	
Secret process	1	Capital: $50 par	
		common, 1,210 sh.	$60,500
		Earned surplus	
		(deficit)	(6,499)
		Shareholders'	
		equity	$54,001
	$66,001		$66,001

If this were to become the year-end balance sheet, the board of directors would find itself in a difficult position. The Company did not pay a cash dividend in the preceding year; it has enough cash on hand to pay up to $6,000 at the end of year six but is prevented (in all but a net worth or a nimble dividend jurisdiction) from legally declaring a dividend because of the earned surplus deficit of $6,499.

(B) At the suggestion of the company's counsel, Peine, Forte & Dure, and after consulting its accountants, Pacioli, Oldcastle & Co., the board of directors decides to meet its problem by reducing the company's stated capital. (Counsel has checked the bank loan documents to make sure they do not prohibit this move.) The local corporation code procedure for "reducing capital" is followed. This procedure usually consists of (i) voting at a directors' meeting to take this action, (ii) in some cases, holding a shareholders' meeting at which the certificate of incorporation is amended by shareholder vote to reduce the par, (iii) filing a certificate of amendment with the state corporation commissioner, and (iv) filing a statement of capital reduction with the same official. Laminated Thumbscrew's shareholders approve the resolution to reduce par from $50 per share to $40 per share and the necessary papers are filed.

(a) *Balance sheet presentation:*

Laminated Thumbscrew, Inc.
Balance Sheet # 10B (giving effect to Transaction 10(A)
and Transaction 10(B))

ASSETS		LIABILITIES	
Cash	$ 6,000	Accounts payable	$ 2,000
Accounts receivable	25,000	Bank loan	10,000
Inventory	30,000	Liabilities	$12,000
Land	5,000		
Secret process	1	SHAREHOLDERS' EQUITY	
		Capital: $40 par	
		common, 1,210 sh.	$48,400
		Capital surplus	12,100
		Earned surplus	
		(deficit)	(6,499)
		Shareholders'	
		equity	$54,001
	$66,001		$66,001

Accounting Note: With the par reduced from $50 to $40 per share, the aggregate stated capital statutorily required drops from $60,500 to $48,400. The balance of $12,100 is declared reduction surplus by the board and is entered under "capital surplus"; by modern practice, it would be entered on the balance sheet as additional paid–in capital.

The reduction of the par is in itself economically meaningless, and, analytically, the market price of the stock should be unaffected. In fact, however, the market may respond; for example, the market may accurately read the par value change as a preliminary to a major asset distribution on the stock, and the stock price may rise as a result.

(b) *Legal capital restraints:*

(i) **Net worth jurisdiction:** shareholder distribution of $54,001 allowable since assets exceed liabilities by $54,001.

    (ii) **Stated capital/surplus jurisdiction:** shareholder distribution of $5,601 allowable in some jurisdictions since assets are $5,601 more than liabilities plus legal capital. Some stated capital/surplus jurisdictions specifically forbid the use of reduction surplus as a basis for distribution. Others permit the use of the reduction surplus, but only if shareholders are notified with the distribution payment that reduction surplus has been charged for the purpose.

    (iii) **Stated capital/earned surplus jurisdiction:** no shareholder distribution allowable since earned surplus is a deficit and the reduction surplus may not be used directly to support a dividend payment. But under modern earned surplus statutes, a reduction surplus *may* be used to offset an earned surplus deficit up to the extent of the deficit, thus helping to put the company in a position to pay future dividends as soon as it has even $1 of earned surplus. (See Transaction 11).

    Further, given the change of par to $40, a distribution of $5,601 to shareholders would be allowed under many earned surplus statutes as a "distribution of capital surplus" so long as shareholders are given notice of the basis for payment and so long as (as here) liquidation preferences of preferred shares are not threatened. Indeed, under many statutes, the charge reflecting such a distribution can (after appropriate shareholder vote) be made directly to *stated* capital, without going through the double step of creating, then charging, the reduction surplus account. And where stands the creditor, for whose protection all this intellectual machinery was built?

    (iv) **Stated capital/surplus or current net profits jurisdiction:** shareholder distribution of at least $5,601 allowable since surplus is $5,601. But is more allowable? See discussion pp. 82–84, supra.

Transaction 11 (Year 6): Reduction Surplus as Offset to Deficit

(A) At the end of year six, the board of directors declares and pays a cash dividend in the amount of $5,601, charging it to the capital surplus (reduction surplus) account.

(a) *Balance sheet presentation:*

Laminated Thumbscrew, Inc.
Trial Balance Sheet # 11A (giving effect to Transaction 11(A))
As at end of Year 6

ASSETS		LIABILITIES	
Cash	$ 399	Accounts payable	$ 2,000
Accounts receivable	25,000	Bank loan	10,000
Inventory	30,000	Liabilities	$12,000
Land	5,000		
Secret process	1	SHAREHOLDERS' EQUITY	
		Capital: $40 par	
		common, 1,210 sh.	$48,400
		Capital surplus	6,499
		Earned surplus	
		(deficit)	(6,499)
		Shareholders'	
		equity	$48,400
	$60,400		$60,400

(B) Both Peine and Pacioli suggest that the appearance of the company's balance sheet could be measurably improved if the capital surplus were used to offset the earned surplus deficit—only a paper entry, but one that erases from the balance sheet that painful public reminder of earlier loss years. The board approves that suggestion.

(a) *Balance sheet presentation:*

Laminated Thumbscrew, Inc.
Balance Sheet # 11B
(giving effect to Transaction 11(A)
and Transaction 11(B))
As at end of Year 6

ASSETS		LIABILITIES	
Cash	$ 399	Accounts payable	$ 2,000
Accounts receivable	25,000	Bank loan	10,000
Inventory	30,000	Liabilities	$12,000
Land	5,000		
Secret process	1	SHAREHOLDERS' EQUITY	
		Capital: $40 par	
		common, 1,210 sh.	$48,400
		Earned surplus	–0–
		Shareholders'	
		equity	$60,400
	$60,400		$60,400

Accounting Note: As a matter of applicable law, even in jurisdictions where capital surplus (reduction surplus) may not be directly charged for a shareholder distribution, it may often be used in this manner to offset a deficit, as was the case under the Model Act (1979).

(b) *Legal capital restraints:*

    (i) **Net worth jurisdiction:** shareholder distribution of $48,400 allowable since assets exceed liabilities by $48,400.

    (ii) **Stated capital/surplus jurisdiction:** no shareholder distribution allowable since assets do not exceed liabilities plus legal capital.

    (iii) **Stated capital/earned surplus jurisdiction:** no shareholder distribution allowable since no earned surplus.

    (iv) **Stated capital/surplus or current net profits jurisdiction:** shareholder distribution of $6,000 allowable; there is no surplus and the corporation lost $7,000 in year six, but it had net profits of $6,000 in year five. See discussion pp. 82–84, supra.

Transaction 12 (Year 7): Paid-in Surplus

At the beginning of year seven, Laminated Thumbscrew sells 100 shares of its $40 par stock at its then-market price of $50 per share, receiving cash of $5,000 in the transaction.

(a) *Balance sheet presentation:*

Laminated Thumbscrew, Inc.
Balance Sheet # 12 (giving effect to Transaction 12)

ASSETS		LIABILITIES	
Cash	$ 5,399	Accounts payable	$ 2,000
Accounts receivable	25,000	Bank loan	10,000
Inventory	30,000	Liabilities	$12,000
Land	5,000	**SHAREHOLDERS' EQUITY**	
Secret process	1	Capital: $40 par	
		common, 1,310 sh.	$52,400
		Capital surplus	1,000
		Earned surplus	–0–
		Shareholders'	
		equity	$53,400
	$65,400		$65,400

Accounting Note: Cash is increased by $5,000, stated capital by $4,000 and a capital surplus of $1,000 is created.

(b) *Legal capital restraints:*

    (i) **Net worth jurisdiction:** shareholder distribution of $53,400 allowable since assets exceed liabilities by $53,400.

    (ii) **Stated capital/surplus jurisdiction:** shareholder distribution of $1,000 allowable since assets are $1,000 more than liabilities plus legal capital.

    (iii) **Stated capital/earned surplus jurisdiction:** no shareholder distribution allowable since no earned surplus. Some statutes permit a capital surplus, such as capital surplus shown above, to be used as a basis for a distribution if notice thereof is given to shareholders.

    (iv) **Stated capital/surplus or current net profits jurisdiction:** shareholder distribution of at least $1,000 allowable since surplus is $1,000. But is more allowable? See Transaction 11B(b)(iv) and discussion pp. 82–84, supra.

Transaction 13 (Year 7):
Stock Repurchase Agreement

During the first six months of year seven, an unusual spurt in business activity produces a $5,000 profit for the company.

(a) *Balance sheet presentation:*

Laminated Thumbscrew, Inc.
Balance Sheet # 13 (giving effect to Transaction 13)

ASSETS		LIABILITIES	
Cash	$10,399	Accounts payable	$ 2,000
Accounts receivable	25,000	Bank loan	10,000
Inventory	30,000	Liabilities	$12,000
Land	5,000	SHAREHOLDERS' EQUITY	
Secret process	1	Capital: $40 par	
		common, 1,310 sh.	$52,400
		Capital surplus	1,000
		Earned surplus	5,000
		Shareholders' equity	$58,400
	$70,400		$70,400

At this point, one of the original investing shareholders dies. Company counsel, Peine, Forte & Dure, reminds the management that, at the time of the company's formation, the original shareholders and the company entered into a stock repurchase agreement under the terms of which the company is given a right of first refusal to buy any or all of the company's shares held in the estate of any deceased shareholder at "the fair market price" of the shares. It is stipulated that the fair market price is $55 per share. Is the company free under the legal capital restrictions to buy in any of the company's outstanding shares—thereby making an asset distribution to a shareholder in respect of his shares— and, if so, how many?

(b) *Legal capital restraints:*

    (i) **Net worth jurisdiction:** share reacquisition of $58,400 allowable since assets exceed liabilities by $58,400.

    (ii) **Stated capital/surplus jurisdiction:** share reacquisition of $6,000 allowable since assets are $6,000 more than liabilities plus legal capital.

    (iii) **Stated capital/earned surplus jurisdiction:** share reacquisition of at least $6,000 allowable, since assets are $6,000 more than liabilities plus legal capital. The "repurchase" is oddly not limited to the $5,000 of earned surplus. In fact, some earned surplus jurisdictions will permit stock repurchases to be made where there is *no* surplus of any kind! Once again, the statutory system fails to block an outpouring of corporate assets into the hands of one or more shareholders, and the creditor's cushion of stated capital proves illusory.

    (iv) **Stated capital/surplus or current net profits jurisdiction:** shareholder distribution of at least $6,000 allowable since surplus is $6,000. But is more allowable? See Transaction 12(b)(iv) and discussion pp. 82– 84, supra.

Legal Note: Stock repurchase agreements (sometimes called "buy-sell" agreements) are an extremely important device for the closely-held corporation. When there is only a handful of shareholders, there is usually no market for the shares, but the estate of a deceased shareholder will typically need cash to pay death expenses. The surviving shareholders will also usually want to protect themselves against an unwelcome stranger as a purchaser of the deceased's shares and may also want, if possible, to retain their respective control percentages vis-à-vis each other. The surviving shareholders can achieve these objectives by buying the shares themselves, of course, but that takes after-tax cash from their own pockets. They would therefore prefer that the same objectives be attained through repurchase of the deceased's shares by the corporation and payment of pre-personal-tax funds out of the corporate treasury into the estate. Stock repurchase agreements are designed to achieve that purpose.

The stock repurchase agreement often provides only for a right of first refusal to buy the deceased's shares to be extended to the corporation and/or the surviving shareholders, but many agreements purport to *require* the corporation, or surviving shareholders, to buy up the shares from the estate. Stock repurchase agreements display considerable variety in their manner of setting the price for the repurchased shares. It is not uncommon for closely-held corporations to carry insurance on the lives of their shareholders to meet the share purchase options or requirements of such agreements.

Share "repurchases" by issuing corporations are not limited to situations where stock repurchase agreements exist. Redemption of preference shares, referred to earlier, are another example. Further, for one reason or another (some unsavory), a corporation's board may wish to have the corporation "buy in" ("buy up", "buy out") the shares of a particular shareholder. Or a publicly-held corporation's management may be moved to "buy in" some of the company's outstanding shares from time to time because the market price is "low". If the corporation is successful in "buying in" shares at a price lower than the liquidating value per share, and the company then liquidates and distributes all its net assets to its remaining shareholders, shareholders who sold their shares "to the corporation" do not share in the liquidation proceeds, and the other shareholders (often including management) are ahead of the game. In principle, the same proposition is true if the company's assets are not liquidated but the discounted capitalized future income stream per share proves greater than the price per share paid to the shareholder who sold his shares "to the corporation".

It is extraordinary that legal capital restraints on stock reacquisitions are in such a state of disarray and require so much legal guesswork. Older cases and statutes did not recognize at all that a purchase by the corporation of its own stock is a form of shareholder distribution from which the "corporation" receives nothing, which is obnoxious to creditors, and which, depending on price, may prejudice or favor shareholders whose shares were not bought in. Many statutes are silent on the matter; some set up special rules on repurchases; some treat them as a kind of "reduction of capital" or liquidating distribution; others treat the reacquisitions like any other shareholder distribution.

Transaction 14 (Year 7): Purchase of Stock for the Treasury

At the end of the first six months of year seven, Laminated Thumbscrew pays out $2,750 in cash to buy in from shareholders 50 shares of its own stock at the market price of $55 per share and the board of directors by resolution designates that the 50 shares shall be held as "treasury stock".

(a) *Balance sheet presentation:*

Laminated Thumbscrew, Inc.
Balance Sheet # 14 (giving effect to Transaction 14)

ASSETS		LIABILITIES	
Cash	$ 7,649	Accounts payable	$ 2,000
Accounts receivable	25,000	Bank loan	10,000
Inventory	30,000	Liabilities	$12,000
Land	5,000	SHAREHOLDERS' EQUITY	
Secret process	1	Capital: $40 par common, 1,310 sh. (50 sh. in treasury)	$52,400
		Capital surplus	1,000
		Earned surplus unrestricted $2,250	
		Restricted by treasury shares 2,750	5,000
		Less: 50 sh. treasury stock	(2,750)
		Shareholders' equity	$55,650
	$67,650		$67,650

Accounting Note: Modern accounting practice recognizes that a corporation's shares in its own hands are not an asset; corporate assets have been reduced by $2,750 by the reacquisition of the stock. As a legal matter, however, treasury shares have not been "retired" or "cancelled". They are still "issued" but not considered "outstanding" (at least for some purposes), and they continue to be reflected in the stated capital figure. In the accounting treatment shown here, these elements are recognized. In addition, earned surplus available for shareholder distributions is shown to be restricted by a reserve in the amount of the purchase price of the shares. In the example given, the transaction is made explicit by restricting the earned surplus in the amount of the purchase price. That treatment is not, however, required by current accounting principles and other accounting treatments are possible. The treasury shares might, for instance, be shown at par. Or, before restricting the earned surplus, it might be permissible to make a first charge against the capital surplus account, at least to the extent of $15 for each share acquired, the excess of the purchase price per share over the stated capital (par value) per share. Another possibility would be to charge the capital surplus account only $10 for each share acquired (and the balance to earned surplus) since in the most recent share issuance of more than 55 shares (see Transaction 12), $10 per share was allocated to capital surplus. The statutes usually offer no specific guidance. See Accounting Research Bulletin 43, chs. 1A and 1B; APB No. 6, ¶¶ 12–13.

(b) *Legal capital restraints:*

   (i) **Net worth jurisdiction:** shareholder distribution of $55,650 allowable since assets exceed liabilities by $55,650.

   (ii) **Stated capital/surplus jurisdiction:** shareholder distribution of $3,250 allowable since assets are $3,250 more than liabilities plus legal capital.

   (iii) **Stated capital/earned surplus jurisdiction:** shareholder distribution of $2,250 allowable since unrestricted earned surplus is $2,250. (The local statute may not contain the refinement of "restricted earned surplus" in which case perhaps $5,000 is available for dividends since the balance sheet continues to show earned surplus as $5,000.)

   (iv) **Stated capital/surplus or current net profits jurisdiction:** shareholder distribution of $6,000 allowable since surplus is $6,000. But is more allowable? See discussion pp. 82–84, supra.

Transaction 15 (Year 7): Sale of "Treasury Shares"

Three months later, at a time when the market price of Laminated Thumbscrew stock has risen to $60 per share, the board of directors authorizes the sale of 20 shares of the company's 50 shares of treasury stock and the shares are sold by the corporation for $1,200 cash.

(a) *Balance sheet presentation:*

Laminated Thumbscrew, Inc.
Balance Sheet # 15 (giving effect to Transaction 15)

ASSETS		LIABILITIES	
Cash	$ 8,849	Accounts payable	$ 2,000
Accounts receivable	25,000	Bank loan	10,000
Inventory	30,000	Liabilities	$12,000
Land	5,000	SHAREHOLDERS' EQUITY	
Secret process	1	Capital: $40 par common, 1,310 sh. (30 sh. in treasury)	$52,400
		Capital surplus	1,000
		Capital surplus— treasury stock sales	100
		Earned surplus unrestricted $3,350	
		Restricted by treasury shares 1,650	5,000
		Less: 30 sh. treasury stock	(1,650)
		Shareholders' equity	$56,850
	$68,850		$68,850

Accounting Note: By the accounting treatment shown, cash is increased by the $1,200 sale price of the 20 shares, stated capital is left unaffected, unrestricted earned surplus is restored to the extent of the $1,100 that the company had paid for the 20 shares, the $100 difference between the company's purchase price (see Transaction 14) and the resale price of the 20 shares is entered as capital surplus, and the two offsetting treasury stock items are reduced from $2,750 (50 shares @ $55 per share) to $1,650 (30 shares @ $55 per share). Modern accounting would not recognize the $100 as a "profit" to be added to earned surplus.

Note that throughout these treasury share transactions, regardless of asset outflows from the corporation's treasury to shareholders, and asset inflows from shareholders to the corporate treasury, the legal stated capital figure remains frozen and wholly unreflective of what is going on. This is because it refers to all outstanding shares and treasury shares are traditionally conceived to be "issued" but not "outstanding".

(b) *Legal capital restraints:*

    (i) **Net worth jurisdiction:** shareholder distribution of $56,850 allowable since assets exceed liabilities by $56,850.

    (ii) **Stated capital/surplus jurisdiction:** shareholder distribution of $4,450 allowable since assets are $4,450 more than liabilities plus legal capital.

    (iii) **Stated capital/earned surplus jurisdiction:** shareholder distribution of $3,350 allowable since unrestricted earned surplus is $3,350. See also Transaction 14(b)(iii).

Is the $100 capital surplus item derived from the purchase and sale of the treasury shares available for dividend purposes? Though accountants maintain that the $100 gain is not an income increment but an increase in capital surplus, is it clear that it falls outside a not untypical statutory definition of earned surplus—"net profits, income, gains and loss"?

    (iv) **Stated capital/surplus or current net profits jurisdiction:** shareholder distribution of $6,100 allowable since surplus is $6,100. But is more allowable? See discussion pp. 82–84, supra. Query: Does the $100 "gain" contribute to current "net profits" for purposes of these statutes?

Transaction 16 (Year 7): Retirement of "Treasury Shares"

A short time later (prior to the end of year seven), the board of directors by resolution "retires" the remaining 30 shares of treasury stock to the status of authorized but unissued stock.

(a) *Balance sheet presentation:*

Laminated Thumbscrew, Inc.
Balance Sheet # 16 (giving effect to Transaction 16)

ASSETS		LIABILITIES	
Cash	$ 8,849	Accounts payable	$ 2,000
Accounts receivable	25,000	Bank loan	10,000
Inventory	30,000	Liabilities	$12,000
Land	5,000	SHAREHOLDERS' EQUITY	
Secret process	1	Capital: $40 par	
		common, 1,280 sh.	$51,200
		Capital surplus	1,000
		Earned surplus	4,650
		Shareholders' equity	$56,850
	$68,850		$68,850

Accounting Note: As shown, on retirement of the 30 shares that had been purchased for $1,650, $1,200 (30 shares @ $40 par) is charged against the stated capital account, $100 is charged against "Capital surplus—treasury stock sales," eliminating that item, and the remaining $350 is charged against earned surplus; the matching entries restricting earned surplus disappear.

Expressing these entries in another way, the treasury share offset of $1,650 appearing on Balance Sheet # 15 is eliminated, $1,200 of it being charged against stated capital, $100 against capital surplus, and $350 against earned surplus. In turn, the $1,650 restriction on earned surplus is removed, so that the net effect on unrestricted earned surplus is an increase of $1,300.

Again, alternative accounting treatments might have been possible, such as a charge of $450, or $350, to the general capital surplus account. The statutes give almost no guidance.

Observe carefully the aggregate effect of the acquisition of treasury stock and its retirement. If these transactions are covered by the local legal capital scheme at all, the end product of the full transaction is a reduction of surplus only to the extent that the purchase price of the reacquired shares exceeds the stated capital attributable to them. *That is to say, if the market price of the shares is equal to or less than the stated capital attributable to them, then any number of shares may, through step transactions, be bought in and retired without reducing the surplus account at all.* The assets flow out of the corporate till to the shareholders as their shares are bought up by the company, but the company's balance sheet capability to make shareholder distributions remains as great as before.[5] This process is a "reduction of capital" in the real economic sense—an actual pay-out of corporate assets to shareholders. The legal capital system fails utterly to restrain the outflow of assets to shareholders by this method until the point where further distributions to shareholders would produce a negative net worth. In this sense all statutory legal capital schemes are, ultimately, net worth statutes.

Under the corporation laws of many jurisdictions, the legal retirement of the shares is called a "reduction of capital"; it is not legally effectuated until a statement of reduction of capital is duly filed with the commissioner of corporations and perhaps until other procedural steps are taken.

5. If the purchases of shares from the shareholders are prorated among them in proportion to their holdings, the transactions also leave intact the shareholders' relative equity fraction and voting control.

(b) *Legal capital restraints:*

  (i) **Net worth jurisdiction:** shareholder distribution of $56,850 allowable since assets exceed liabilities by $56,850.

  (ii) **Stated capital/surplus jurisdiction:** shareholder distribution of $5,650 allowable since assets are $5,650 more than liabilities plus legal capital.

  (iii) **Stated capital/earned surplus jurisdiction:** shareholder distribution of $4,650 allowable since earned surplus is $4,650.

  (iv) **Stated capital/surplus or current net profits jurisdiction:** shareholder distribution of $5,650 allowable since surplus is $5,650. But is more allowable? See discussion pp. 82–84, supra.

Transaction 17 (Year 8): Distribution in Kind

During year eight, the board of directors wishes to make a large distribution to shareholders. The company has long held two parcels of land that are carried on the company's books at their initial costs of $350 and $4,650. The latter parcel (no longer used in operations) now has a fair market value of $13,950, and the board, wishing to preserve the corporation's cash, decides to distribute undivided interests in the parcel to the company's shareholders.

(a) *Balance sheet presentation:*

Laminated Thumbscrew, Inc.
Balance Sheet # 17 (giving effect to Transaction 17)

ASSETS		LIABILITIES	
Cash	$ 8,849	Accounts payable	$ 2,000
Accounts receivable	25,000	Bank loan	10,000
Inventory	30,000	Liabilities	$12,000
Land	350	SHAREHOLDERS' EQUITY	
Secret process	1	Capital: $40 par	
		common, 1,280 sh.	$51,200
		Capital surplus	1,000
		Earned surplus	–0–
		Shareholders' equity	$52,200
	$64,200		$64,200

Accounting Note: The land account is reduced by $4,650, and the earned surplus account is charged the same amount, reducing it to zero.[6]

This transaction well illustrates the complete dependence of the legal capital system upon the conventions of accounting and the difference between economic reality and the world of accounting and law. From a creditor's standpoint and an economic perspective, $13,950 in real assets have been taken from the corporate pot and given to shareholders, despite the fact that, as noted at Transaction 16(b), the balance sheet would indicate that a shareholder distribution would (except in a net worth jurisdiction) be limited to $4,650, $5,650 or $5,000.

(b) *Legal capital restraints:*

 (i) **Net worth jurisdiction:** shareholder distribution of $52,200 allowable since assets exceed liabilities by $52,200.

 (ii) **Stated capital/surplus jurisdiction:** shareholder distribution of $1,000 allowable since assets are $1,000 more than liabilities plus legal capital.

 (iii) **Stated capital/earned surplus jurisdiction:** no shareholder distribution allowable since no earned surplus.

 (iv) **Stated capital/surplus or current net profits jurisdiction:** shareholder distribution of at least $1,000 allowable since surplus is $1,000. But is more allowable? See Transaction 13(b)(iv) and discussion pp. 82–84, supra.

Transaction 18 (Year 8):
Increase of Stated Capital by Resolution

Later in year eight, the board of directors votes to increase the company's stated capital by transferring $500 of the capital surplus to stated capital.

---

6. As a result of the distribution, the corporation would, however, have to recognize a $9,300 gain on the parcel for income tax purposes. Internal Revenue Code of 1986 § 311(b). Would that also be viewed as "profits" for purposes of a current net profits statute?

(a) *Balance sheet presentation:*

Laminated Thumbscrew, Inc.
Balance Sheet # 18 (giving effect to Transaction 18)

ASSETS		LIABILITIES	
Cash	$ 8,849	Accounts payable	$ 2,000
Accounts receivable	25,000	Bank loan	10,000
Inventory	30,000	Liabilities	$12,000
Land	350	SHAREHOLDERS' EQUITY	
Secret process	1	Capital: $40 par	
		common, 1,280 sh.	$51,700
		Capital surplus	500
		Earned surplus	–0–
		Shareholders' equity	$52,200
	$64,200		$64,200

(b) *Legal capital restraints:*

(i) **Net worth jurisdiction:** shareholder distribution of $52,200 allowable since assets exceed liabilities by $52,200.

(ii) **Stated capital/surplus jurisdiction:** shareholder distribution of $500 allowable since assets are $500 more than liabilities plus legal capital.

(iii) **Stated capital/earned surplus jurisdiction:** no shareholder distribution allowable since no earned surplus.

(iv) **Stated capital/surplus or current net profits jurisdiction:** shareholder distribution of at least $500 allowable since surplus is $500. But is more allowable? See Transaction 17(b)(iv) and discussion pp. 82–84, supra.

Legal Note: Circumstances are relatively rare in which management may wish to increase stated capital by transfer from other surplus accounts, but they do arise. For present purposes, the key points to note are two. First, an *increase* of the stated capital can be done by a simple vote of the board;[7] reductions of stated capital (except through purchases of shares for the treasury) often require a shareholders' vote in addition to a vote by the board.[8] Second, though it is customary for the stated capital per share of par stock to be equal to the par, the statutes require only that it be equal to, *or greater than,* par; it is not uncommon therefore to find stated capital

7. See, e.g., Del.Gen.Corp.Law § 154.

8. See, e.g., id. § 242(a)(3). Compare id. § 244.

accounts like that shown in Balance Sheet # 18, where the stated capital per share ($40.39) is more than the par.

Transaction 19 (Year 8): Issuance of Preferred Stock

Business improves during year eight, and the company makes $14,000. As its accounts receivable rise, management feels the need for more capital. Thereupon the board and shareholders vote to amend the certificate of incorporation to create a class of preferred stock with a par of $10 per share, a liquidating preference of $100 per share and an annual cumulative dividend of $8 per share; the stock is redeemable by the company at any time at a price of $100 per share. The company sells 100 shares of this preferred stock, and receives for it, $80 cash per share.

(a) *Balance sheet presentation:*

Laminated Thumbscrew, Inc.
Balance Sheet # 19 (giving effect to Transaction 19)
As at end of Year 8

ASSETS		LIABILITIES	
Cash	$10,015	Accounts payable	$ 2,000
Accounts receivable	58,334	Bank loan	10,000
Inventory	17,500	Liabilities	$12,000
Land	350	SHAREHOLDERS' EQUITY	
Secret process	1	Capital: $40 par	
		common, 1,280 sh.	$51,700
		$8 preferred, $10	
		par, 100 sh.	1,000
		Capital surplus:	
		Common	500
		Preferred	7,000
		Earned surplus	14,000
		Shareholders'	
		equity	$74,200
	$86,200		$86,200

Accounting Note: The stated capital of the new preferred is entered at $1,000 (100 shares at $10 par) and the remaining $7,000 received is entered as capital surplus; it would have been possible for the board to designate as stated capital for the preferred any number between $1,000 and $8,000. Note that a separate stated capital account is created and shown for each class of stock, as required by modern accounting practice. Less often required by corporation statutes, the accounting treatment above also creates a separate capital surplus account for each class; the reason will appear in the next paragraph. $8,000 is added to cash, which had been depleted by operations since Transaction 18.

(b) *Legal capital restraints:*

With two classes of stock outstanding, it now becomes necessary to inquire separately for each class whether distributions may be made to the holders.

I. Preferred

In general, the statutes on legal capital are more lenient in their restrictions on the distribution of dividends on preferred stock, unless the company would thereby be rendered insolvent. Corporate managements usually insist that the company be free under its bond indentures to pay preferred dividends as they accrue; they do so to preserve the credit image of the company, to give some reality to the putative preferred position of the senior stock, and to head off remedial protective action by the holders of preferred, as by electing directors in the event of non-payment of preferred dividends. The same arguments have led to weakening of the statutes restricting preferred dividends.[9]

If a company under the statute of a particular state cannot legally pay dividends on its common stock because of insufficient earned surplus, but can legally do so on its preferred, may not the board issue some low par or no par preferred shares as a "stock dividend" to common shareholders in proportion to their holdings of common and thereafter merrily pay out corporate assets to them as preferred dividends free of the legal capital statutes? How should preferred stockholders try to protect against this possibility?

II. Common

All distributions on the common stock of the company are now subject to the prior contractual claims and restraints of the preferred stock.

Otherwise:

(i) **Net worth jurisdiction:** common shareholder distribution of $74,200 allowable since assets exceed liabilities by $74,200.

(ii) **Stated capital/surplus jurisdiction:** common shareholder distribution of $21,500 allowable since assets are $21,500 more than liabilities plus legal capital.

9. See Model Act (1979) § 46 (last paragraph).

Legal Note: In accordance with most if not all legal capital statutes, this calculation draws no distinction between the stated capitals and surpluses of the separate classes. If, however, the balance sheet test is applied by class of stock, then one would deduct from the $21,500 an additional $7,000 (the paid-in surplus of the preferred), leaving a total of $14,500 available for common stock distributions.

The implications of this point are of importance. This can be readily seen if the facts above are changed to assume that the *only* surplus on the balance sheet is the $7,000 paid-in surplus created through the issue of the preferred. Would the management then be free to pay out dividends to the common and charge that surplus? If so, the result is that the new preferred holders will have "invested" dollars in the corporate enterprise only to see them paid out to the holders of securities ranking junior to them. That will not make the preferred shareholders happy.

The point also has other facets. When it comes time to pay the annual $8 dividend on the preferred, may (should) that dividend be charged against the earned surplus account? If so, will not the common shareholder now contend that such a charge will have the effect of (a) unfairly paying dividends on the preferred out of earned surplus created prior to the issuance of the preferred and (b) reducing the company's future capacity to pay dividends to the common and that, therefore, the preferred dividends should be charged against the preferred's capital surplus? [10] And what about the possibility of charging the common's capital surplus for the preferred dividends?

No statutory legal capital scheme is sufficiently sophisticated or worked through to deal with such questions, nor indeed can it be without resort to a complexity that far outbalances any gains from it. Yet corporate lawyers and accountants must provide definitive answers to such questions as the company does business in the ordinary course.

(iii) **Stated capital/earned surplus jurisdiction:** shareholder distribution of $14,000 allowable since earned surplus is $14,000.

(iv) **Stated capital/surplus or current net profits jurisdiction:** shareholder distribution of $21,500 allowable since surplus is $21,500. See discussion pp. 82–84, *supra.*

10. Or, if the statute permits, a direct charge against stated capital, to preserve earned surplus for the common?

Transaction 20 (Year 9): Present and Future Stock Issuance (No Par Stock; Convertible Debentures; Subscriptions; Warrants; Options; "PIKs" and "Poison Pills")

As Laminated gains momentum, the board of directors effects a number of financial capital transactions in year nine. The market price of the $40 par common has meantime dropped to $25. (These five transactions all have elements in common that can profitably be compared with each other. For that reason, and for conciseness in presentation here, the five transactions are grouped together and reflected in the single balance sheet, Balance Sheet # 20.)

(1) The company buys, for stock, all the assets (and assumes all the liabilities) of a small enterprise. Laminated's certificate of incorporation is amended to provide for a separate class of common stock that is in all respects pari passu to the outstanding $40 par common except that it is non-voting and is no par. The board authorizes the issuance of 250 shares of the no par stock for the net assets of the selling company; the assets acquired (all real estate) are valued by the Laminated board of directors at a fair market value of $18,000 and the liabilities at $13,000, for a net of $5,000. The board resolves that the stated capital for the 250 outstanding shares of no par stock is to be $2,000 and the balance of $3,000 is to go to capital surplus.

> **Legal Note:** If the value of the net assets purchased was in fact $5,000, as the board's resolution asserts, the price paid for the no par common was $20 per share. Under the doctrine of "equitable contribution", was that transaction fair to the holders of the $40 par common which was selling at $25 at the time? What would one need to know to decide? E.g.: What would have been the cost to Laminated of alternative capital? Did the real estate purchased have a unique value to Laminated? Are there any risks of additional hidden liabilities? Does the fact that the $40 par common can vote and the no par common cannot justify issuing the no par stock for a price that is less than the par value of the voting stock and also less than the current market value of the voting stock? How much less?

Accounting Note: The accounting entries for this transaction are:

Dr. Land	$18,000	
Cr. Accounts payable		$13,000
Cr. Stated capital, no par common, 250 sh.		2,000
Cr. Capital surplus, no par common		3,000

(2) Requiring additional capital, the management of Laminated sells, for $20,000 in cash, $20,000 face amount of 9¼% ten-year convertible debentures. Under the terms of the debentures, the holder may at any time convert a $1,000 face amount debenture into 30 shares of the company's $40 par common stock.

Legal Note: As a matter of logical analysis (not necessarily actual market behavior), a rational holder of one of these $1,000 debentures, which pay interest of $92.50 per annum, will (apart from tax considerations) convert it into 30 shares of Laminated $40 par common stock if (a) the market value of the common rises above $33.33 ($1,000 divided by 30) and there is a resale market for it; or (perhaps) if (b) the dividend on a share of common comes to exceed $3.08 ($92.50 divided by 30) per annum and promises to continue to do so; or if (c) the average annual growth of the per share value, plus dividends, exceeds $3.08 per share and promises to continue to do so.

Under the doctrine of "equitable contribution", were the terms of the convertible debentures fair to the existing holders of $40 par common, which at the time had a market price of $25?

Accounting Note: When a $1,000 debenture is converted into 30 shares of $40 par common, the company's liabilities will be reduced and its stated capital must be increased to reflect the issue of the new shares. But the figures do not match evenly. On the conversion of a debenture, the company's liabilities will be reduced by $1,000 but stated capital will have to be increased by $1,200 with respect to the 30 newly-issued shares. Arguably, nothing need be done about this until the time of conversion. But some accountants would say, with logic on their side, that at the time the debentures are first issued, a surplus account should be restricted by $200 for each debenture in anticipation of the ultimate conversion and of the charge that will at that time have to be made to a surplus account to make up the stated capital deficiency. Thus, the accounting entries made on the issue of the convertible debentures are:

Dr. Cash	$20,000
Cr. 9¼% Conv. Debentures, 10 yrs.	$20,000

and, in addition, enter under a surplus account a $4,000 reserve under a surplus account, with a footnote reading: "Restricted reserve for conversion of 9¼% Conv. Debentures to $40 par common stock, $4,000."

(3) The management persuades the holders' of the outstanding $40 par common to subscribe to an additional 500 shares of the same class, but they will not agree to a subscription price greater than $25 per share.

> **Legal Note:** If the applicable corporation statute provides for preemptive rights, and the certificate of incorporation of Laminated Thumbscrew does not exclude them, each $40 par common shareholder must be given an opportunity to subscribe to the new issue in proportion to the number of such shares he holds.

> On the other hand, it can only be a mad world that would say that a corporation with an earned surplus that would comfortably ground a distribution to its common shareholders should reduce that capacity when it succeeds in persuading new investors to subscribe to purchase new shares and to put *more* assets into the corporation—but that is the result if the subscription price is less than par. This transaction is a subscription agreement to buy stock in the future, and not a present purchase; the subscription price will be required to be paid in and the stock certificates issued whenever the board calls upon the subscribers for payment. For reasons grounded in history, however, stock subscribed is considered to be issued stock for purposes of capital accounting and the legal capital statutes. There are a number of anomolies about this convention, the most bizarre of which is that if (as is not the case here) the subscription price is greater than par, then the effect of the subscription will be to create a corporate receivable, to increase the stated capital to the extent of the par, *and* to create a capital surplus (!). In this way a paper transaction, that involves no payment of assets into the corporate treasury, could be used in a balance sheet surplus jurisdiction to provide a surplus basis for legally distributing corporate assets to common shareholders.

> In the case given, however, the problem is different. The subscription price of $25—which is dictated by market realities—runs flatly afoul of the fundamental concept of par—that, unless bankruptcy is impending, the purchas-

ers of newly-issued stock must pay in an amount equal to or greater than par. The board of directors and shareholders could, of course, simply amend the certificate of incorporation again to reduce the par, as in Transaction 10. But there may be another way to go or at least another argument to run. As noted with regard to Transaction 8, the shares issued in a stock dividend are simply issued "against" surplus. Similarly, in the case of shares issued on conversion of the debentures, as just discussed, part or all of the stated capital can be made up by simply charging a surplus account. Why can this not also be done in the case of "watered stock" (stock that is issued for less than par) where the company has a sufficient surplus to enable it to make up a sufficient stated capital entry by simply charging the surplus account? Laminated Thumbscrew decides to try this in its handling of the new stock subscriptions. The accounting entries are:

Dr. Subscriptions receivable,
$40 par common, 500 sh. @ $25 $12,500

Dr. Earned surplus   7,500

Cr. Stated capital, $40 par common, 500 sh. $20,000

(4) Laminated Thumbscrew's management also goes to its preferred shareholders with an offering of stock warrants. Under the terms of these warrants, the holder may buy from the company one share of its $8 preferred stock, $10 par value, at any time within the next year at a price of $75. The market price of the preferred at the time of the sale of the warrants is $65. The management succeeds in selling 1,000 of these warrants, but is only able to obtain a price of $1 per warrant.

Accounting Note: In the world of corporate finance, the warrant is a close family relation of the convertible debenture, and at least a cousin of the subscription, but the accounting convention with regard to warrants is different. Sale of these warrants will not lead to a balance sheet entry for the preferred stock that may ultimately be issued on exercise of the warrants; the only balance sheet entry will be a reference to the warrants themselves, with a footnote giving the details of the terms. If the warrant purchase price of the stock were below par, would the answer be different? And if the price of the preferred reaches, or approaches, $75—the price above which a warrant holder would find it to his economic advantage to exercise his warrant—will the accountants begin to require an entry on the balance sheet for the preferred stock to be sold through the warrants?

The accounting entries (apart from explanatory footnote) are:

Dr. Cash $1,000

Cr. Warrants outstanding $1,000

Note on "PIKs": During the high-flying days of the late 1980s, some companies issued so-called "payment in kind" ("PIK") preferred stock. The issuer of such stock has the option for a designated period of time to pay dividends in additional shares of the same class rather than in cash. Eventually, the PIK period ends and the issuer is required to begin paying dividends in cash but during the PIK period the security is analogous to a zero-coupon bond that accumulates interest without payment in cash. (In fact, there are PIK debt securities as well as PIK preferred stock.) The PIK rights are structured so that the shareholder can expect to receive more value in PIK shares than he would otherwise have expected to receive in interest, at least during the PIK period. Since in the absence of available surplus the issuer would be prevented by the applicable legal capital statute from issuing PIK shares, PIK preferred stock is always low par or no par stock. See also Transaction 8.

(5) A committee of the board of directors, acting pursuant to a vote of shareholders approving a management stock option plan, issues a block of incentive stock options to the company's four key executives. Under the terms of these options, each executive may at any time within the ensuing five years, if still in the employ of the company, purchase up to 50 shares of the company's $40 par common stock at a price of $35 per share.

Legal Note: Former Federal tax incentives for executive stock options are gone for now but options continue to have some appeal as a compensation tool since they increase the executive's equity position in the company and conserve assets of the corporation by rewarding the executive off the financial statements through dilution of the value of the shares of shareholders.

Accounting Note: Unlike the other transactions involving potential future stock issues, the accounting convention is that the grant of the stock options does not lead to any entry on the balance sheet.

Future exercise by Laminated Thumbscrew's executives of their options to purchase $40 par shares at a price of $35 per share will obviously not comply with the classical requirement that no less than par be paid. But the issuance of the option itself is not a violation of the statute. As for the future, it is the hope of the management that when an executive option is exercised, and a share issued, the accounting entries can be handled by

debiting some surplus account for the difference (which
account? and if there is no surplus account?):

Dr. Cash	$35	
Dr. Surplus	5	
Cr. Stated capital,		
$40 common		$40

Note on "Poison Pills": During the 1980s, many publicly-
.held corporations sought to discourage hostile takeovers,
i.e., changes in control not approved by the board of
directors. Particularly favored were techniques that
could be implemented without stockholder approval.
Among those is the so-called "poison pill". Euphemisti-
cally denominated "stock purchase plans", these mechanisms are designed to deter prospective acquirers from
making a bid for control without first negotiating with
the board of directors.

Following is a simplified model of the mechanism of a poison
pill. It does not purport to be a description of a modern
plan, its only purpose being to reveal the working principles involved in such a plan so the reader can discern the
legal capital issues it raises. The reader who is interested
will find in footnote 11 adjustments that bring the model
closer to the real world.

Suppose that the board of directors of X Co. declares and
distributes as a dividend on each of its outstanding common shares a "Right" to purchase an additional common
share. The board makes a reasonable guesstimate of the
"long term" value of a common share and sets that
amount as the amount that the Right holder must pay in
to X Co. in order to purchase one common share—the
"Exercise Price". As the Exercise Price set is considerably above the current market price per share at the time
of the Right distribution, a Right holder has no incentive
to exercise his Right at the present time.

But the Right has other more interesting provisions. By its
terms, if any person, P, should, at any future time within
the term of the Right, come to acquire shares entitling P
to more than a designated percentage of the total voting
power of X Co. (say, 30%), then a holder of a Right—*other
than P*—will have the option to purchase *two* shares of
the common stock of X Co. for the Exercise Price that
theretofore would have brought him only one share. This
new right is said to "flip in" to X Co. The obvious effect
of this provision is to discourage any P from acquiring
more than 30% of the voting power of X Co.

To illustrate: If the present market price of an X Co. common
share (and also its net worth per share) is $9, and there

are 100 shares outstanding, and the Exercise Price of each Right was set at $11, and P acquires 31 shares (31%) at an average a price of $10, and all holders of common shares exercise their Rights (except P, whose Rights, because of his status as an acquiring person, are non-exercisable), then the arithmetical results will be the following: The total shares outstanding increase from 100 to 238 (100 + (69 × 2)); P's 31% holding is diluted to 13% (31 divided by 238); X Co.'s net worth per share rises by $759 (69 × $11); the net worth per share declines from $9 to $6.97 (as $759 is paid in and 138 more shares are issued); and P's 31 shares for which he paid $310 are now worth only $216.07 (assuming they continue to trade at net worth per share).

The board's bargaining leverage vis à vis a world of potential Ps lies in its power to "redeem" the Rights—to "pull the pill". By the terms of the Rights the board can cancel the Rights, and if P's proposed terms for acquiring control of X Co. (and his identity?) are satisfactory to the board, the board will likely do so, thereby removing the barrier blocking P. To the extent all this works, the poison pill will have done its job of compelling P to deal with the board, forestalling any direct offer by P to shareholders.

As expanded in the margin,[11] real world poison pills are more complex and typically contain refinements to deal with

---

11. In practice, unless X Co. has available an unusually large number of authorized but unissued common shares, the poison pill plan will usually use, not common shares but, instead, authorized but unissued "preferred stock" and grant Rights to purchase shares of a new class of preferred stock. The terms of the new class are set by the board acting under statutory and charter authorization to fill in the terms of the class (often called "blank-check preferred"). The matter would have to go shareholder vote if more shares had to be authorized; so the Rights are issued in units of small fractions (often 1/100th of a preferred share)—with each such fractional share of the new preferred having the same voting rights as a whole share of common, plus small additional dividend and liquidation rights. Often the Rights have no efficacy at all until or unless P's acquisition of the designated percentage of control (typically, between 10% and 20%) triggers the flip-in. Finally, the Rights distributed will also include "flip-over" rights to purchase shares of the common stock of any ac-

quiring survivor company in a merger with X Co. with a value equal to twice the Exercise Price. (Since virtually all takeovers require such a merger as a step in the transaction, the "flip-over" rights are designed to survive that event, impose upon the unwelcome suitor a large liability to the Rights holders that he must meet despite the merger, and thus discourage him at the outset from thinking he can go ahead without the blessing of the X Co. board.) The scope of enforceability of poison pill plans is the subject of much current litigation. Generally, courts have upheld poison pills except where state statutes prohibit discriminating among shareholders. Compare *Moran v. Household International, Inc.*, 500 A.2d 1346 (Del.1985); *Dynamics Corp. of America v. CTS Corp.*, 805 F.2d 705 (7th Cir.1986) (interpreting Indiana and Delaware law); *Georgia–Pacific Corp. v. Great Northern Nekoosa Corp.*, 727 F.Supp. 31 (D.Me.1990); with *Amalgamated Sugar Co. v. NL Industries, Inc.*, 644 F.Supp. 1229 (S.D.N.Y.1986) (applying New Jersey law).

varieties of constraints arising out of the particular circumstances. Enough has been said, however, to hint at the array of legal capital questions kicked up by poison pill plans.

Suppose Laminated Thumbscrew's board adopts a poison pill plan. What should be the accounting treatment of the Rights on issuance as a dividend? Are they like warrants (see (4), supra) or options (see, supra)? Currently, under generally accepted accounting principles, they are treated like options, i.e., no entry is made on the balance sheet (although reference is made to them in the notes to the balance sheet). State law typically does not differ in this respect. But what is to be entered in the capital accounts at the point of "flip-in" when the rights accrue to acquire Laminated Thumbscrew shares at one-half of their market value? And "par value" concepts in this environment are as relevant as hooped skirts; the whole topic is simply avoided by designating the preferred as no par or *de minimis* par.

*   *   *   *   *   *   *   *   *

(a) *Balance sheet presentation:*

The five transactions grouped as Transaction 20 and the correlative accounting entries listed above produce the following balance sheet:

Laminated Thumbscrew, Inc.
Balance Sheet # 20 giving effect to Transaction 20
As at end of Year 9

ASSETS		LIABILITIES	
Cash	$ 31,015	Accounts payable	$ 15,000
Subscriptions re-		Bank loan	10,000
ceivable—$40		9¼% Conv. Deben-	
par common,		tures, 10 yrs.	20,000
500 sh. @ $25	12,500	Liabilities	$ 45,000
Accounts receivable	58,334	SHAREHOLDERS' EQUITY	
Inventory	17,500	Capital:	
Land	18,350	$40 par common,	
Secret process	1	1,780 sh.	$ 71,700
		No par common,	
		250 sh.	2,000
		$8 preferred	
		$10 par, 100 sh.	1,000
		Warrants [1]	1,000
		Capital surplus:	
		$40 par common	500
		No par common	3,000
		$8 preferred	7,000
		Earned surplus:	
		Restricted [2] $4,000	
		Unrestricted 2,500	
			6,500
		Shareholders'	
		equity	$ 92,700
	$137,700		$137,700

1. Outstanding, 1,000 warrants, issued at $1 per warrant, each entitling the holder to purchase 1 share of $8 preferred stock, $10 par value, at $75 at any time within the ensuing year.

2. Restricted reserve for conversion of 9¼% Conv. Debentures to 600 shs. of $40 per common stock.

(b) *Legal capital restraints:*

I. Preferred

See discussion at Transaction 19.

II. Common

(An aside: Although the no par stock subscribed for is "issued" for technical reasons of legal capital accounting, it will not, of course, be "outstanding" for purposes of receiving dividend payments.[12])

12. Is it "outstanding" for purposes of voting rights? computations of shareholder quorums? computations of class voting requirements, etc.?

(i) **Net worth jurisdiction:** common shareholder distribution of $92,700 allowable since assets exceed liabilities by $92,700.[13]

(ii) **Stated capital/surplus jurisdiction:** assuming (without asserting) the $1,000 for warrants outstanding is treated as stated capital, shareholder distribution of $17,000 allowable since assets are $17,000 more than liabilities plus legal capital. The balance sheet statutes accord no special recognition to the accountants' entry restricting the earned surplus account by $4,000 in anticipation of the future conversion of the debentures. But would a modern court? And should a careful lawyer?

(iii) **Stated capital/earned surplus jurisdiction:** shareholder distribution of $6,500 is statutorily allowable since earned surplus is $6,500. But of this amount, $4,000 is restricted by the accounting entry anticipating conversion of the convertible debentures. It is likely that an earned surplus statute would be interpreted to take such restrictions into account and would limit the allowable distribution to $2,500.

(iv) **Stated capital/surplus or current net profits jurisdiction:** shareholder distribution of $17,000 allowable since surplus is $17,000. See discussion pp. 82–84, supra. Is there any argument that the $1,000 entry for Warrants should be treated as surplus?

13. Suppose, as an analytic exercise, that the board now decides in a net worth jurisdiction to distribute to shareholders all assets except the $45,000 required to pay its creditors—decided, in short, to liquidate. Assume, too, that the conversion privilege of the debentures, the warrants and the stock options all lapse or are cut off. Assume that the subscriptions for the 500 shares of $40 par common are called, and, as agreed, $12,500 is paid in. Assume, finally, that the actual liquidating values of the company's assets are equal to their book value, so there will be $92,700 to be distributed. Of this, $10,000 must go to pay the $100 per share liquidating preference of the 100 shares of preferred. The remaining $82,700 must be divided among the 1,780 shares of $40 par common and the 250 shares of no par common since they rank pari passu on liquidation. $82,700 ÷ 2,030 = $40.73 per share. In this circumstance, it will clearly advantage the earlier shareholders for the board not to call the new subscriptions, since the new subscribers will pay in only $25 per share and promptly receive back $40.73. If the subscriptions are not called, this will reduce corporate assets available for distribution by $12,500 to $70,200, but will reduce the common shares outstanding to 1,280, so that the pro rata distribution per share will increase to $54.84.

Does this analysis establish that $25 per share was too low a price for the subscriptions and "unfair" to the existing shareholders under the principle of equitable contribution? Or that the subscribers were foolish, since the board will only call if the stock sinks in price?

Legal Note: In the interest of simplicity, it has been assumed that Laminated Thumbscrew's lawyer, accountant and board of directors set up the $4,000 provision for the convertible debentures as a restriction on the earned surplus account. But it is worth considering that the restriction (if made at all) might have been offset against one or more capital surplus items. If, for example, the capital surplus item for the preferred stock were to be restricted to provide a source of stated capital for the common shares issued on conversion of the debentures, the result would be to preserve earned surplus and thus make it possible to make cash payments on junior stock that would be charged against sources invested by senior stock.

Transaction 21 (Year 10): Transactions between Corporation and Shareholders

In year ten, the fortunes and prospects of Laminated Thumbscrew steadily improve as it makes a profit of $11,000, the $40 par common rises on the market to $36 per share, the no par common rises to $32 and the $8 preferred goes up to $76.

A. The following share transactions then take place:

(1) The board of directors calls the outstanding $40 par common stock subscriptions, the subscribers pay in the $12,500, and the certificates for the 500 shares are issued to the purchasers.

Accounting Note: The entries are:

Dr. Cash	$12,500	
Cr. Stock subscription		$12,500

No entry is needed for stated capital since it was made when the subscriptions were entered into.

(2) The holders of all the convertible debentures convert their $20,000 in debt instruments to 600 shares of common stock.

Accounting Note: The entries are:

Dr. Debentures	$20,000	
Dr. Earned surplus	4,000	
Cr. Stated capital,		
$40 par common		$24,000

The entry restricting earned surplus by $4,000 is eliminated, and the number of outstanding $40 par common shares is increased to 2,380.

(3) The holders of 100 of the outstanding warrants exercise their right to buy shares of the $8 preferred at a price of $75 per share; the other 900 warrants lapse.

Accounting Note: The entries are:

Dr. Cash	$ 7,500	
Cr. Stated capital, $8 preferred $10 par		$ 1,000
Cr. $8 preferred capital surplus		6,500

* * * *

Dr. Warrants	$ 1,000	
Cr. $8 preferred capital surplus		$ 1,000

The number of outstanding $8 preferred shares is increased to 200.

(4) The president and vice president of Laminated Thumbscrew exercise their options to buy 10 shares of $40 par common for $35 per share.

Accounting Note: The entries are:

Dr. Cash	$ 350	
Dr. Earned surplus	50	
Cr. Stated capital, $40 par common		$ 400

The number of outstanding $40 par common shares is increased to 2,390. See discussion at Transaction 20(5).

Legal Note: In most jurisdictions a careful lawyer would be reluctant to give an opinion that these ten shares are "fully paid and non-assessable" despite the proper appearance of the stated capital account since each of these shares was clearly issued for less than par.[14] But then so were the shares that were issued on conversion of the debentures, and the shares issued "against surplus" in the stock dividend, etc., etc. There is no relief from internal inconsistencies in the statutory stated capital system. The lawyer could at least assure the purchasing executives that their actual risk of liability is both very remote and narrowly limited.

B. Following on these share transactions, the board of directors makes the following distributions to shareholders:

(1) The company pays the annual dividend of $8 per share on the 200 shares of outstanding $8 preferred stock.

Accounting Note: What surplus should be charged for this $800 distribution? Since the management would prefer to keep earned surplus available for common stock dividends, it decides to charge the preferred dividend to the capital surplus account attributable to the $8 preferred. In a stated capital/surplus jurisdiction, the corporation's

---

14. See, e.g., Del.Gen.Corp.Law § 157. But see Md.Gen.Corp.Law § 2–203(e).

lawyer would approve the legality of this action. The accounting entries are:

Dr. Capital surplus
$8 preferred $ 1,600
Cr. Cash $ 1,600

(2) The company pays a dividend of $5 per share on the 2,390 outstanding shares of $40 par common and the 250 shares of no par common.

Accounting Note: It is assumed that the cash and earned surplus accounts were increased by the $11,000 profit for the year. The accounting entries for the dividends are:

Dr. Earned surplus $13,200
Cr. Cash $13,200

See Legal Note below with regard to this transaction.

(3) The company redeems 50 of the 200 outstanding shares of $8 preferred stock at the redemption price of $100 per share.

Accounting Note: The accounting entries are:

Dr. Stated capital,
$8 preferred $ 500
Dr. $8 preferred
capital surplus   4,500
Cr. Cash $ 5,000

How do creditors like this redemption transaction? How do common shareholders like it? How do the preferred shareholders who were redeemed like it? How do preferred shareholders whose shares were not redeemed like it?

(a) *Balance sheet presentation:*

Laminated Thumbscrew, Inc.
Balance Sheet # 21 (giving effect to Transaction 21)
As at end of Year 10

ASSETS		LIABILITIES	
Cash	$ 42,565	Accounts payable	$ 15,000
Accounts receivable	58,334	Bank loan	10,000
Inventory	17,500	Liabilities	$ 25,000
Land	18,350	SHAREHOLDERS' EQUITY	
Secret process	1	Capital: $40 par common, 2,390 sh.	$ 96,100
		No par common, 250 sh.	2,000
		$8 preferred, $10 par, 150 sh.	1,500
		Capital surplus:	
		$40 par common	500
		No par common	3,000
		$8 preferred	8,400
		Earned surplus	250
		Shareholders' equity	$111,750
	$136,750		$136,750

(b) *Legal capital restraints:*

I. Preferred

See discussion at Transaction 19.

II. Common

(i) **Net worth jurisdiction:** common shareholder distribution of $111,750 allowable since assets exceed liabilities by $111,750.

(ii) **Stated capital/surplus jurisdiction:** shareholder distribution of $12,150 allowable since assets are $12,150 more than liabilities plus legal capital.

Legal Note: The above distributive transactions illustrate some of the questions that arise regarding which surplus account should be charged when a distribution is made. Laminated Thumbscrew at this stage has two classes of common stock and one of preferred. In a jurisdiction allowing dividends to be charged to capital surplus, may dividends on one class be charged to capital surplus attributable to the other? If one class has a capital surplus account, and another does not, should dividends on the former be charged to its capital surplus in order to preserve support for dividends for the class that has no such surplus? Note that the present case is simpler than many in that the two classes of common are *pari passu* in respect of dividends and liquidation; interest conflicts between the holders of the two classes would be much greater if dividends could be paid to one class while being skipped for the other. For ease and clarity in the above example, the common stock dividend was entered as a charge to earned surplus, the most conservative option.

    (iii) **Stated capital/earned surplus jurisdiction:** shareholder distribution of $250 allowable since earned surplus is $250.

Note: Now consider the situation as a practical business matter. Is there any conceivable business reason why common shareholder distributions *should* be limited to an infinitesimal $250 in the case of this successful profitable enterprise that has a gaudy equity/debt ratio of 4.5, cash equal to nearly twice its total liabilities, a current ratio (current assets to current liabilities) of 7.9, a quick ratio of 3.9 (cash, marketable securities and receivables to liabilities), and at least one asset (the secret process) that is probably undervalued on the books?

The most fundamental criticism of the legal capital structure is not that it is shot through with analytic flaws—which it is—but that it operates arbitrarily, wholly unrelated to sensible business considerations, as the above situation illustrates.

    (iv) **Stated capital/surplus or current net profits jurisdiction:** shareholder distribution of $12,150 allowable since surplus is $12,150. See discussion pp. 82–84, supra.

Transaction 22 (Year 11): Corporation Combination; Purchase Accounting and Pooling of Interests Accounting

In year eleven, the management of Laminated Thumbscrew learns that it might be possible for the company to acquire another company, Iron Maidenform, Inc. Maidenform is in trouble. After many successful years under the leadership of a strong executive, the recently-deceased founder, the company's board has not been able to find or agree upon a successor, and the family shareholders are at swords' points. Maidenform has lost money for the last two years and is cash-short. The management of Laminated Thumbscrew believes, however, that Maidenform has some undervalued but developable assets, and that the two enterprises are promisingly complementary. A striking additional feature of Maidenform is that, despite recent losses, its balance sheet carries a substantial earned surplus. Its balance sheet is as follows:

Iron Maidenform, Inc.

ASSETS			LIABILITIES	
Cash	$ 5,000		Accounts payable	$ 17,000
Accounts receivable	20,000		Bank loan	8,000
Inventory	15,000		Liabilities	$ 25,000
Equipment	25,000		SHAREHOLDERS' EQUITY	
Land	35,000		Capital: $50 par common, 1,000 sh.	$ 50,000
			Earned surplus	25,000
			Shareholders' equity	$ 75,000
	$100,000			$100,000

Unlike the case of Laminated, there is no public market for the closely-held Maidenform stock; as can be seen, Maidenform's book value per share is $75 per share. The book value of each of Laminated's 2,390 shares of $40 par common and 250 shares of no par common (after allotting $15,000 to the liquidation value of the $8 preferred) is $36.65; as its affairs have prospered, its market price has climbed to $50 per share. Laminated's board decides to propose a transaction in which Laminated shares will be exchanged for Maidenform shares. Many factors go into the negotiation of a stock exchange ratio, predominantly the comparative bargaining power of the parties. The parties execute a letter of intent which leads to an agreement that each share of Maidenform stock will be entitled to receive 1.4 shares of Laminated $40 par common. To acquire Maidenform, therefore, Laminated will have to issue 1,400 additional shares of its $40 par common. All Maidenform shareholders vote to approve the agreement. Laminated thereupon issues to them 1,400 shares of its $40 par common which, in effect, is exchanged for their Maidenform stock.

> **Legal Note:** The description of this transaction has been written so as not to characterize or specify the legal means through which combination is effected. There are several mechanical ways by which it can be done. Three of them are relevant here as they involve share issuance.

> **Purchase of assets for shares:** As in Transaction 20(1), Laminated Thumbscrew can issue stock to Maidenform in exchange for all its assets and liabilities.[15] Thereupon Maidenform might retain the stock

---

15. For a greater number of shares, Laminated might instead acquire only the assets, leaving the liabilities with the seller, but there are complications to that procedure, including some risk that unpaid creditors of the seller might be able to pursue the purchaser regard-

as its only asset; or it might sell it on the market and use the proceeds to continue in some other business; or it might dissolve and distribute in liquidation the Laminated shares to its own shareholders. Shareholders voting against the transaction would be entitled, upon compliance with certain statutory procedures, to exercise "appraisal rights" and receive cash in the amount of the "fair value" of their shares.

Merger: The two companies might effect a statutory merger. Upon vote of both boards of directors and both groups of shareholders,[16] one company would be designated as the continuing company (here, Laminated) and the other as the terminating company (here, Maidenform). By operation of the corporation statute, upon effectiveness of the merger, all the assets and liabilities of Maidenform would become assets and liabilities of the continuing company and all assenting shareholders of Maidenform would become shareholders of the continuing company. Shareholders voting against the merger would be entitled to appraisal rights.

Exchange of stock: In an exchange of stock, Laminated would offer shareholders of Maidenform to exchange Laminated shares for their Maidenform shares and upon the exchange Maidenform would be a subsidiary of Laminated. Non-exchanging shareholders would remain, as minority shareholders, unless eliminated in a subsequent transaction.

Since any of these three mechanisms can be employed by either of the two companies, there are six such structural options.[17]

Accounting Note: Purchase Method: Transaction 20(1) describes the purchase of the assets and liabilities of another corporation in exchange for an issue of stock by Laminated Thumbscrew. The accounting for that kind of transaction is straight-forward. The board of directors of

less of the contract between seller and buyer.

16. Some corporation statutes provide that a shareholder vote is not required if the number of shares issued by the acquiring corporation is less than a certain percentage (e.g., 20%) of the number of shares of the same class. E.g., Del.Gen.Corp.Law § 251(f).

17. Other avenues also exist to achieve the same economic result. For example, Laminated could make a cash tender offer to shareholders of Maidenform, either for cash or a combination of such and securities. Or

through a statutory consolidation, both Laminated and Maidenform could terminate, their assets and liabilities could be transferred to a newly-formed corporation, and assenting shareholders of both terminating companies would automatically become shareholders of the new company; dissenters would be entitled to appraisal rights. Or, by a three-party combination, either Laminated or Maidenform could create a 100% subsidiary, X Company, and then combine X Company and the other company by any of the above routes.

the issuing company determines a fair value for the shares being issued and for the assets and liabilities acquired. An appropriate entry is made in the stated capital account for the shares issued, and if the net value of the assets and liabilities acquired is determined by the board to be more than the stated capital entry, the remainder is credited to a capital surplus account. Appropriate entries are then made on the balance sheet for the tangible and determinable assets acquired. If there is a difference between the valuation of the stock issued and the net fair value of assets and liabilities acquired, it is entered on the purchaser's books as "goodwill".[18] Under modern practice, this goodwill will be amortized ("written off") against earnings over a reasonable period, not in excess of 40 years. The book value of the acquired assets and liabilities as they appeared on the seller's books is often immaterial.

Let it be assumed that the Laminated–Maidenform combination is to be accounted for as though it were such a purchase. The purchase price for the net assets and liabilities acquired is determined by the Laminated board to be $70,000, i.e., 1,400 shares times their current market price of $50 per share. The new liabilities assumed are $25,000, so the assets to be added to the Laminated balance sheet must total to $95,000 if a write-off of goodwill is to be avoided. In allocating this amount among all assets except cash, the board of directors assesses the value of each item on the Maidenform balance sheet, as it is taken on to Laminated's books. It finds Maidenform's book values to be inflated. The board concludes that the accounts receivable acquired should be reduced to $15,000; that the inventory is worth only $5,000; that the equipment should be reduced to $20,000; and that the land should be reduced to $30,000; this leaves $20,000 to be entered as goodwill. These figures are considered to be assets on Laminated's balance sheet.[19] On the liability side of the balance sheet, the newly-assumed liabilities are accepted as is and increase the total liabilities by $25,000; stated capital for the $40 par common is increased by $56,000 (1,400 shares times $40 par) and capital surplus attributable to the $40 par common is increased by the balance of $14,000. The balance sheet then reads as follows:

18. Modern accounting practice would prefer the far-clearer term "excess of cost over actual assets acquired", but "goodwill" is still in common use.

19. In actual practice, this type of valuation and allocation is usually performed by the buyer in advance of the acquisition. Often the allocation is written into the acquisition agreement.

(a) *Balance sheet presentation:*

Laminated Thumbscrew, Inc.
Balance Sheet # 22A (giving effect to Transaction 22)
Accounting by Purchase Method

ASSETS		LIABILITIES	
Cash	$ 47,565	Accounts payable	$ 32,000
Accounts receivable	73,334	Bank loan	18,000
Inventory	22,500	Liabilities	$ 50,000
Equipment	20,000	**SHAREHOLDERS' EQUITY**	
Land	48,350	Capital: $40 par	
Goodwill	20,000	common, 3,790	
		sh.	$152,100
Secret process	1	No par common,	
		250 sh.	2,000
		$8 preferred, $10	
		par, 150 sh.	1,500
		Capital surplus:	
		$40 par common	14,500
		No par common	3,000
		$8 preferred	8,400
		Earned surplus	250
		Shareholders'	
		equity	$181,750
	$231,750		$231,750

(b) *Legal capital restraints:*

I. Preferred

See discussion at Transaction 19.

II. Common

(i) **Net worth jurisdiction:** shareholder distribution of $181,750 allowable since assets exceed liabilities by $181,750.

(ii) **Stated capital/surplus jurisdiction:** shareholder distribution of $26,150 allowable since assets are $26,150 more than liabilities plus legal capital.

(iii) **Stated capital/earned surplus jurisdiction:** shareholder distribution of $250 allowable since earned surplus is $250.

(iv) **Stated capital/surplus or current net profits jurisdiction:** shareholder distribution of $26,150 allowable since surplus is $26,150. See discussion pp. 82–84, supra.

Accounting Note: Pooling of Interests: An alternative way of looking at the corporate combination leads to an alternative accounting method, the so-called "pooling of interests" method. The combinatory transaction may be regarded as an arrangement between two shareholder groups rather than a transaction between two corporate entities. If a combination is effected by issuing common stock, each stockholder group partially gives up its exclusive interest in assets which its corporation formerly held but receives a partial interest in assets formerly held by the other corporation. The shareholders may be said to "pool their interests". From this premise and perspective, it is contended that the financial statements of the component companies in the combination should be "pooled". When the "pooling of interests" method of accounting is used, the recorded assets and liabilities of the constituent companies are simply carried forward to the combined corporation at their recorded amounts; that is, the transaction is not used as an occasion for placing an accounting value on the shares issued nor for allocating that value on the books among the assets acquired. Correspondingly, no goodwill item is created on the combined balance sheet. Not only are the balance sheets combined in this manner through the use of the "pooling of interests", but current income statements are also combined, and income statements for prior years are restated to show such a combination.

The plausibility of the "pooling of interests" concept can be most easily seen when the formal form of the combination is a "consolidation" (although in practice this legal form is seldom used), that is, a combination in which both shareholder groups surrender their stock and receive in exchange the stock of a new corporation into which the two former corporations are combined. But the fact that one of the corporations usually issues its stock in exchange for that of the other does not alter the substance of the transaction. Thus, the pooling of interests technique may apply equally to business combinations in which one or more companies become subsidiary corporations, or one company transfers its net assets to another, or each company transfers its net assets to a newly-formed corporation. One or more combining companies may be subsidiaries of the issuing corporation after the combination is consummated. Dissolution of the combining company is not a condition for applying the pooling of interests method; if the newly-acquired subsidiary is continued in existence and the other conditions for pooling are met, the pooling of interests method governs the process by which the financial statements of the subsidiary are consolidated with those of the parent.

Let it be assumed that the Laminated–Maidenform combination is to be accounted for by the pooling of interests method. The asset side of the balance sheet of Laminated is augmented by the recorded values that appeared on the asset side of the Maidenform balance sheet. Similarly, the liabilities are transferred. But stated capital on Laminated's balance sheet must be increased by $56,000 (1,400 shares times $40 par) to reflect the newly-issued shares. The Maidenform balance sheet carried a $50,000 stated capital, and this is "transferred" first to make up the required stated capital of the combined enterprise. But what of the other $6,000 needed? To supply this amount, some surplus account or accounts must be charged. It is probably acceptable to charge one or more capital surplus accounts for this purpose—whether or not originally on the balance sheet of the continuing or the terminating company, and whether or not attributable to the class of shares being newly issued. But assuming the most conservative avenue is taken, and the $6,000 is charged to earned surplus, the result is as follows:

(a) *Balance sheet presentation:*

Laminated Thumbscrew, Inc.
Balance Sheet # 22B (giving effect to Transaction 22)
Accounting by Pooling of Interests Method

ASSETS		LIABILITIES	
Cash	$ 47,565	Accounts payable	$ 32,000
Accounts receivable	78,334	Bank loans	18,000
Inventory	32,500	Liabilities	$ 50,000
Equipment	25,000	SHAREHOLDERS' EQUITY	
Land	53,350		
Secret process	1	Capital: $40 par common, 3,790 sh.	152,100
		No par common, 250 sh.	2,000
		$8 preferred, $10 par, 150 sh.	1,500
		Capital surplus:	
		$40 par common	500
		No par common	3,000
		$8 preferred	8,400
		Earned surplus	19,250
		Shareholders' equity	$186,750
	$236,750		$236,750

Legal Note: Note that whether the $6,000 is charged to capital surplus account or an earned surplus account, once more an example is provided where shares are issued "against" surplus. See the discussion at Transaction 20(3).

(b) *Legal capital restraints:*

I. Preferred

See discussion at Transaction 19.

II. Common

(i) **Net worth jurisdiction:** shareholder distribution of $186,750 allowable since assets exceed liabilities by $186,750.

(ii) **Stated capital/surplus jurisdiction:** shareholder distribution of $31,150 allowable since assets are $31,150 more than liabilities plus legal capital.

(iii) **Stated capital/earned surplus jurisdiction:** shareholder distribution of $19,250 allowable since earned surplus is $19,250. If the $6,000 required to increase stated capital had been charged to capital surplus accounts, the earned surplus account would be $6,000 higher, or $25,250.

(iv) **Stated capital/surplus or current net profits jurisdiction:** shareholder distribution of $31,150 allowable since surplus is $31,150. See discussion pp. 82–84, supra. If Iron Maidenform had had current net profits, they would have been "transferred" to Laminated Thumbscrew under the pooling of interests method of accounting and, depending upon their amount, might have provided the basis for an even greater distribution. See id.

Note: Balance Sheets # 22A and # 22B should be carefully compared. They will be found to be quite different, not only as to capital and surplus structure but also in the composition of their asset accounts, with consequent impacts (principally because of the treatment of "goodwill") on the company's future earnings statements.

For present purposes, the key point to notice from this transaction as accounted for by the pooling of interests method is that Laminated Thumbscrew has succeeded in developing approximately $19,000 (or perhaps $25,000) in earned surplus by doing no more than issuing more shares of its own stock. If Iron Maidenform had had current earnings, Laminated Thumbscrew would have acquired those too. The enterprise acquired by Laminated Thumbscrew is, at least for the present, a money loser with an inflated balance sheet. Nonetheless, the transaction has now put Laminated Thumbscrew in a position where it may, even in the most stringent jurisdiction, pay out to its shareholders a minimum of $19,250.

Note, too, that the transaction could have been handled so as to transfer earned surplus onto the Laminated balance sheet with no charge to capital surplus or earned surplus. If, instead of $40 par stock, no par or low par shares had been issued to the former Iron Maidenform shareholders, stated capital with regard to the shares issued could have been set by the board of directors at say, $50,000, the same as the stated capital of Iron Maidenform, and the $6,000 charge could have thus been avoided. Indeed, if in that transaction the increment required to be made to stated capital had been set at *less* than $50,000, the difference would have gone on to Laminated Thumbscrew's balance sheet as some new form of additional capital surplus. Finally, another possibility might have been to run the merger in the opposite direction, leave Iron Maidenform as the surviving corporation and issue no par or low par stock of Maidenform, transferring to its balance sheet the large, stated capital figure on the Laminated Thumbscrew balance sheet.

In many situations, it is evidently advantageous to an acquiring company to account for a corporate combination on the pooling of interests basis. In the heady days of the go-go funds and of high-flying conglomerates in the mid-1960s, a key factor was the flood of acquisitions that were accounted for on this basis, with a resultant pile-up of earnings and earned surplus bought with newly-issued stock and other more elaborate paper. The reasons for these acquisitions were not related to a desire to circumvent legal capital constraints on shareholder distributions. The stacked-up earnings emerging from pooling combinations demonstrated to a credulous market that the issuer was, and continued to be, a "growth company" whose stock was deserving of a high price-earnings ratio, whose price per share rose correspondingly, and whose ability was thereby increased to issue more new shares as the medium of exchange to bring into the conglomerate the income and earned surplus of still more corporations that did not enjoy as high a price-earnings ratio.[20] When the reaction came

20. To be more complete: The active acquisition-minded companies were perceived by the market as "growth companies" and therefore had high price-earnings multiples, but their technologies, or competition, had developed to a point where their growth in earnings was leveling off. In order to sustain the growth image, these companies leveraged their stock prices against companies that had good earnings but low price-earnings multiples. Thus, if Company X had 1,000,000 shares outstanding, earned $1,000,000 per year and sold on the market for 40 times earnings, while Company Y was earning $100,000 per year but was valued on the market at 20 times earnings, or $2,000,000, Company X could negotiate to acquire Company Y for approximately 50,000 of X's shares (leaving out the liquidity and dilution factors). The newly-issued 50,000 shares would, after the transaction, generate for Company X $100,000 per year in new earnings, or $2 per new share issued. In general, the $100,000 in new earnings added $4,000,000 to the market value of the shares of Company X. Thus, after the acquisition, Company X could expect its market value to rise to $44,000,000 and, with 1,050,000 shares outstanding, the stock would rise from $40 per share to around $42. Meanwhile, the former shareholders of Company Y would have received a listed, marketable, "growth" security on a tax-free exchange basis to replace what, typically, had been a non-growth, closely-held stock. Hence, everyone was happy. But the transaction had done nothing to alleviate the basic non-growth character of the acquirer, and

with the market declines of the late-1960s, closer attention was brought to bear on the practice of pooling of interests accounting, and a great debate raged among accountants, lawyers, and other interested parties on the question whether the pooling of interests method should ever be allowable, and, if so, under what conditions. The publication in 1970 of Opinion 16 (Business Combinations) by the Accounting Principles Board of the American Institute of Certified Public Accountants has, for the time being, put the matter at rest.[21] This is not a proper place to review the 47–page Opinion 16, though language from it has been drawn on *passim* in summary form here. But it may be said that the Board drew a great line, like the Pope in the Treaty of Tordesillas, holding that both the purchase method and the pooling of interests method have their places, but that there can never be a choice between them—if in a particular transaction one is right, then the other is wrong. That approach required the Board to specify in detail which kinds of transactions fall on which side of the line, and that is why the Opinion reads like 47 pages of Internal Revenue Service Regulations. (To satisfy the curious reader, the Laminated Thumbscrew–Iron Maidenform transaction falls in the class of transactions that under Opinion 16 must be accounted for by the pooling of interests method.)

As a final observation, as noted above, under the typical corporation statute, shareholders of the terminating company (and perhaps of the continuing company) who vote against a merger or transfer of assets have the right to pursue a meticulous procedure called appraisal rights and require the continuing company to pay

there was usually no reason to suppose that the newly-acquired $100,000 of earnings flow would grow substantially either. Indeed, as acquisition followed acquisition, it often happened that the newly-acquired earnings dropped, for the managements of the conglomerates found that they were unable to manage properly the diverse businesses they had acquired and that they were also unable to enlist dedicated, continuous and enthusiastic management efforts from the former owners and managers of the businesses acquired.

The acquiring conglomerate had to have pooling of interests accounting to avoid the goodwill factor on its balance sheet. Usually the price for the selling company had to be sweetened somewhat to consummate the deal; thus, in the example above, 60,000 shares of Company X would have been a more typical price. In that case, if the fair value of the assets of Company Y transferred to the books of Company X had been equal to $2,000,000, an additional $400,000 (10,000 shares at $40 per share) would have to be accounted for as goodwill. If, in addition, the fair value of the assets of the acquired company was relatively low, an even larger goodwill item would have had to be entered on the books of the acquiring company if the pooling of interests accounting method had not been available for use. The goodwill item looks bad on the acquirer's balance sheet since it implies that the issuer's stock is not really worth $40, or that the selling company is overpriced; the accountants will require the goodwill to be amortized over time, thereby reducing the earnings of the acquirer; the amortization is not deductible for tax purposes; the result would be that the newly-acquired earnings would be depressed, and the whole purpose of the deal would be frustrated.

21. But just barely: Opinions of the Board require a two-thirds vote; in the case of Opinion 16, twelve members assented and six dissented.

them in cash the fair market value of their shares.[22] This payment of dissenters' rights is a distribution of corporate assets to
shareholders and may entail very large sums; but once again the
statutory legal capital constraints do not constrain, since payments of dissenters' rights are everywhere exempt from them and
creditors are again left to watch as dollars flow out of the corporate treasury to junior security holders.

Transaction 23 (Year 11): Dissolution and Liquidation

During year eleven, a small syndicate of investors acquires
virtually all the shares of Laminated Thumbscrew, and for a
number of business and tax reasons decides to dissolve the corporation, sell off its assets, and distribute the proceeds to the
shareholders. This is voted by the board of directors and shareholders and a certificate of corporate dissolution is thereupon filed
with the corporation commissioner.

(a) *Balance sheet presentation:*

Same as Balance Sheet # 22B. The filing of the dissolution
certificate does not affect the balance sheet, though the fact of
its filing may be footnoted.

(b) *Legal capital constraints:*

All jurisdictions: shareholder distributions are allowable in
an amount equal to the net market value of the net assets
of the company, as they are liquidated. The dollar
amount cannot be taken from the book figures since the
total value of the assets distributed will usually be determined by the real market value of the corporate assets as
they are sold off and turned into liquid proceeds.[23] For
example, what value, if any, will the secret process have
in liquidation?

Upon the filing of the certificate of dissolution, every jurisdiction becomes a net worth jurisdiction and nothing more.
Dissolution automatically renders the local legal capital
statute irrelevant. The board of directors, as it officiates
in the liquidation and distribution of the enterprise assets, is of course mandated to pay off the corporation's
creditors first. And if the board distributes assets to the
shareholders without paying the corporation's creditors,
the board members themselves may be held liable by the

22. See Manning, *The Shareholder's
Appraisal Remedy: An Essay for Frank
Coker,* 72 Yale L.J. 223, 265 (1962).

23. This sentence is qualified by
"usually" because occasionally a corporate asset will be distributed in undivid-

ed interests to the shareholders, or securities held by the corporation will be
divided and distributed; in these instances there is no realization of a market value for the assets distributed.

creditors. But so long as the board meets that requirement, it is no longer inhibited by legal capital constraints
from making asset distributions to shareholders. Note,
too, that though the creditors come "first" in their claim,
the board is not required to pay them all first chronologically before making distributions to shareholders so long
as the creditors are ultimately paid.

And so, at the end of the day, and as the assets are being
distributed to the shareholders as the creditors wait in
line—as in *Wood v. Dummer*—the modern legal capital
statutes become inoperative by their own terms. But that
is not surprising. As was stated at the beginning of this
book so many pages ago, the problem to which the legal
capital doctrines are directed is how to control shareholder distributions by a *going* enterprise.

Second Part

THE REVISED MODEL BUSINESS CORPORATION ACT—LEVELLING THE LABYRINTH

Subpart One

THE REVISED MODEL ACT— EXPOSITION

Long overdue change has at last come to the field of legal capital.

In 1975 California struck out into new territory in the financial provisions of its new General Corporation Law as they substantially reconstructed the traditional edifice. Shares need no longer be denominated as par or no par, the revisers commenting that "a statement of 'par value' is not prohibited; it will simply have no legal significance. . . ."[1] As for the concept of treasury shares, shrift has seldom been so short as that accorded by the revisers as they say: "In most respects, treasury shares are merely a historical curiosity."[2] Distributions to shareholders may be made to the extent that retained earnings are available *or* certain ratios of certain assets to certain liabilities (and current assets to current liabilities) are met.[3]

The 1980s also saw a variety of less extensive changes in the pay-in and pay-out provisions of the corporation laws of other states, including Ohio[4] and Kansas[5].

The headline news of the 1980s in this field, however, was the overturn of the legal capital provisions of the Model Business Corporation Act—the basis of the corporation laws of approximately 35 states.

---

1. Cal.Gen.Corp.Law § 202(d), Comment.

2. *Id.,* § 510, Comment.

3. *Id.,* § 500. This statute apparently originated in a statute regulating application of surplus resulting from reduction of stated capital. See Deering's Cal.Civ.Code § 348(b) (1937); compare id. § 346 (regulating payment of dividends). See also Hills, Model Corporation Act, 48 Harv.L.Rev. 1334, 1341–42 (1935). Alaska has a statute similar to Cal.Gen.Corp.Law § 500. Alaska Stat. § 10.06.358 (1989). One must maintain a certain skepticism as to whether indenture-like ratio provisions are warranted in a general corporation statute or will prove administrable. The most likely outcome, one fears, is that such provisions will prove too technical for many purposes and too primitive for others. And it is hard to muster confidence in state courts as accounting tribunals.

4. Ohio Gen.Corp.Law § 1701.33 (1985).

5. Kan.Stat.Ann. § 17–6402 (1988).

176

Chapter I

INTRODUCTION

The initial—and the biggest—shock to hit the staid edifice of the Model Act came in 1980. In that year, a sweeping set of coordinated amendments to the Model Act demolished the traditional legal capital scheme. 1984 saw further substantial amendment, rewriting and consolidation as the entire Model Act was revised for the first time in 35 years to produce the Revised Model Business Corporation Act (the "Revised Model Act"). Then in 1987 more sandpapering touches were applied to the new shareholder pay-in and pay-out provisions of the Revised Model Act.

The new provisions of the Revised Model Act are the product of literally thousands of hours of intensive joint work by dozens of experienced corporation lawyers from law firms, corporate counsel offices and law faculties who have over the past 12 years or more made up the Committee on Corporate Laws—the Committee of the Business Law Section of the ABA that is charged to be the generator, keeper and revisor of the Model Act.[1] The revision process has had the further benefit throughout of consultation with members of the accounting and finance communities.

The result of these events and labors is that the Revised Model Act presents to the world of the 1990s a shiny, new, carefully-fashioned, refined set of integrated provisions on shareholder pay-in and shareholder pay-out reflecting modern thought and practice in corporation law, finance and accounting.

At this writing, Arkansas, Georgia, Indiana, Iowa, Kentucky, Mississippi, North Carolina, Oregon, Pennsylvania, South Carolina, Tennessee, Virginia, Washington, Wisconsin and Wyoming have already adopted the Revised Model Act. Other states, e.g. Maryland, while not adopting the Revised Model Act in its entirety, have enacted its shareholder pay-out provisions. Further, it would not be surprising if additional states that are not, and are not likely to become, Model Act states will, in respect of shareholder pay-in and pay-out, follow the lead of the new provisions of the Revised Model Act.

Given these circumstances, a focussed review of those provisions of the Revised Model Act is warranted. It follows.

1. Disclosure being the order of the day in contemporary corporation law, let it be disclosed that the author was an active participant in the 1980, 1984 and 1987 labors of the Committee.

Source and Citation Note: A number of materials and sources are relevant to such a review.

- Accompanying the major amendments to the Model Act made in 1980 was a Report of the Committee on Corporate Laws. It appears at 34 *Bus.Law.* 1867 (1979). That Report is here cited as "1980 Report".

- Accompanying each section of the Revised Model Act, issued in 1984, is correlative Official Comment, cited here as "O.C.1984."

- Accompanying the 1987 amendments to two relevant sections of the Revised Model Act was a Report of the Committee on Corporate Laws. It appears at 42 Bus. Law. 259–269 (1986). That Report includes, in respect of the two sections amended (Sections 6.40 and 8.33), corresponding Official Comment; in addition that Report reproduced (and somewhat refined) the entire Official Comment to those two sections. Official Comment appearing in that Report is cited here as "O.C.1987"; text of that Report other than Official Comment is here cited as "1986 Report".

- For present purposes, six Sections of the Revised Model Act are key. Governing share issuance and shareholder pay-in are Sections 6.21, 6.22 and 6.23. Regulating shareholder pay-outs is Section 6.40. Regulating acquisition by a corporation of its own shares is Section 6.31.

Those five sections, together with their related Official Comment, are set out in the Appendix to this book. The sixth section is Section 8.33, governing the liability of directors for making an unlawful distribution. The full text of that provision and its Official Comment are included in the discussion that follows here.

The reader should refer to the Appendix where indicated. In fact, the interested reader would do well to read the Appendix as a whole. It is not long, and as statutory text goes, the prose is, while not exactly racy, surprisingly readable.

* * *

The opening of the 1980 Committee Report comes right to the point. Boldly planting its flag, the Report commences:

The amendments to the financial provisions of the Model Business Corporation Act (the 'Model Act') reflect a complete modernization of all provisions of the Model Act concerning financial matters, including (a) the elimination of the outmoded concepts of stated capital and par value, (b) the definition of 'distribution' as a broad term governing dividends, share repurchases and similar actions that should be governed by the same standard, (c) the reformulation of the statutory standards governing the making of distributions, (d) the elimination of the concept of treasury stock, and (e) the making of a number of technical and conforming changes which are necessary or advisable in connection with the basic revisions.

It has long been recognized by practitioners and legal scholars that the pervasive statutory structure in which 'par value' and 'stated capital' are basic to the state corporation statutes does not today serve the original purpose of protecting creditors and senior security holders from payments to junior security holders, and may, to the extent security holders are led to believe that it provides some protection, tend to be misleading. In light of this recognized fact, the Committee on Corporate Laws has, as part of a fundamental revision of the financial provisions of the Model Act, deleted the mandatory concepts of stated capital and par value. . . .

* * *

The Committee also concluded that the concept of treasury stock should be eliminated, and that reacquired shares should automatically be restored to the status of authorized but unissued stock, unless the articles prohibit reissuance. This is based upon the judgment that treasury stock should have no meaningful or valid status of any substance, particularly in view of the elimination of par value, and stated capital, and of surplus as a measuring limitation. . . .[2]

As can be seen, these are no small tinkerings. The 1980 revisions of the Model Act yanked out by the roots every tendril of the doctrines discussed earlier in this book. Like an old Soviet encyclopedia dealing with a political "unperson", it eliminated almost every reference to par, and eradicated all references to stated capital, treasury shares, surpluses, and all their fearsome progeny.

The subsequent Revised Model Act has done the clean-up work in this arena.

What then is left to be said about the treatment of this topic in the Revised Model Act? Quite a lot.

---

2. 1980 Report, 34 Bus.Law. at 1867–69.

Chapter II

REGULATING THE SHAREHOLDER'S CONTRIBUTION

Matters have, indeed, become a lot simpler.

A. AUTHORIZATION OF SHARES

As in the past, the Revised Model Act provides that the articles of incorporation must prescribe the classes of shares and the number of shares of each class that the corporation is authorized to issue.[1] Very wide (but not total) latitude is provided to shape the terms and provisions of each class of shares.[2]

B. PAR

If one is of a mind to designate a "par value" for the authorized shares, he is free to do so,[3] but it is without legal consequence.

C. SHAREHOLDER'S PAY-IN OBLIGATION

1. Character of Consideration

There are no longer restrictions on the *character* of the consideration received by the corporation for the issued shares. For purposes of buying shares, John Rockefeller's promissory note and Barbra Streisand's contract for a future concert performance are now recognized as the valuable economic assets that everyone but lawyers always knew they were.

2. Amount of Consideration

There is no longer a concept of "par" and no statutorily-imposed minimum price at which shares must be issued. Therefore there can be no "watered stock"—shares issued for less than an arbitrarily-fixed price. The share purchaser is obligated by contract to pay in to the corporation for his shares whatever he agreed to pay in. No more.[4]

---

1. Rev.Model Bus.Corp. Act. §§ 2.02(a)(2), 6.01(a).

2. Id., § 6.01.

3. Id., § 2.02(b)(2)(iv). See 1980 Report at 1887 for discussion of status of par provisions in articles of incorporation of pre-existing corporations.

4. Read closely, Section 6.21(c) calls upon the board of directors to make a determination "[b]efore the corporation issues shares" that the consideration to be received for the shares is adequate. The Section goes on to say that if the board determines that the consideration is adequate, that concludes any enquiry

180

3. Equitable Contribution

The Revised Model Act recognizes the true nature of the problem raised by an issuance of shares at too low a price—the problem of equitable contribution. "The price at which shares are issued is primarily a matter of concern to other shareholders whose interests may be diluted if shares are issued at unreasonably low prices or for overvalued property."[5]

It is a key responsibility of the board to exercise serious business judgment as to the adequacy of consideration received by the corporation for shares issued. If directors do not meet that responsibility, they are answerable to existing shareholders for failing to meet the standard of performance set for directors by the most important section in the Revised Model Act—Section 8.30, prescribing the basic duties of directors.

4. Share Dividends

Section 6.23 eradicates the legal capital fictions that have been concocted to explain "payment" for "share dividends". The Official Comment to that Section says straightforwardly and quite correctly, "A share dividend is solely a paper transaction: No assets are received by the corporation for the shares and any 'dividend' paid in shares does not involve the distribution of property by the corporation to its shareholders." The Section therefore provides outright that a corporation may issue shares as share dividends without receiving any consideration.

* * *

And that is about all there is to say about regulation of the *issuance* of shares by the Revised Model Act. (The Revised Model Act has a great deal more to say, of course, about the legal attributes and features of shares and the rights and obligations of shareholders.)

as to the liability of the share purchaser to pay anything more. But what if the board does not make that determination until later? Or at all? The third party purchaser's own obligation should not hang in doubt in dependence upon the board's action or inaction in that regard; and no court reading the context of the statute and Official Comment as a whole should reach a contrary conclusion. Unfortunately, however, the grammatical structure suggests that in the event of board delay or non-action, the purchaser might not have an absolute statutory shield protecting him against a claim that he should pay in more assets than he contracted for.

And Section 6.22(a) does little to clarify the situation when it declares that the purchaser is not liable with respect to the shares "except to pay the consideration for which the shares were *authorized* to be issued. . . ." (Emphasis added.) To remove all doubt, the careful practitioner representing the buyer would be well advised to require that he receive evidence of a determination of adequacy and authorization of issue by the board *before* the closing of the share purchase.

5. Rev. Model Bus.Corp. Act § 6.21, Official Comment.

Chapter III

REGULATING DISTRIBUTIONS TO SHAREHOLDERS

A. DISTRIBUTION

Whatever the form of transaction, any asset flow from the corporation's coffers to shareholders as such that is not matched by an equivalent asset inflow is a distribution.[1] Every form of share purchase or redemption is thus a distribution; a share dividend, correspondingly, is not. All "distributions" are treated equally by the Revised Model Act.

B. INSOLVENCY—EQUITY SENSE

Section 6.40(c)(1) retains the mandate that "[n]o distribution may be made if, after giving it effect . . . the corporation would not be able to pay its debts as they become due in the usual course of business. . . ." This incorporates the concept of insolvency as classically defined by the courts of Chancery. As a restatement of Justice Story's opinion in *Wood v. Dummer*,[2] it is unchallengeable as a matter of policy.

Note, however, the discussion below of its implementation.

C. ADJUSTED NET WORTH TEST

The second test that a corporate distribution must meet is set forth in Section 6.40(c)(2). It mandates an adjusted net worth balance sheet test.

Fundamentally, the Section provides simply for a net worth balance sheet test as it states that "[n]o distribution may be made if, after giving it effect . . . the corporation's total assets would be less than the sum of its total liabilities. . . ." The Section makes one adjustment to that calculation, however; if the corporation has outstanding shares with preferential rights on liquida-

---

1. Section 1.40(6) defines "distribution" to mean "a direct or indirect transfer of money or other property (except its own shares) or incurrence of indebtedness by a corporation to or for the benefit of its shareholders in respect of any of its shares. A distribution may be in the form of a declaration or payment of a dividend; a purchase, redemption, or other acquisition of shares; a distribution of indebtedness; or otherwise."

2. See discussion at pp. 30–33, supra.

tion, the dollar amount of those rights is, for this purpose, to be deemed a "liability".[3]

The differences between this adjusted balance sheet test and traditional legal capital statutes are dramatic.

To recall to the reader, in legal capital statutes the structural design for regulating distributions to shareholders is to:

> (1) arrive at a dollar number as the balance sheet net worth (assets minus liabilities) of the corporation;
>
> (2) divide up the net worth section of the balance sheet into a number of separate prescribed conceptual bins—stated capital and surplus accounts;
>
> (3) post dollar numbers into each of those bins, more or less in accordance with murky ground rules set more or less independently by statutes, courts, lawyers and accountants; and,
>
> (4) employ the various dollar numbers in the separate bins as legal yardsticks for regulating (various kinds of) distributions of corporate assets to (various kinds of) shareholders as such.

In the Revised Model Act, the structural design for regulating distributions to shareholders is to:

> (1) arrive at a dollar number as the balance sheet adjusted net worth of the corporation (assets minus liabilities, counting as a liability the liquidation claims of any outstanding senior preference shares); and,
>
> (2) employ that single dollar number as the legal yardstick for regulating any distribution of corporate assets to any shareholder as such.

Thus, the Revised Model Act calls for no concept of stated capital or any other kind of capital account. It does not require differentiation among kinds of surplus. And it does not differentiate between capital and surplus accounts. But it does add substance to the prior liquidation claim of the holder of preference shares by according him *pro tanto* the same protection that the statute gives to a creditor of the corporation.

Now, of course, a corporation's management, or its board of directors, or its accountants, or a regulatory agency or whoever may choose or insist that the corporation fix a par for its shares; or may assign "stated capital" entries on the balance sheet for this or that class of shares or share transaction; or may create any other subdivisions within the southeast net worth corner of the

---

3. See Appendix, O.C.1987, § 6.40
Preferential Dissolution Rights and the
Balance Sheet Test.

balance sheet that happen to appeal to them. But for purposes of assessing the legality of a distribution to shareholders, all those things matter not.

D. WHY TWO TESTS?

In the course of the years of debate within the Committee on Corporate Laws dealing with regulation of shareholder distribution, it was suggested by some that any balance sheet test is inherently so deficient that the new Section 6.40 should drop it and contain the equity insolvency test, solo. Proponents of that view pointed out that the corporation law of Massachusetts has never contained any regulation of shareholder distribution other than the equity insolvency rule and creditors of Massachusetts corporations seem none the worse for it.

An insight to some of the considerations that entered into the ensuing debate can be gleaned from a reading of the following excerpt from the Official Comment to Section 6.40:

Equity Insolvency Test

As noted above, older statutes prohibited payments of dividends if the corporation was, or as a result of the payment would be, insolvent in the equity sense. This test is retained, appearing in section 6.40(c)(1).

In most cases involving a corporation operating as a going concern in the normal course, information generally available will make it quite apparent that no particular inquiry concerning the equity insolvency test is needed. While neither a balance sheet nor an income statement can be conclusive as to this test, the existence of significant shareholders' equity and normal operating conditions are of themselves a strong indication that no issue should arise under that test. Indeed, in the case of a corporation having regularly audited financial statements, the absence of any qualification in the most recent auditor's opinion as to the corporation's status as a "going concern," coupled with a lack of subsequent adverse events, would normally be decisive.

It is only when circumstances indicate that the corporation is encountering difficulties or is in an uncertain position concerning its liquidity and operations that the board of directors or, more commonly, the officers or others upon whom they may place reliance under section 8.30(b), may need to address the issue. Because of the overall judgment required in evaluating the equity insolvency test, no one or more "bright line" tests can be employed. However, in determining whether the equity insolvency test has been met, certain judgments or assumptions as to the future course of the corporation's business are customarily justified, absent clear evidence to the contrary. These include the likelihood that (a) based on existing and contemplated demand for the corporation's products or services, it will be able to generate funds over a period of time sufficient to satisfy its existing and reasonably anticipated obligations as they mature, and (b) indebtedness which matures in the near-term will be refinanced where, on the basis of the corporation's financial condition and future prospects and the general availability of credit to businesses similarly situated, it is reasonable to assume that such refinancing may be accomplished. To the extent that the corporation may be subject to asserted or unasserted contingent liabilities, reasonable judgments as to the likelihood, amount, and time of any recovery against the corporation, after giving consideration to the extent to which the corporation is insured or otherwise protected against loss, may be utilized. There may be occasions when it would be useful to consider a cash flow analysis, based on a business forecast and budget, covering a sufficient period of time to permit a conclusion that known obligations of the corporation can reasonably be expected to be satisfied over the period of time that they will mature.

Can a board of directors with any confidence make such futuristic analyses and judgments? Over how many months, years or decades ahead are they to be called upon to do so? Can a lawyer opine on the application of that standard in a particular corporate business situation? Put differently, suppose it were to be the rule that every distribution can be challenged at any future time when, the corporation having gone broke, someone chooses to contend that the board (and its lawyers) should have foreseen that dollars earlier distributed to shareholders ought to have been held back for creditors; then, and in that case, would it not be necessary to develop in effect an elaborate body of rules, procedures and limitations to reconcile the multiple considerations involved?

After all, there can be no fixed answer—only a balancing answer—possible in response to the single issue to which these statutes—and this book—are addressed. As stated at page 33, supra, "The problem of limiting distributions to shareholders arises fundamentally out of the economic pressure to make some distributions to shareholders while some creditors' claims remain outstanding and unpaid. That condition arises from the reality of the ongoing enterprise operating over time." Seen in hindsight, mistakes are inevitable. As a matter of practical business, and of practical legal administration, every bankruptcy cannot be allowed to trigger a spate of claims that distributions made in the past were improper. Most commentators (including this one) and all foreign observers find courts in the United States already too willing to tolerate lawsuits in business matters based on the cheap wisdom of retrospection.

Everyone knows that any species of balance sheet-based test carries with it the deficiencies that are inherent in the often artificial conventions of accounting rules. Nonetheless, a balance sheet test provides a reference point to which executives, boards, bankers and lawyers can look as they try to get on with their jobs. And that reference point has been accepted as well by the courts.

Virtually all corporation statutes say that a distribution must meet both the equity test and the local balance sheet-derived test. In the usual commercial situation in real life, however, the criterion that is daily employed by everyone to assess the legality of a proposed distribution is balance sheet-based. That action taken in good faith will in fact be upheld, even if the corporation later encounters economic disaster. In the rare and extreme case, where management's conduct does not meet the sniff test as it has shovelled out assets to the common shareholders to the injury of creditors but did so in conformity with the balance sheet-based rules, the court has available to it, and can be expected to resort to, application of the equity insolvency standard. But what would be the consequence if the equity insolvency standard were to be the *only* standard rather than a fall-back "bad-case" standard and thus required to carry the full burden of creditor protection against profligate distributions to shareholders? Would that compel development of a corpus of rules to deal with prospective unknowables and unascertainables implied by the Official Comment quoted above?

The Committee concluded to leave both the protective standards in the Revised Model Act.

E. VALUATION

Any balance sheet-based measurement is dependent upon the valuation practices and accounting principles employed. Section 6.40 leaves a lot of leeway. Rejecting the option of mandating "generally accepted accounting principles" ("GAAP"), the Section requires only that the accounting system used be reasonable in the circumstances. Going further still, subsection (d) permits the board of directors to base its determination of compliance with subsection (c) "on a fair valuation or other method that is reasonable in the circumstances." [4]

4. See Appendix, O.C.1987, § 6.40
Balance Sheet Test: Generally accepted
accounting principles; Other principles.

F. MISCELLANEOUS PROVISIONS

The practitioner will find certain technical aspects of the new Section 6.40 extremely helpful since they address and resolve practical problems that hitherto had no satisfactory answers and are unsuited for gradual case law solution. For example, Section 6.40(e) presents a carefully worked set of rules for setting the point in *time* when the effect of a distribution is to be measured.[5] Section 6.40(f) addresses the priority in claim of an instrument of indebtedness distributed to shareholders.[6] Record dates are the topic of Subsection (b).[7] Added in 1987, Subsection (g) prescribes the method for applying the Section 6.40 formula in the case of a particular type of contingent debt security.[8]

These provisions do not merit attention until one has a real problem on his desk. They are cited here primarily to illustrate the dramatic qualitative contrast between the new Revised Model Act and the jurisprudential fog that has traditionally blanketed this field.

G. LIABILITY FOR UNLAWFUL DISTRIBUTIONS

The topic of director liability for improper distribution to shareholders is addressed in the Revised Model Act by Section 8.33.

No other provision of the Revised Model Act imposes a specific liability upon directors, all acts of directors being blanketed by the responsibility provisions of Section 8.30. Speaking strictly analytically, there is no need for any other liability standard targeted on a single type of infraction of duty. But, perhaps primarily for historical reasons, it was concluded to continue a special liability provision—Section 8.33—for non-compliance with the rules of Section 6.40 on improper distributions to shareholders. But that decision bore with the concomitant necessity to mesh with precision the two separate liability provisions.

The task appears to have been accomplished by Section 8.33. That Section and comment are marked by extraordinary finesse; to those who, like this author, have worked in these vineyards, quite recognizable is the intellectual stamp of the nation's most serious scholar of this subject. The features of the solution are of such fine grain as to defy summarization. For that reason, the text of Section 8.33, with Official Comment, follows in full.

---

5. See Appendix, O.C.1987 § 6.40 Time of Measurement; Application to Reacquisition of Shares: Time of Measurement.

6. Id., Application to Reacquisition of Shares: Priority of debt distributed directly or incurred in connection with a reacquisition of shares.

7. Id., Record Date.

8. Id., Application to Reacquisition of Shares: Treatment of certain indebtedness.

§ 8.33 LIABILITY FOR UNLAWFUL DISTRIBUTIONS

(a) A director who votes for or assents to a distribution made in violation of section 6.40 or the articles of incorporation is personally liable to the corporation for the amount of the distribution that exceeds what could have been distributed without violating section 6.40 or the articles of incorporation if it is established that he did not perform his duties in compliance with section 8.30. In any proceeding commenced under this section, a director has all of the defenses ordinarily available to a director.

(b) A director held liable under subsection (a) for an unlawful distribution is entitled to contribution:

   (1) from every other director who could be held liable under subsection (a) for the unlawful distribution; and

   (2) from each shareholder for the amount the shareholder accepted knowing the distribution was made in violation of section 6.40 or the articles of incorporation.

(c) A proceeding under this section is barred unless it is commenced within two years after the date on which the effect of the distribution was measured under section 6.40(e) or (g).

§ 8.33 OFFICIAL COMMENT

Although the revisions to the financial provisions of the Model Act have simplified and rationalized the rules for determining the validity of distributions (see section 6.40), the possibility remains that a distribution may be made in violation of these rules. Section 8.33 provides that if it is established that a director failed to meet the standards of conduct of section 8.30 and voted for or assented to an unlawful distribution, the director is personally liable for the portion of the distribution that exceeds the maximum amount that could have been lawfully distributed. It also expressly preserves for a director all defenses which would ordinarily be available, notably the common law business judgment rule.

The explicit reference to the availability of defenses ordinarily available to a director was not contained in the Model Act sections that were predecessors of section 8.33, and may well be unnecessary. This declaration was included in the current text for two reasons. First, section 8.33 is the only provision in the Model Act specifying liability for directors in the event of failure to comply with the statute (specifically section 6.40), and the absence of the declaration might have provided the basis for an argument that the standards for section 6.40 were different than in other cases, a result not intended by the Model Act. Second, the declaration was inserted to make section 8.33 congruent with the intent of section 8.30(d), and the Official Comment thereunder, which states that the director is automatically shielded from liability if his compliance with section 8.30 is established and that the application of the business judgment rule need only be considered if compliance with the standard of conduct set forth in section 8.30 is not established.

A director who is compelled to restore the amount of an unlawful distribution to the corporation is entitled to contribution from every other director who could have been held liable for the unlawful distribution. The director may also recover the amounts paid to any shareholder who accepted the payments knowing that they were in violation of the statute. A shareholder who receives a payment not knowing of its invalidity is entitled to retain it. Although no attempt has been made in the Model Act to work out in detail the relationship between this right of recoupment from shareholders and the right of contribution from assenting directors, it is expected that a court will equitably apportion the obligations and benefits arising from the application of the principles set forth in this section.

Section 8.33(c) limits the time within which a proceeding may be commenced against a director for an unlawful distribution to two years after the date on which the effect of the distribution was measured. Although a statute of limitations provision is new to the Model Act, a substantial minority of jurisdictions have provisions limiting the time within which an action may be brought on account of an unlawful distribution.

The special attention traditionally accorded by corporation statutes to the topic of improper distribution of assets to stockholders is echoed in the 1990 amendment adding Section 2.02(b)(4) to the Revised Model Act. That section permits the articles of incorporation to include a provision eliminating or limiting the liability of a director to the corporation or its shareholders for money damages; but that general authority has its limiting exceptions—one of which is "a violation of Section 8.33 . . . ."[9]

As a side comment to Section 8.33, although the two-year statute of limitations provision in Subsection (c) does not say so in so many words, the only sensible interpretation to put upon it is that it applies only to an action by the corporation (or shareholder or creditor?) against an offending director and does not bar a subsequent action over by him for contribution from fellow directors.

9. Committee on Corporate Laws, *Changes in the Revised Model Business Corporation Act—Amendment Pertain-* *ing to the Liability of Directors,* 45 Bus. Law. 695, 702 (1990).

Chapter IV

ABOLITION OF TREASURY SHARES

The pay-out of assets by the corporation to acquire its own shares is, of course, a "distribution" under Section 1.40(6) of the Revised Model Act and must comply with the requirements of Section 6.40.

In earlier corporate practice and vocabulary, the shares involved in this transaction by the corporation were looked upon as reified "things", and the transaction was seen as the purchase of an asset. It was generally recognized, though, that something was a bit odd about this particular "asset". Nineteenth century jurisprudence resolved the problem by declaring that the "acquired shares" were "held in the treasury" and, though still "issued", were no longer "outstanding". Shares residing in this limbo-land could be plucked out and "resold" by the board of directors; or the board of directors could "retire" them to the status of "authorized but unissued shares"; or the board could "cancel" them, thereby reducing the number of authorized shares.

No one today views any of this talk as anything but conceptual word-juggling, a historical curiosity.[1] It is easy and tempting in a world of rapid change for each generation to consider its fathers, and their fathers' fathers, to have been dimwitted if not downright cretinous. But one should not be overready to dismiss the judges and law practitioners of the day of Justice Story as nincompoops, however garbled their invented notions of "treasury shares". Most often, yesterday's answers that appear unsophisticated today arose out of different premises, or less experience, or different objectives or a different context. So it was with "treasury shares". That fiction was an ingenious practical solution to a key operational problem of the day. As noted in earlier discussion, the concept of "treasury shares" was a makeshift ameliorant to the artificial paralysis of "par", offering a way to permit shares to be sold at their market value. And in that day, double-entry bookkeeping was as unknown as the computer.

Very likely our children's children will entertain a low regard for the mental capacity of those of us who happen to be adults in the 1990s. Certainly our daily doings are providing a lot of evidence tending to support that conclusion; but it is to be hoped that those who come later will not be too harsh in their judgment

---

1. See pp. 192, 196–97, infra.

of our poor efforts to understand and deal with the new world around us—especially our first efforts.

But, forgivable or not at the time of their inception, "treasury shares" are today simply humbug. The Model Act in 1980 finally said so out loud and Section 6.31 of the Revised Model Act concurs. It provides in subsection (a) that: "A corporation may acquire its own shares and shares so acquired constitute authorized but unissued shares." By traditional vocabulary, all "treasury shares" continued to be "issued shares"; thus, as the quoted language eliminates any possibility of a limbo category lying in between "authorized but unissued" and "outstanding", its effect is to eliminate the concept of "treasury shares" by wiping out the premise upon which it rested.

The balance of Section 6.31 deals with the procedure for reducing the number of authorized shares to the extent of the shares "reacquired".

Part of the Official Comment to Section 6.31 warrants quotation:

> One concept eliminated by the 1980 amendments was that of treasury shares. The status of once-issued but reacquired shares was an uneasy one under the traditional statutes. It was universally recognized that a corporation's shares in its own hands are not an asset any more than authorized but unissued shares. As an economic matter payments made by a corporation to repurchase its own shares must be viewed as a distribution of corporate assets by the corporation rather than as an acquisition of an asset. Further, conventional statutes gave treasury shares an intermediate status between issued and unissued: they were treated as outstanding shares for some purposes, and they could be resold or disposed of by the corporation (presumably) without regard to restrictions that might be imposed on the original issuance of shares by the corporation. Finally, the accounting treatment for treasury shares was complex, confusing, and to some extent unrealistic since the capital accounts often did not reflect transactions in treasury shares.
>
> Under the 1980 revisions of the financial provisions in the Model Act the concept of treasury shares is unnecessary. Authorized but unissued shares of the corporation may be issued on the same basis and with the same freedom as treasury shares under earlier statutes. Attorneys' opinions on the legality of the issuance of shares under the revised Model Act will therefore be unaffected by the elimination of the technical distinction between original shares and treasury shares. A possible exception to these statements is that the

concept of treasury shares may have permitted listed companies to save modestly on stock exchange listing fees in some cases that may not be available under the [r]evised Model Act provisions.

The Third Part, infra, discusses some possible repercussions of this important statutory change.

It is worthy of note that throughout the Revised Model Act the word "stock" has disappeared in favor of the word "shares". The change is more than a drafting nicety. Outgoing with that change is the last vestige of the etymological echo of the word "stock" as being an asset of the corporation.[2] And incoming with the word "share" is the accurate perception that vis à vis the corporation, the interest held by an equity investor is not a "thing" like a theater ticket and not a reified claim like the fixed obligation of a bond; it is instead a *ratio*, an undivided fractional interest shared with changing numbers of other holders in a changing aggregate of economic values.

If someone donates to a corporation a theater ticket or the corporation's own outstanding promissory note, the corporation's assets are increased. If someone donates to a corporation one of its own shares, the corporation's assets are not increased—only the value of the fractional interest of each of the other shareholders is increased. If the concept of "shares" had been understood from the beginning and not become blurred by the extraneous notion of "stock" as an asset, the "historical curiosity" of "treasury stock" would have never have been given birth.

* * *

Thus endeth the review of the contribution and distribution provisions of the Revised Model Act. For illustrations of the Revised Model Act's distribution provisions in action, see Subpart Two, following.

2. See pp. 32–33, supra.

Subpart Two

THE REVISED MODEL ACT—
ILLUSTRATIONS

As discussed in Subpart One of this Second Part, the distributions provisions (Section 6.40) of the Revised Model Act are an adjusted net worth statute. The one adjustment made by Section 6.40 is to include (unless the articles of incorporation provide otherwise) the aggregate dissolution preferences on outstanding senior shares as liabilities in calculating the corporation's net worth. Thus, a corporation will be permitted to make a distribution only to the extent that its assets exceed the sum of its liabilities *plus* (unless the articles provide to the contrary) the aggregate of dissolution preferences on stock that is senior to the class of shares for which the proposed distribution is being tested.

As applied to the transactions reviewed in the First Part, Subpart Two (and assuming no contrary provision in the articles of incorporation of Laminated Thumbscrew, Inc.), Section 6.40 of the Revised Model Act yields the following results:

Transactions 1 through 18: Same as in Net Worth Jurisdiction. No preferred stock having been issued in any of these transactions, the dissolution preference adjustment of Section 6.40(c)(2) is inapplicable.

Transaction 19: Common shareholder distribution of $64,200 allowable since assets ($86,200) exceed by that amount the sum of liabilities ($12,000) and dissolution preference of $100 per share on the 100 outstanding shares of preferred stock ($10,000).

Transaction 20: Common shareholder distribution of $82,700 allowable since assets ($137,700) exceed by that amount the sum of liabilities ($45,000) and dissolution preference of $100 per share on the 100 outstanding shares of preferred stock ($10,000).

Transaction 21: Common shareholder distribution of $96,750 allowable since assets ($136,750) exceed by that amount the sum of liabilities ($25,000) and dissolution preference of $100 per share on the 150 outstanding shares of preferred stock ($15,000).

Transactions 19–21: Note that Section 6.40(c)(2) permits the articles of incorporation to provide that senior dissolution preferences shall not be included in calculating amounts available for distribution.

Transactions 22 and 23: Same as in Net Worth Jurisdiction. See Transactions 1 through 18, supra.

Third Part

STATE OF PLAY—1990: YESTERDAY AND TOMORROW AS CONTEMPORARIES

As we enter the last decade of this millennium, what is the current state of play with regard to the law regulating shareholder pay-in and pay-out?

1. Certainly the situation is far better than it has been at any time before. One can only be grateful for the progress made, particularly in the 1980s. But the battle line is quite ragged.

At the present time, the field is occupied by:

- a handful of states that have adopted the Revised Model Act and the 1987 amendments;

- some states that have adopted the Revised Model Act but not the 1987 amendments;

- some states with the former Model Act, including the 1980 amendments;

- many states with the former Model Act but without the 1980 amendments;

- many states (including some of the most important states of incorporation) with their own version of corporation laws, the shareholder pay-in and pay-out provisions of which fall into four or five different categories—all of them antiques;

- all of the above floating in an opaque sea of 150 years of inconsistent, incoherent and incomprehensible judicial doctrine.

2. Whether many more states will follow the lead of the Revised Model Act is an open question. The changes may well strike many practitioners and legislators as so conceptually radical that they may balk. It is conceivable, even, that the proposed changes may lead some persons for the first time to examine the degree of protection afforded to creditors by the present legal capital system and to discover that it is a Swiss cheese made up mainly of holes; some persons might be moved by that observation to move in exactly the opposite legislative direction in an effort to put in place a new statutory system that would seek to give creditors a stronger position.

194

3. The more interesting question is just how the legal and accounting professions—and ultimately the courts—will adapt to the Revised Model Act where it is enacted into law. The Revised Model Act cannot prevent lawyers, accountants and corporate financial officers—and courts—from thinking in traditional terms of "stated capital". Many will find it difficult to take seriously mere statutory efforts to obliterate their doctrinal learning at a stroke.

The author's grandfather—a reflective and courtly member of the Kentucky bar—went to his grave at venerable years, declaring with undiminished conviction that the merger of Law and Equity was a terrible mistake, that rules of Law and principles of Equity remain immutably distinct, just as they have always been, and that the only consequence of the "merger" of Law and Equity has been that now there are no good common law lawyers any more and no good equity practitioners either.

To many experienced readers of corporate balance sheets, it will come as a distinct shock to discover suddenly that as a legal matter the southeast corner may henceforth carry only an entry for shareholders' equity—with no distinctions drawn between "stated capital" accounts and surpluses of myriad kinds, and with no elaborate entries for "treasury shares". Indeed, one may predict with some confidence that many practitioners will simply keep on in their old ways for years to come—their commitment to ancient doctrine unwavering.

4. The relationship between the fields of law and accounting in this area is interesting too.

From one perspective, the corporation statute declares only what the purchasing shareholder must pay for his shares and how large a distribution may lawfully be made to shareholders. The statutes presume to say nothing as to how corporations, or their accountants, shall keep their books or prepare their financial statements.

From another perspective, the situation looks quite different. The matter of treasury shares affords the best illustration. The Revised Model Act—and since 1980 its predecessor Model Act—have provided that there is no such thing as treasury shares. As the accountants have, or have not, in recent years, gone through varieties of gyrations in moving numbers around in the capital accounts, they have either been doing it in accordance with the particular state legal capital scheme—or they have not. The accountants are free to do as they will, regardless of the local statute—but the consequence may be that if the entries they post are dictated by a system that is not concordant with the local statutory one, then the numbers and groupings they post on a corporation's financial statements are useless to the poor CFO to review or to the lawyer who is being asked to opine on the validity of a proposed distribution to shareholders.

Unwelcome as it may be, the ineluctable logic of the situation is that if the accountants are *not* keeping score in the same way as the applicable state statute, the lawyer will only be able to opine on the statutory compliance of a given distribution by developing a second set of balance sheet numbers that do reflect the applicable statutory scheme.

5. Government regulators occasionally slice across the field in some mindless or unfathomable orbit of their own. For example, the Securities and Exchange Commission requires an issuer of shares of preferred stock with an involuntary liquidation preference that "exceeds the par or stated value thereof" to file "an opinion of counsel as to whether there are any restrictions upon surplus by reason of such excess and also as to any remedies available to security holders before or after payment of any dividend that would reduce surplus to an amount less than the amount of such excess." [1]

The unexceptionable general purpose of this requirement is, of course, to compel disclosure to preference shareholders of possible restrictions on dividend payments to them. Unfortunately for practitioners, however, the language of the regulation is bent and garbled to the point of incomprehensibility—as is so often the case with statutes and judicial statements in this tangled snarl. The point at hand, however, is only to note that the viruses bred over generations in the stated capital doctrines of the states have now wormed their way into Washington, D.C.

6. The uninitiated would likely expect to encounter a sophisticated understanding at the stock exchanges of their stock in trade, stock. But when he actually takes stock of the situation, he will find that the exchanges in their listing operations continue to be uncritical believers in "treasury stock" and in the image of a share of stock as a reified thing like a theater ticket. In that perspective, there are only so many seats and so many tickets. Some such notion underlies the whole idea that "these particular shares" of a company are "listed" (i.e., are in the orchestra), while "those shares" of the same class of the same company are not (i.e., are in the balcony). It will not prove easy for the folks at the stock exchanges to wrap their minds around the implications of the new reality that the law says that there *are* no treasury shares. Where in the world did the listing go? Coming to

1. S.E.C. Reg. S–K, Item 601(b)(7), 17 C.F.R. § 229.601(b)(7).

understand a share as a ratio rather than a thing is not likely to
go down easily at the stock exchanges.

7. Two ghosts continue to lurk in the wings, as they have all
along: the tangential, or overlapping, perimeters of the Revised
Model Act, the Bankruptcy Act and state fraudulent conveyance
statutes. The Official Comment to Section 6.40 glances at the
problem and then hurries on, saying,

> The revised Model Business Corporation Act estab-
> lishes the validity of distributions from the corporate law
> standpoint under section 6.40 and determines the poten-
> tial liability of directors for improper distributions under
> sections 8.30 and 8.33. The federal Bankruptcy Act and
> state fraudulent conveyance statutes, on the other hand,
> are designed to enable the trustee or other representative
> to recapture for the benefit of creditors funds distributed
> to others in some circumstances. In light of these diverse
> purposes, it was not thought necessary to make the tests
> of section 6.40 identical to the tests for insolvency under
> these various statutes.

8. Of a certainty, there are out there somewhere a million
private contracts that in one way or another—rationally or irrationally—touch upon, or are touched by, conceptual references to
par, stated capital, earned surplus, treasury stock and other terms
in the large lexicon of legal capital. Those contracts have not
been vitiated or banned or outlawed. But as time passes, they will
float farther and farther way from current statutory usage and
modern corporate practice. As such, their interpretation will
become less predictable—as has happened with the skills once
required to write a bill in equity or an artful conveyance of
enfeoffment.

In anticipation of that future, foresighted corporate counsel
will—beginning today—stop using the dying concepts of legal
capital as building blocks for his constructions.

*   *   *

So, there is still much to do.

But who would want a life without much to do?

APPENDIX

Changes in the Revised Model Business Corporation Act —Amendments Pertaining to Distributions

This Appendix contains the full text of Sections 6.40 and 8.33 of the Revised Model Business Corporation Act, marked to show changes made in 1987 as published in *The Business Lawyer* in November, 1986. 42 Bus.Law. 259 (1986).

§ 6.40 DISTRIBUTIONS TO SHAREHOLDERS

(a) A board of directors may authorize and the corporation may make distributions to its shareholders subject to restriction by the articles of incorporation and the limitation in subsection (c).

(b) If the board of directors does not fix the record date for determining shareholders entitled to a distribution (other than one involving a ~~repurchase~~ purchase, redemption, or other ~~reacquisition~~ acquisition of the corporation's shares), it is the date the board of directors authorizes the distribution.

(c) No distribution may be made if, after giving it effect:

(1) the corporation would not be able to pay its debts as they become due in the usual course of business; or

(2) the corporation's total assets would be less than the sum of its total liabilities plus (unless the articles of incorporation permit otherwise) the amount that would be needed, if the corporation were to be dissolved at the time of the distribution, to satisfy the preferential rights upon dissolution of shareholders whose preferential rights are superior to those receiving the distribution.

(d) The board of directors may base a determination that a distribution is not prohibited under subsection (c) either on financial statements prepared on the basis of accounting practices and principles that are reasonable in the circumstances or on a fair valuation or other method that is reasonable in the circumstances.

(e) Except as provided in subsection (g), the effect of a distribution under subsection (c) is measured:

(1) in the case of distribution by purchase, redemption, or other acquisition of the corporation's shares, as of the earlier of (i) the date money or other property is transferred or debt incurred by the corporation or (ii) the date the shareholder ceases to be a shareholder with respect to the acquired shares;

198

(2) in the case of any other distribution of indebtedness, as of the date the indebtedness is distributed; and

(3) in all other cases, as of (i) the date the distribution is authorized if the payment occurs within 120 days after the date of authorization or (ii) the date the payment is made if it occurs more than 120 days after the date of authorization.

(f) A corporation's indebtedness to a shareholder incurred by reason of a distribution made in accordance with this section is at parity with the corporation's indebtedness to its general, unsecured creditors except to the extent subordinated by agreement.

(g) Indebtedness of a corporation, including indebtedness issued as a distribution, is not considered a liability for purposes of determinations under subsection (c) if its terms provide that payment of principal and interest are made only if and to the extent that payment of a distribution to shareholders could then be made under this section. If the indebtedness is issued as a distribution, each payment of principal or interest is treated as a distribution, the effect of which is measured on the date the payment is actually made.

§ 6.40 OFFICIAL COMMENT

The reformulation of the statutory standards governing distributions is another important change made by the 1980 revisions to the financial provisions of the Model Act. It has long been recognized that the traditional "par value" and "stated capital" statutes do not provide significant protection against distributions of capital to shareholders. While most of these statutes contained elaborate provisions establishing "stated capital," "capital surplus," and "earned surplus" (and often other types of surplus as well), the net effect of most statutes was to permit the distribution to shareholders of most or all of the corporation's net assets—its capital along with its earnings—if the shareholders wished this to be done. However, statutes also generally imposed an equity insolvency test on distributions that prohibited distributions of assets if the corporation was insolvent or if the distribution had the effect of making the corporation insolvent or unable to meet its obligations as they were projected to arise.

The financial provisions of the revised Model Act, which are based on the 1980 amendments, sweep away all the distinctions among the various types of surplus but retain restrictions on distributions built around both the traditional equity insolvency and balance sheet tests of earlier statutes.

1. *The Scope of Section 6.40*

Section 1.40 defines "distribution" to include virtually all transfers of money, indebtedness of the corporation or other property to a shareholder in respect of the corporation's shares. It thus includes cash or property dividends, payments by a corporation to purchase its own shares, distributions of promissory notes or indebtedness, and distributions in partial or complete liquidation or voluntary or involuntary dissolution. Section 1.40 excludes from the definition of "distribution" transactions by the corporation in which only its own shares are distributed to its shareholders. These transactions are called "share dividends" in the revised Model Business Corporation Act. See section 6.23.

Section 6.40 imposes a single, uniform test on all distributions. Many of the old "par value" and "stated capital" statutes provided tests that varied with the type of distribution under consideration or did not cover certain types of distributions at all.

2. *Equity Insolvency Test*

As noted above, older statutes prohibited payments of dividends if the corporation was, or as a result of the payment would be, insolvent in the equity sense. This test is retained, appearing in section 6.40(c)(1).

~~For an on going business enterprise the equity insolvency test requires that decisions be based on a cash flow analysis that is itself based on a business forecast and budget for a sufficient period of time to permit a conclusion that known obligations of the corporation can reasonably be expected to be satisfied over the period of time that they will mature. It is not sufficient simply to measure current assets against current liabilities, or determine that the present estimated "liquidation" value of the corporation's assets would produce sufficient funds to satisfy the corporation's existing liabilities.~~

~~In determining whether a corporation is, or as a result of a proposed distribution would be rendered, insolvent, the board of directors may rely on information supplied by the officers of the corporation. It is not necessary for them to know of the details of the cash flow analysis of the proposed distribution involves no significant risk of equity insolvency.~~

In most cases involving a corporation operating as a going concern in the normal course, information generally available will make it quite apparent that no particular inquiry concerning the equity insolvency test is needed. While neither a balance sheet nor an income statement can be conclusive as to this test, the existence of significant shareholders' equity and normal operating conditions are of themselves a strong indication that no issue should arise under that test. Indeed, in the case of a corporation having regularly audited financial statements, the absence of any qualification in the most recent auditor's opinion as to the corporation's status as a "going concern," coupled with a lack of subsequent adverse events, would normally be decisive.

It is only when circumstances indicate that the corporation is encountering difficulties or is in an uncertain position concerning its liquidity and operations that the board of directors or, more commonly, the officers or others upon whom they may place reliance under section 8.30(b), may need to address the issue. Because of the overall judgment required in evaluating the equity insolvency test, no one or more "bright line" tests can be employed. However, in determining whether the equity insolvency test has been met, certain judgments or assumptions as to the future course of the corporation's business are customarily justified, absent clear evidence to the contrary. These include the likelihood that (a) based on existing and contemplated demand for the corporation's products or services, it will be able to generate funds over a period of time sufficient to satisfy its existing and reasonably anticipated obligations as they mature, and (b) indebtedness which matures in the near-term will be refinanced where, on the basis of the corporation's financial condition and future prospects and the general availability of credit to businesses similarly situated, it is reasonable to assume that such refinancing may be accomplished. To the extent that the corporation may be subject to asserted or unasserted contingent liabilities, reasonable judgments as to the likelihood, amount, and time of any recovery against the corporation, after giving consideration to the extent to which the corporation is insured or otherwise protected against loss, may be utilized. There may be occasions when it would be useful to consider a cash flow analysis, based on a business forecast and budget, covering a sufficient period of time to permit a conclusion that known obligations of the corporation can reasonably be expected to be satisfied over the period of time that they will mature.

In exercising their judgment, the directors are entitled to rely, under section 8.30(b) as noted above, on information, opinions, reports, and statements prepared by others. Ordinarily, they should not be expected to become involved in the details of the various analyses or market or economic projections that may be relevant. Judgments, further, must of necessity be made on the basis of information in the hands of the directors when a distribution is authorized. See section 8.30. They should not, of course, be held responsible as a matter of hindsight for unforeseen developments. This is particularly true with respect to assumptions as to the ability of the corporation's business to repay long-term

obligations which do not mature for several years, since the
primary focus of the directors' decision to make a distribution
should normally be on the corporation's prospects and obligations
in the shorter term, unless special factors concerning the corporation's prospects require the taking of a longer term perspective.

3. Relationship to the Federal Bankruptcy Act and Other Fraudulent Conveyance Statutes

The revised Model Business Corporation Act establishes the
validity of distributions from the corporate law standpoint under
section 6.40 and determines the potential liability of directors for
improper distributions under sections 8.30 and 8.33. The federal
Bankruptcy Act and state fraudulent conveyance statutes, on the
other hand, are designed to enable the trustee or other representative to recapture for the benefit of creditors funds distributed to
others in some circumstances. In light of these diverse purposes,
it was not thought necessary to make the tests of section 6.40
identical to the tests for insolvency under these various statutes.

4. Balance Sheet Test

Section 6.40(c)(2) requires that, after giving effect to any
distribution, the corporation's assets equal or exceed its liabilities
plus (with some exceptions) the dissolution preferences of senior
equity securities. Section 6.40(d) authorizes asset and liability
determinations to be made for this purpose on the basis of either
(1) financial statements prepared on the basis of accounting practices and principles that are reasonable in the circumstances or (2)
a fair valuation or other method that is reasonable in the circumstances. The determination of a corporation's assets and liabilities and the choice of the permissible basis on which to do so are
left to the judgment of its board of directors. In making a
judgment under section 6.40(d), the board may rely under section
8.30(b) upon opinions, reports, or statements, including financial
statements and other financial data prepared or presented by
public accountants or others.

Section 6.40 does not ~~incorporate technical accounting terminology and specific accounting concepts. Accounting terminology
and concepts are constantly under review and subject to revision
by the Financial Accounting Standards Board, the American Institute of Certified Public Accountants, the Securities and Exchange
Commission, and others. In making determinations under this
section, the board of directors may make judgments about accounting matters, taking into account its right to rely upon professional
or expert opinion and its obligation to be reasonably informed as
to pertinent standards of importance that bear upon the subject at
issue.~~ utilize particular accounting terminology of a technical

nature or specify particular accounting concepts. In making determinations under this section, the board of directors may make judgments about accounting matters, giving full effect to its right to rely upon professional or expert opinion.

In a corporation with subsidiaries, the board of directors may rely on unconsolidated statements prepared on the basis of the equity method of accounting (see American Institute of Certified Public Accountants, APB Opinion No. 18 (1971)) as to the corporation's investee corporations, including corporate joint ventures and subsidiaries, although other evidence would be relevant in the total determination.

a. Generally accepted accounting principles

The directors will normally be entitled to use generally accepted accounting principles and to give presumptive weight to the advice of professional accountants with respect to their application. But section 6.40 only requires the use of accounting practices and principles that are reasonable in the circumstances, and does not constitute a statutory enactment of generally accepted accounting principles. The widespread controversy concerning various accounting principles, and their continuous reevaluation, suggest that a statutory standard of reasonableness, rather than of generally accepted accounting principles, is appropriate. The Model Act does not reject generally accepted accounting principles; on the contrary, it is expected that their use will be the basic rule in most cases. The statutory language does, however, require informed business judgment applying particular accounting principles to the entire circumstances that exist at the time.

The board of directors should in all circumstances be entitled to rely upon reasonably current financial statements prepared on the basis of generally accepted accounting principles in determining whether or not the balance sheet test of section 6.40(c)(2) has been met, unless the board is then aware that it would be unreasonable to rely on the financial statements because of newly-discovered or subsequently arising facts or circumstances. But section 6.40 does not mandate the use of generally accepted accounting principles; it only requires the use of accounting practices and principles that are reasonable in the circumstances. While publicly-owned corporations subject to registration under the Securities Exchange Act of 1934 must, and many other corporations in fact do, utilize financial statements prepared on the basis of generally accepted accounting principles, a great number of smaller or closely-held corporations do not. Some of these corporations maintain records solely on a tax accounting basis and their financial statements are of necessity prepared on that basis. Others prepare financial statements that substantially reflect gen-

erally accepted accounting principles but may depart from them
in some respects (e.g., footnote disclosure). These facts of corporate life indicate that a statutory standard of reasonableness,
rather than stipulating generally accepted accounting principles
as the normative standard, is appropriate in order to achieve a
reasonable degree of flexibility and to accommodate the needs of
the many different types of business corporations which might be
subject to these provisions, including in particular closely-held
corporations. Accordingly, the revised Model Business Corporation Act contemplates that generally acceptable accounting principles are always "reasonable in the circumstances" and that other
accounting principles may be perfectly acceptable, under a general
standard of reasonableness, even if they do not involve the "fair
value" or "current value" concepts that are also contemplated by
section 6.40(d).

b Other principles

If a corporation's financial statements are not presented in
accordance with generally accepted accounting principles, a board
of directors should normally consider the extent to which the
assets may not be fairly stated or the liabilities may be under-
stated in determining the aggregate amount of assets and liabilities.

Section 6.40(d) specifically permits determinations to be made
under section 6.40(c)(2) on the basis of a fair valuation or other
method that is reasonable in the circumstances. Thus the statute
authorizes departures from historical cost accounting and sanc-
tions the use of appraisal and current value methods to determine
the funds amount available for distributions. No particular
method of valuation is prescribed in the statute, since different
methods may have validity depending upon the circumstances,
including the type of enterprise and the purpose for which the
determination is made. For example, it is inappropriate in most
cases to apply a "quick-sale liquidation" method value to value an
enterprise in most cases, particularly with respect to the payment
of normal dividends. On the other hand, a "quick-sale valuation
liquidation" valuation method might be appropriate in certain
circumstances for an enterprise in the course of liquidation or of
reducing its asset or business base by a material degree. In most
cases, a fair valuation method or a going-concern basis would be
appropriate if it is believed that the enterprise will continue as a
going concern.

In determining the value of assets, all of the assets of a
corporation, whether or not reflected in the financial statements
(e.g., a valuable executory contract), should be considered.

Ordinarily a corporation should not selectively revalue assets. It should consider the value of all of its material assets, whether or not reflected in the financial statements (e.g., a valuable executory contract). Likewise, all of a corporation's material obligations ~~and commitments~~ should be considered and revalued ~~quantified~~ to the extent appropriate and possible. In any event, section 6.40(d) ~~imposes upon the board of directors the responsibility of applying~~ calls for the application under section 6.40(c)(2) of a method of determining the aggregate amounts of assets and liabilities that is reasonable in the circumstances.

Section 6.40(d) also refers to some "other method that is reasonable in the circumstances." This phrase is intended ~~inserted~~ to comprehend within section 6.40(c)(2) the wide variety of possibilities that might not be considered to fall under a "fair valuation" or "current value" method but might be reasonable in the circumstances of a particular case.

5. *Preferential Dissolution Rights and the Balance Sheet Test*

Section 6.40(c)(2) provides that a distribution may not be made unless the total assets of the corporation exceed its liabilities plus the amount that would be needed to satisfy any shareholders~~'~~'s superior preferential rights upon dissolution if the corporation were to be dissolved at the time of the distribution. This requirement in effect treats preferential dissolution rights of ~~classes or series of~~ shares for distribution purposes as ~~equivalent to~~ if they were liabilities ~~rather than as equity interests~~ for the sole purpose of determining the amount available for distributions, and carries forward analogous treatment of shares having preferential dissolution rights from earlier versions of the Model Act. In making the calculation of the amount that must be added to the liabilities of the corporation to reflect the preferential dissolution rights, the assumption should be made that the preferential dissolution rights are to be established pursuant to the articles of incorporation, ~~(or resolution creating a series having preferential rights)~~ as of the date of the distribution or proposed distribution. The amount so determined must include arrearages in preferential dividends if the articles of incorporation ~~or resolution~~ require that they be paid upon the dissolution of the corporation. In the case of shares having both a preferential right upon dissolution and ~~additional~~ other nonpreferential rights, only the preferential ~~portion of~~ rights should be taken into account. The treatment of preferential dissolution rights of classes of shares set forth in section 6.40(c)(2) is applicable only to the balance sheet test and is not applicable to the equity insolvency test of section 6.40(c)(1). The treatment of preferential rights mandated by this section may always be eliminated by an appropriate provision in the articles of incorporation.

6. *Time of Measurement*

Section 6.40(e)(3) provides that the time for measuring the effect of a distribution for compliance with the equity insolvency and balance sheet tests for all distributions not involving the reacquisition of shares or the distribution of indebtedness is the date of authorization, if the payment occurs within 120 days following the authorization; if the payment occurs more than 120 days after the authorization, however, the date of payment must be used. If the corporation elects to make a distribution in the form of its own indebtedness, under section 6.40(e)(2) the validity of that distribution must be measured as of the time of distributions, unless the indebtedness qualifies under section 6.40(g).

Section 6.40(e)(1) provides a different rule for the time of measurement when the distribution involves a reacquisition of shares. See ~~Part 8A~~ below, Application to Reacquisition of Shares—Time of measurement.

7. *Record Date*

Section 6.40(b) fixes the record date (if the board of directors does not otherwise fix it) for distributions other than those involving a ~~repurchase or~~ reacquisition of shares as the date the board of directors authorizes the distribution. No record date is necessary for a ~~repurchase or~~ reacquisition of shares from one or more specific shareholders. The board of directors has discretion to set a record date for a ~~repurchase or~~ reacquisition if it is to be pro rata and to be offered to all shareholders as of a specified date.

Application to ~~Repurchases or Redemption~~ Reacquisition of Shares

The application of the equity insolvency and balance sheet tests to distributions that involve the purchase, ~~or~~ redemption, or other acquisition of the corporation's shares creates unique problems; section 6.40 provides a specific rule for the resolution of these problems as described below.

Time of measurement

Section 6.40(e)(1) provides that the time for measuring the effect of a distribution under section 6.40(c), if shares of the corporation are reacquired, is the earlier of (i) the payment date, or (ii) the date the shareholder ceased to be a shareholder with respect to the shares, except as provided in section 6.40(g).

b. *When tests are applied to redemption-related debt*

In an acquisition of its shares, a corporation may transfer property or incur debt to the former holder of the shares. The case law on the status of this debt is conflicting. However, share repurchase agreements involving payment for shares over a period of time are of special importance in closely-held corporate enterprises. Section 6.40(e) provides a clear rule for this situation: the legality of the distribution must be measured at the time of the issuance ~~or~~ of incurrence of the debt, not at a later date when the debt is actually paid, except as provided in section 6.40(g). Of course, this does not preclude a later challenge of a payment on account of redemption-related debt by a bankruptcy trustee on the ground that it constitutes a preferential payment to a creditor.

c. *Priority of debt distributed directly or incurred in connection with a ~~redemption~~ reacquisition of shares*

Section 6.40(f) provides that indebtedness created to ~~purchase~~ acquire the corporation's shares or issued as a distribution is on a parity with the indebtedness of the corporation to its general, unsecured creditors, except to the extent subordinated by agreement. General creditors are better off in these situations than they would have been if cash or other property had been paid out for the shares or distributed (which is proper under the statute), and no worse off than if cash had been paid ~~out to the shareholders~~ or distributed and ~~which was~~ then lent back to the corporation, making the shareholders (or former shareholders) creditors. The parity created by section 6.40(f) ~~therefore~~ is logically consistent with the rule established by section 6.40(e) that these transactions should be judged at the time of the issuance of the debt.

Treatment of certain indebtedness

Section 6.40(g) provides that indebtedness need not be taken into account as a liability in determining whether the tests of section 6.40(c) have been met if the terms of the indebtedness provide that payments of principal or interest can be made only if and to the extent that payment of a distribution could then be made under section 6.40. This has the effect of making the holder of the indebtedness junior to all other creditors but senior to the holders of all classes of shares, not only during the time the corporation is operating but also upon dissolution and liquidation. It should be noted that the creation of such indebtedness, and the related limitations on payments of principal and interest, may create tax problems or raise other legal questions.

Although section 6.40(g) is applicable to all indebtedness meeting its tests, regardless of the circumstances of its issuance, it is anticipated that it will be applicable most frequently to permit the reacquisition of shares of the corporation at a time when the deferred purchase price exceeds the net worth of the corporation. This type of reacquisition will often be necessary in the case of businesses in early stages of development or service businesses whose value derives principally from existing or prospective net income or cash flow rather than from net asset value. In such situations, it is anticipated that net worth will grow over time from operations so that when payments in respect of the indebtedness are to be made the two insolvency tests will be satisfied. In the meantime, the fact that the indebtedness is outstanding will not prevent distributions that could be made under subsection (c) if the indebtedness were not counted in making the determination.

§ 8.33 LIABILITY FOR UNLAWFUL DISTRIBUTIONS

(a) ~~Unless he complies with the applicable standards of conduct described in section 8.30, a~~ A director who votes for or assents to a distribution made in violation of ~~this Act~~ section 6.40 or the articles of incorporation is personally liable to the corporation for the amount of the distribution that exceeds what could have been distributed without violating section 6.40 ~~this Act~~ or the articles of incorporation if it is established that he did not perform his duties in compliance with section 8.30. In any proceeding commenced under this section, a director has all of the defenses ordinarily available to a director.

(b) A director held liable under subsection (a) for an unlawful distribution ~~under subsection (a)~~ is entitled to contribution:

(1) from every other director who ~~voted for or assented to the distribution without complying with the applicable standards of conduct described in section 8.30~~ could be held liable under subsection (a) for the unlawful distribution; and

(2) from each shareholder for the amount the shareholder accepted knowing the distribution was made in violation of ~~this Act~~ section 6.40 or the articles of incorporation.

(c) A proceeding under this section is barred unless it is commenced within two years after the date on which the effect of the distribution was measured under section 6.40(e) or (g).

§ 8.33 OFFICIAL COMMENT

Although the revisions to the financial provisions of the Model Act have simplified and rationalized the rules for determining the validity of distributions (see section 6.40), the possibility remains that a distribution may be made in violation of these rules. Section 8.33 provides that if it is established that a directors ~~who~~ failed to meet the standards of conduct of section 8.30 and voted for or assented to an unlawful distribution, the director is ~~are~~ personally liable for the portion of the distribution that exceeds the maximum amount that could have been lawfully distributed. It also expressly preserves for a director all defenses which would ordinarily be available, notably the common law business judgment rule.

The explicit reference to the availability of defenses ordinarily available to a director was not contained in the Model Act sections that were predecessors of section 8.33, and may well be unnecessary. This declaration was included in the current text for two reasons. First, section 8.33 is the only provision in the Model Act specifying liability for directors in the event of failure to comply with the statute (specifically section 6.40), and the absence of the declaration might have provided the basis for an argument that the standards for section 6.40 were different than in other cases, a result not intended by the Model Act. Second, the declaration was inserted to make section 8.33 congruent with the intent of section 8.30(d), and the Official Comment thereunder, which states that the director is automatically shielded from liability if his compliance with section 8.30 is established and that the application of the business judgment rule need only be considered if compliance with the standard of conduct set forth in section 8.30 is not established.

A director who is compelled to restore the ~~that~~ amount of an unlawful distribution to the corporation is entitled to contribution from every other director who ~~voted for or assented to~~ could have been held liable for the unlawful distribution. ~~In addition,~~ The director may also recover the ~~any~~ amounts paid to any shareholders who accepted the payments knowing that they were in violation of the statute. A shareholder who receives a payment not knowing of its invalidity is entitled to retain it. Although no attempt has been made in the Model Act to work out in detail ~~in the Model Act~~ the relationship between this right of recoupment from shareholders and the right of contribution from assenting directors, it is expected that a court will equitably apportion the obligations and benefits arising from the application of the principles set forth in this section.

Section 8.33(c) limits the time within which a proceeding may be commenced against a director for an unlawful distribution to two years after the date on which the effect of the distribution was measured. Although a statute of limitations provision is new to the Model Act, a substantial minority of jurisdictions have provisions limiting the time within which an action may be brought on account of an unlawful distribution.

*

INDEX

References are to Pages

†